The Therapy Industry

THE THERAPY INDUSTRY

The Irresistible Rise of the Talking Cure, and Why It Doesn't Work

Paul Moloney

PlutoPress
www.plutobooks.com

First published 2013 by Pluto Press
345 Archway Road, London N6 5AA

www.plutobooks.com

Distributed in the United States of America exclusively by
Palgrave Macmillan, a division of St. Martin's Press LLC,
175 Fifth Avenue, New York, NY 10010

British Library Cataloguing in Publication Data
A catalogue record for this book is available from the British Library

ISBN   978 0 7453 2987 1   Hardback
ISBN   978 0 7453 2986 4   Paperback
ISBN   978 1 8496 4876 9   PDF eBook
ISBN   978 1 8496 4878 3   Kindle eBook
ISBN   978 1 8496 4877 6   EPUB eBook

Library of Congress Cataloging in Publication Data applied for

This book is printed on paper suitable for recycling and made from fully managed
and sustained forest sources. Logging, pulping and manufacturing processes are
expected to conform to the environmental standards of the country of origin.

10   9   8   7   6   5   4   3   2   1

Typeset from disk by Stanford DTP Services, Northampton, England
Simultaneously printed digitally by CPI Antony Rowe, Chippenham, UK and
Edwards Bros in the United States of America

Contents

Acknowledgements

For their continual encouragement and editorial advice I would like to give special thanks to Carol Morris, Dave Crook and David Castle.

I would also like to express my gratitude for the assistance of Jan Bostock, John Cartmell, John Cromby, Clive Chimonides, Bob Diamond, William Epstein, Val Gillies, Dave Harper, Carl Harris, Guy Holmes, Paul Kelly, Sue Mahoney, Barry McInnnes, Penny Priest, Kieran Lord, Zounish Rafique, David Smail, David Smith, Jan Soffe-Casswell, Biza Stenfert Kroese, Fran Taylor, Mike Tupling and Fran Walsh.

Finally, I must gratefully acknowledge the help of a grant from the British Society of Authors.

Dedicated to the memories of Mark Rapley,
and of my grandmother, Gladys, and of my father, Roy

Introduction:
The Light at the End of the Tunnel?

The sense of control, hopefulness, and comfort [is] common to many forms of psychotherapy ... Through the adoption of a set of organizing principles or a coherent world-view, the patient comes to see a 'light at the end of the tunnel'.

R.J. De Rubeis and colleagues[1]

Therapeutic assumptions and jargon have spread into our lives – from school to university to workplace, from the health advice clinic to the prison, and to popular entertainment programmes where experts advise lonely people how to attract a partner, or parents how to be better ones. These specialists seek to persuade us that our troubles stem, not from the world in which we live, but from our lack of insight into ourselves and from our failure to take responsibility for what we think, feel and do. All might be well if their ideas were better grounded in science than their forerunners from even 50 years ago. The main task of this book is to show that this is not the case.

In the western world, treatments for the mad, the disturbed and the undesirable have been in continual flux down the centuries, and perhaps most rapidly in the last two. At the beginning of the second millennium, the majority of mental health professionals are acquainted only with the more recent treatments, or with as much of them as are deemed relevant to their occupational niche. They have little time or incentive to question the scientific – much less philosophical – basis of what they are doing. A historical view, however, soon shows that it has always been a mixture of fashion, political upheaval, institutional demands, and competition between rival professions and interest groups that have shaped how misery and madness have been treated, and regarded. Science, understood as the attempt to learn from systematic observation, has come a very long way behind. Insights such as these are perhaps the hardest to grasp. After all, psychologists and therapists are trained and accredited by prestigious universities and colleges, they are relatively well paid and they write books and speak confidently of their theories and techniques. As often as not, they try to pass this ebullience on to their clients. When it comes to trying to glimpse the emptiness at the heart of the therapy industry, however, the importance of a questioning, historical outlook cannot be overstated. The first chapter of this book – 'Misery, Mind Cures and Fashion' – accordingly tries to give a brief, critical overview of some of the main currents in psychiatry and psychotherapy since the late nineteenth century, leading on to an evaluation of the status of these fields in the twenty-first.

Despite the popularity of therapy, it is psychiatry that remains the most powerful mental health profession, the older and wealthier sibling against which all of the others must measure themselves – whether in envy, admiration, or contention. But as Chapter 2 shows, the psychiatric map of the disturbed mind – as little more than the by-product of faulty genes and of wayward biochemistry – is itself a distortion, brought about by the overweening confidence of its creators, and by the power that they enjoy in prescribing drugs for the treatment (more often the management) of distress. There is nothing like tablets and injections for conferring a spurious reality to the 'mental illnesses' that they are ostensibly designed to tackle. If the science of psychiatry is shaky, then this has not stopped hordes of its practitioners, with a few psychologists for company, from stepping forward to create new forms of deviance. For the shy and the socially awkward, for the restless and the disruptive, or for those who are merely 'odd' – a host of stigmatising diagnostic labels await. The consequences are far reaching. Outside of the Shangri-La world of media celebrity, social tolerance for eccentricity is narrowing.

If psychiatrists have fostered an impoverished and one-dimensional view of the patient, then have the talking therapists done any better? Some of these practitioners at least have seen the richness and uniqueness of the sufferer's subjective experience, and how it echoes what their world has done to them. Too many of them, however, have assumed that, given the right therapeutic advice and techniques, their clients will be able to muster wide powers of determination, unlocking what amounts to their own 'inner CEO', who will take charge of their troubles. When contrasted with what 50 years of laboratory and social research have been suggesting about the limits to human self-awareness and freedom, however, this picture starts to look as myopic as its psychiatric counterpart. In 1959, the sociologist C. Wright Mills described the gap between what people say and what they actually do as *the* central problem of the social sciences.[2] These words remain true today. For the therapists, there is room for a lot more humility in their claims to understand, cure and console.

Indeed, this boils down to a fundamental issue of the value of what therapists do, a subject about which they have long been defensive, and cannot answer a deceptively simple question: *does therapy work?* Despite many years of research into the effects of psychological treatment, the standards of investigation are still so poor that it is hard to say with confidence just how helpful or unhelpful therapy might be. This conclusion applies even to the evidence quoted in such authoritative tones in the UK central government's National Institute of Clinical Excellence (NICE) database and to the clinical guidelines issued by the American National Institute of Mental Health. Careful scrutiny of even the best of the research literature suggests that, because of the powerful placebo effects involved in this kind of treatment, and the historical failure of most researchers to adequately control for them, then all of the main psychological therapies are of marginal helpfulness at best, and are probably ineffective.

The practices and prescriptions of modern-day psychologists may be much closer than believed to the nostrums of the medical profession before the modern era: a time when a soothing touch counted most, when patients often had strong views about the correct dose of laudanum for their illnesses, and when he or she who paid the piper called the tune. The main difference between current psychological practice and nineteenth-century medicine is that Victorian doctors would frankly acknowledge the uselessness of most of their remedies, at least in private. Their patients knew that health was precarious and life often short, and they seldom expected great results.[3]

If the psychological therapies do not do what they are supposed to do, then it is worth asking why. After all, most of them amount to distillations of our common-sense notions of how people change any aspect of their conduct, by making a decision to act differently, and then sticking with it. One reason might be that many of us are locked in tough or demoralising circumstances that do not admit of change, despite what our therapist tells us. Another reason, complementary to the first, might be that some of us have been seriously mistreated by other people earlier on in our lives, and, at the level of unvoiced feelings, can no more forget this than we can forget to speak our native tongue. The distressed person therefore is not so much ill as hurt by what others have done to or withheld from them. Some of the ways in which this might happen are explored in Chapter 5, which draws upon a long tradition of research into the likely social causes of misery and of madness.

Rather than acknowledging the power of the distressed person's situation in their ills, and much less seeking to change it, the talking therapists have focused mainly upon adjusting people to their circumstances. Their ideas and methods, or 'technologies of the self',[4] have come to seem natural and useful, but in this aim of control, their ambitions are not so different from those of the psychiatrists. They are offering a more palatable or even seductive medicine, but medicine just the same. Chapter 6 examines both the diffusion of therapeutic thinking into western society and some of the unhelpful consequences for how we see ourselves and our struggles, taking a critical look at a range of fields, including education, refugee management, offender rehabilitation, and the promotion of health and well-being.

At root, the justification for most of these applications of talking treatment is economic. Perhaps the biggest and boldest example of this kind of thinking is the UK government's 'Improving Access to Psychological Therapies' (or IAPT) project. Designed to bring psychological therapy on demand to almost anyone who wants it, IAPT was also conceived with the larger ambition of improving the happiness of the general population and of taking the long-term depressed and anxious off the sickness benefit rosters, and back into paid employment: the assumption being that therapy, and then work, will make them free. However, as Chapter 7 shows, this scheme is deeply flawed in its conception and execution, not least in its naïve embrace of cognitive behavioural therapy (CBT) as the answer, not just to the psychologists' prayers, but to everyone else's.

Indeed, the IAPT scheme came about, in part, because it was proposed by the members of a metropolitan elite, who had the ear of government. As in any other industry, talking therapists find themselves in a marketplace, where they must set out their stall and continually upgrade and distinguish their services and products. In this marketplace, they must also maintain their appeal to the government agencies and individuals who purchase their services, as Chapter 8 illustrates, in its discussion of the latest fads, including 'happiness psychology' imported from the United States, and mindfulness practices – borrowed, with unseemly haste – from South East Asian religious traditions, and especially from Mahayana Buddhism.

For anyone who might have hoped that the therapy professions are all about scrupulous science and good faith, then the picture built up so far cannot be an encouraging one. Nevertheless, some practitioners have been unable to ignore the huge gap between what the theories say should be happening, and what both their clinical experience and their knowledge of the wider field of social science is telling them. In their different ways, these writers point to what might be called an alternative approach, long ignored by the therapy industry, an approach that takes account of both the weight of the world upon people's lives, and the limits of what can be achieved through therapeutic (or any other kind) of talk. Not all of these thinkers would see themselves as dissidents, nor are they all in full mutual agreement. However, their work shares enough common ground to stake the outlines of what is arguably a more scientific psychology. One that avoids the serious mistake of treating the mind as a disembodied will, or as an information processor, and which gives instead a central role to the feelings that entangle us, inextricably, with our surroundings.

And for many people – perhaps most – this world has recently become a colder and more uncertain place. A series of stock market failures have caused huge economic and social disruption throughout large parts of the globe, including many so-called 'developed' nations that not long ago looked secure and prosperous. On both sides of the Atlantic, the super-rich are gaining and flaunting fortunes on a scale not seen since the days of the British Empire, while social inequality of all kinds has been on the increase. At the end of the first decade of the new century, in the United States, one in seven households lacked secure supplies of food,[5] and astonishingly, close to one in four American children lived in them.[6] In Britain, at least a quarter of all children remained below the poverty line. Some of the poor were working, but mainly in exploitative low-wage conditions and with little chance of moving upward into a better way of life. Hairdressing was the fastest growing British job of the 1990s, and in the early twenty-first century, the share of the UK population working as domestic servants is the same as in the nineteenth. For many, the prospects of falling into personal poverty or chronic debt are more plausible and more to be feared than they were a generation ago.[7]

In circumstances like these, when governments are keen to offer us therapy and to lecture us about how to attain 'happiness', then we surely need to be more sceptical, and to start looking elsewhere for answers to our most urgent problems. As far as the science and practice of talking treatment are concerned, a fundamental rethink of the whole field is required. This is important, because the therapy industry sells us illusions about our ability to better our lives through individual effort. These illusions fit rather conveniently with the neoliberal strictures of working life and consumption, by which we are assessed, and ever more so, on our willingness to embrace change and our adaptability for personal makeover – and psychological therapy is the internal makeover, par excellence.

As a global civilisation, the prospects for survival into the following century do not look good. Rather than comforting illusions, we need as much clear thinking as we can muster. This Introduction began with a brief statement of the therapist's credo: the need to make sure that the client stays optimistic about their progress, with the hope of improvement conceived as the alluring glow at the end of our collective tunnel. If we continue to listen to the false promises of the therapy industry, and, even more, of the political interests that it too often (if inadvertently) represents, then the glimmer at the end of our collective tunnel might turn out to be the light – not of salvation – but of an oncoming train.[8]

Part I

Evaluating Psychological Techniques

1
Misery, Mind Cures and Fashion

So persuasive is the power of the institutions that we have created that they shape not only our preferences, but our sense of possibilities.

Ivan Illich[1]

At the start of the eighteenth century, if you raged at voices that no one else could hear, saw things that nobody else could see, especially if you annoyed or frightened other people at the same time, then your sufferings could be construed as demonic possession, brain fever, or as the just deserts for your moral backsliding. You might find yourself detained in the public madhouse, regarded as not far above a wild animal. You would most likely be tamed and managed with varying degrees of harshness or, if you were luckier, with the stern compassion of the philanthropist.

As the Enlightenment gathered pace, medical explanations of madness began to compete with supernatural ones, and fee-paying asylums were built across the land in out-of-the-way places. Some of these institutions were little better than the warehouses for the 'feeble minded' that went before. Others aimed to restore sanity with a mixture of crafts and manual labour, fresh country air, communal living, personal cleanliness and Christian instruction. This regime came to be known as 'moral management', its architects mainly laymen – and very often Quakers. The profits were not as high as for other industries but they could be substantial. By the mid-nineteenth century, the moral managers found themselves in competition with the alienists or 'mad doctors', medical men who saw madness as the outward sign of tainted hereditary, or of degenerate habits. They asserted solid scientific knowledge and expertise in the treatment of the brain, and believed that gathering the afflicted together under one roof would lead to a new understanding of insanity and to its eventual cure.[2] These claims to a unique scientific insight into madness were questionable, even by the lights of mid-nineteenth-century medicine. Lay observers had argued for a hidden logic behind the delusions of 'madness', as, for example, fantasies that grew from excessive passions or that served to deny the humiliation and disappointment that blighted some peoples' lives.[3] In the end, however, none of these arguments mattered, because the alienists could back their claims with the professional status of medicine and a Royal Charter. They fast succeeded in ousting the moral managers and their well-intentioned amateurism.[4]

Asylums also served a larger purpose within the new industrial order. In the new factories and workshops, there was a growing need for docile and dependable workers, prepared to turn up on time and do as they were told. For the labouring classes, the uncertainties and brutalities of rural life had at least been familiar ones, but the new urban existence imposed a unique blend of rootlessness and anonymity. As the smoky, warren-like cities and towns grew, so the poorest districts became packed with factory labourers. These were places of sprawl, overcrowding, noise and filth. The products of the Industrial Revolution included hundreds of thousands of disturbed people, as well as millions of tons of cotton and steel. The asylums joined with the prisons and workhouses to make a great system that ensnared the feckless and the indigent and that, without any deliberate intent, none the less served as a warning to anyone tempted to stray from their daily drudgery. At the close of the eighteenth century, there were only around 40 asylums in England and Wales; 60 years later, there were over 400, most of them crammed with the urban poor.[5]

Outside of the asylum walls, the Victorian middle classes suffered mental ailments of their own. In Europe and North America, many middle-class women were prone to insomnia, sleeplessness, fatigue, phobias and more rarely (but spectacularly) to trance-like states and to flights of ecstasy or paralysis that had no physical explanation. These disturbances had long been ascribed to the mobile female womb. But this account of 'hysteria' had fallen out of favour by the 1870s, because it could not be squared with the new anatomical and functional knowledge of the nervous system. Widely viewed instead as signs of the obvious weakness of the female sex and of their overwrought nerves, these 'symptoms' can be more accurately seen as an unconscious rebellion against the gilded cage of respectable middle-class femininity. Clinical treatments – which at their most extreme included barbaric genital surgery or enforced confinement – were in truth an effective means for keeping women in their place.[6] It was not that men lacked 'neurotic tendencies'. Rather, the bewhiskered elders of the medical community had long ignored, downplayed, or misdiagnosed the emotional torment that they sometimes saw in their male patients. The economic and political rise of the middle classes (and of the white man's claim to racial and cultural superiority in the age of empire) had been founded upon a singular vision of strong, self-possessed and rational manhood: not to be undermined by medical recognition of 'rampant neurotic weakness in the male sex'.[7]

Nevertheless, by the closing decades of the nineteenth century, it became harder to deny that a great number of men were also suffering from psychological problems, largely in the guise of irritability, anxiety and lassitude that could echo the recalcitrant mental and physical exhaustion – or chronic fatigue syndrome – that is a familiar (and controversial) diagnosis, in the early twenty-first century. Once again, no biological cause was apparent, but this did not prevent these symptoms from quickly coming to be seen as the condition of 'neurasthenia', as formulated by the Manhattan physician George Miller Beard.[8] The demands of modern civilization, Beard declared, especially the pressures of commercial leadership and intellectual work, were straining the nerve fibres of businessmen, administrators, academics, bookkeepers, solicitors and the like. Neurasthenia became a popular diagnosis because it enabled the growing number of male 'hysterics' to be viewed in a dignified and even heroic light, the casualties of their own success as striving go-getters in the world of corporate enterprise. None of this prevented their wives and daughters eventually being diagnosed with it too, notwithstanding the huge overlap between the symptoms of this condition and those of hysteria. It was certainly in the interests of neurologists, psychiatrists and even religious and ethical thinkers to promote this catch-all illness – because it endorsed their authority and expertise, and gave the last two groups an up-to-date language in which to talk about the evils of the modern age.[9]

Meanwhile, the sufferer might receive a cornucopia of treatments – from hypnosis, and moral instruction to physical therapies, including massage, bathing, rest cures and 'galvanic stimulation' – but one treatment that grew in popularity was psychoanalysis. As a set of theories and techniques, it chimed with the risqué conviction of the educated classes that sexual repression contributed to mental disorder. Psychoanalysis offered an altogether more intriguing and dramatic take upon personal troubles, and had the added benefits of absorbing every symptom of neurasthenia into its own landscape – under the heading of 'neurosis'.[10] Above all, psychoanalysis purported to offer a cure for hysteria, as illustrated by the dramatic account by Freud and his colleague Josef Breuer, of Breuer's work with the patient that they named 'Anna O' (real name: Bertha

Pappenheim), an account that subsequent scholarship has shown to be entirely mythical. Pappenheim in fact remained so disturbed after seeing Breuer that she had to be quickly re-institutionalised into a Swiss sanitarium, the first of several such episodes, and she continued to experience her symptoms for years afterwards.[11]

Originally a doctor and a neurologist by training, the young Freud turned his attention to the causes of mental illness, especially the hysterical paralyses that were afflicting middle-class women in mid-nineteenth-century Vienna and throughout Europe and the United States. Freud made himself an understudy of the French physician Charcot at the Saltpêtrière Institute in Paris, where this charismatic teacher used hypnotism to restore seemingly paralysed patients back to normality. Charcot suspected that sexual and emotional tensions underlay many of these illnesses. Back in Vienna, Freud had experimented with cocaine and even nasal surgery as potential cures for mental disturbance, but under Charcot he became increasingly interested in the idea that the surface symptoms of mental illness might be the patient's way of concealing unconscious desires and conflicts from themselves as much as from everyone else.[12] Drawing upon clinical observation and the idea of developmental stages from embryology, he began to formulate his famous tripartite theory of the mind – divided into the super-ego, the ego and the id; this scheme has been colourfully, if irreverently, described as a dark cellar, in which a well-bred spinster and a sex-crazed monkey grapple in combat, refereed by a nervous bank clerk.[13]

Freud's favoured treatment method required the patient or analysand to express whatever came into their head. This technique of 'free association' often required them to lie down on a couch, although things were not always this formal and Freud sometimes analysed people while they were seated, or even while they were walking with him through the Austrian countryside, in the case of his disciple, Ferenczi.[14] Wherever the analysis took place, the task of the analyst was to decode the client's uncensored utterances for the hidden symbols that offered clues to their unconscious conflicts. The resulting dose of truth would banish the need for further painful repression and evasion, or neurotic misery, leaving the analysand free to get on with a life of 'ordinary unhappiness'. Freud always claimed that these analytic skills were arcane and self-taught in the unique instance of their author, but otherwise to be mastered by undergoing an expensive course of analysis once or more a week, for several years and beyond. This, combined with Freud's initial insistence that each analyst be a medical doctor (a view that he relaxed somewhat in his later years), ensured that the whole world of analytic training and practice was available only to the wealthiest of individuals. Freud proffered psychoanalysis as an experimental and investigative procedure, a route to self-knowledge and control more than a cure for misery.[15] However, this did not prevent him from crediting himself as the cause of sudden improvements in the condition of his patients, should they occur, or from eschewing the benefits that came with psychoanalysis being perceived as a branch of medicine.

The popularity of psychoanalysis helped to dispel the idea of neurasthenia as a literal form of wear-and-tear upon the hardware of the brain, and it cast a similar question mark over hereditarian views of mental illness, displacing them with an entirely functional view of disturbance, as a breakdown in mental organisation. Less well remarked upon was psychoanalysis's penchant for directing attention away from the world that gave rise to personal ills, in favour of a journey into the inward depths of the psyche.

The First World War and its aftermath contributed to these changing views of emotional illness. This conflict was unusual for the huge numbers of psychological casualties, and for the officer class being among those who suffered the highest rates of breakdown. It would have been unthinkable to blame these ills upon the inherited weaknesses of these elite men, and in search of a convincing explanation, psychiatrists were forced to look to the horrors of trench warfare.[16] Electric shock treatment had been tried on some of these hapless casualties, but to little effect, other than as perceived punishment. The ideas of Freud suggested new and seemingly more humane remedies, including psychoanalytic therapy for shell-shock victims, pioneered by psychiatrists like A.J. Brock and W.H. Rivers, at Craiglockhart War Hospital for Officers, in what is now a suburb of Edinburgh.[17]

In the interwar years, the Freudian doctrine was disseminated and developed by his followers, who split into numerous warring schools, almost every one of them declared apostate by the master. These have been given the generic term 'psychodynamic' psycho-therapies. Famously, the Swiss analyst Carl Jung rejected Freud's atheism, and his view that neurosis was the result of sexual repression or trauma. In a more humanistic vein, Jung saw the search for personal wholeness and integrity – or 'individuation' – as the key to most psychological distress. He thereby added a focus on spirituality into a psychoanalytic practice that pointed toward the wisdom and healing power of the collective unconscious. This was the repository of all of the mythological symbols and yearnings of humankind and of the 'archetypes' – recurrent images and themes that surfaced in dreams and visions and that, according to Jung, addressed the clients' dilemmas. The archetypes had power to restore lost meaning and vitality, if only the client would heed their advice. Jung's interest in non-western cultures and in arcane subjects like alchemy have given his ideas an enduring appeal to New Age thinkers in the twenty-first century, notwithstanding his fondness for seeing Africans and other non-white 'races' as essentially childlike, and his publicly pronounced views on Jewish mental and emotional life during the 1930s, which sometimes veered rather too close to those of the Nazi regime.[18]

It is often said that wars lead to cultural and social innovation, and so it has proved with the talking treatments. The large numbers of casualties from the Second World War gave birth to group psychoanalytic therapy, the more economical batch treatment of several soldiers at once, pioneered at institutions like the Northfield Hospital in Birmingham, and Mill Hill, in London.[19] Freudian-inspired treatments spread into the fields of child and family guidance at a slow and piecemeal rate in the years between the wars; but more swiftly in the decades after the Second World War, as welfare states established themselves throughout western Europe, and American insurance-based health care turned toward outpatient treatment for disturbed or unruly children.[20] The object relations school of analysis, developed by British practitioners such as Melanie Klein and Ronald Fairbairn, was well suited to these changes, because it held that cure could be achieved through building good relations with others (with what Freud had termed the 'objects' of unconscious desires) rather than via the management of internal drives. This outlook chimed well with growing scientific curiosity about infant development, as the foundation for adult personality and well-being. Exponents like Donald Winnicott and John Bowlby emphasised the importance of the environments in which children are reared, the emotional unity of mother and child, and the need for consistent care and nurture, themes that did not appear much in Freud's account. Both of these clinicians advised the British government about the potentially harmful effects of the separation of evacuated children from their mothers; their concerns echoing contemporary male anxieties that women, who had run the factories during the war, should now be returning back to the home, where they supposedly belonged. This emphasis on the importance of maintaining 'secure emotional attachments' has found its way into many strands of current psychodynamic treatment, where the therapist strives to provide a place of safety, a 'secure base', in which the client can express and come to terms with their deepest fears, and perhaps mend their latent capacities for emotional attachment and trust, that had been frayed or broken in their formative years. This concern with emotional protection can extend to the minutiae of therapy, including the requirement that the client and therapist always meet in the same room and at the same hour.[21]

By contrast, American psychoanalytic psychology – largely the product of the diaspora of central European analysts before the Second World War – retained the traditional Freudian focus upon the enclosed world of the individual psyche. In this 'Ego psychology', the task of therapy was to help the individual to adjust better to prevailing social conditions via the strengthening of the super-ego, in essence, through the application of will power. Though psychodynamic therapy in the United States fell into decline from the early 1970s,[22] this belief in the apparent desirability and ease of self-transformation has diffused into a wide range of other therapies in the US, and beyond.

This spread of psychological thinking and techniques ensured that, by the 1950s, neurosis came to be diagnosed across all levels of society, tightening its grip upon the popular and professional imagination.[23] (The language of neurasthenia or of 'weakened nerves' lingered on in the popular culture of the West: in films, novels and commercial 'nerve tonic' remedies, only to re-emerge in late twentieth-century maladies such as 'stress', 'burn-out' and 'Chronic Fatigue Syndrome'.) The idea of neurosis permitted a wide range of feelings, emotions and conduct to be corralled under the rubric of a single illness that everyone felt they could recognise. More tellingly, it fixed happiness, contentment and optimism as standards to which all should aspire, just as it transmuted sadness and discontent from the ordinary elements of human life into forms of sickness such as 'depression', in need of professional ministration. This duty to stay well had never been entirely a matter for the doctors. For the two thousand years since Hippocrates and Galen,[24] adequate rest, regular and sufficient diet, exercise, and the avoidance of worry were seen as the prerequisites of a healthy body and mind. What was new was the requirement that each citizen be willing to seek out and follow the advice of the experts, on the basis of each having some form of mental vulnerability or disorder – whether actual, or latent.

Meanwhile, the asylums continued to deal with the most downtrodden and disturbed; their stock in trade consisting of the psychotic, the elderly and the intellectually impaired, as well as refractory youth, the sexually deviant and the destitute. Across the world, new experimental 'treatments' were tried out, most often for the putative disease of schizophrenia: for example, insulin coma therapy, ECT and lobotomy. The doctors told themselves that their patients were usually improved, if not cured.[25] The personal consequences of these new and drastic treatments were often terrible indeed.

The late 1950s and early 1960s saw early moves toward community care – a small trickle of patients leaving the asylums that was to become a flood in the last quarter of the century. These events are often attributed to the introduction of new classes of psychiatric drugs –the so-called major tranquillisers, which supposedly made room for a life beyond the asylum grounds, without need of straitjackets and padded cells. In hindsight, however, the community care movement had more to do with a gathering scepticism about the benefits of institutions, coupled with a rising belief in the importance of maximum personal choice and freedom. Across a 20-year period starting from 1960, it became acceptable to blame society for every type of difficulty, including mental illness. The briefly fashionable theories of the psychiatrist R.D. Laing and of the behaviourist psychologists such as B.F. Skinner were in tune with widespread questioning of the political establishment and its grip upon the lives of ordinary people, especially amongst the young. When combined with the critiques of the civil liberties lobby and of the opponents of institutional care, a new window was created through which madness could be viewed, not as a permanent and bizarre affliction, but as an understandable response to a disordered world.

From this new vista, the opening up of the asylums seemed natural and inevitable, although not everyone was so idealistic. There is little doubt that many of the politicians who endorsed 'care in the community' did so because it offered a cheaper alternative to the labour-intensive warehousing of the insane. Nevertheless, the overall outcome was clear, organic notions of serious mental illness were increasingly questioned and biomedical psychiatry, regnant since the nineteenth century, was suddenly on the defensive.

In parallel with these changes, the 1960s also witnessed the continued expansion of psychoanalytic and other therapies in Europe and the United States, in the spheres of mental health care and education and guidance. Social workers and probation officers could describe themselves as applied psychoanalysts.[26] It was in this period that clinical psychologists, originally based in the big hospitals, started to move out into health centres and other community venues, to offer treatment to people suffering from anxiety, phobias and low mood.

Clinical psychologists differ from psychiatrists in that they have not usually studied medicine, though before their training some of them may have worked in other health care professions, and all of them possess undergraduate and postgraduate degrees in psychology. In the UK, clinical psychology has always been closely linked with the National Health Service and dates almost from its inception, when an alliance between academic psychologists interested in the treatment of neurosis and leading psychiatrists, in search of competent technicians to develop and administer diagnostic and mental tests that might help to legitimate their work, led to the creation of the first training course in this subject: at the Maudsley Hospital, under the guidance of Hans Eysenck. Both of these disciplines came to share a preference for the classification and measurement of human behaviour, for viewing mental disorder as saying more about the afflicted individual than about their situation, and distaste for what many saw as woolly psychoanalytic thinking.[27]

These similarities were most obvious when, in the 1950s, the psychologists, still based in the hospital clinics, began to create therapies that derived from the work of theorists such as Ivan Pavlov, a Russian physiologist and B.F. Skinner, an American psychologist who endeavoured to develop a scientific approach to the study of human behaviour. For these practitioners, the study and analysis of thoughts and feelings was unscientific, because they could not be directly observed.[28] In line with scientific materialist doctrines, the behavioural psychologists, as they called themselves, saw consciousness as an epiphenomenon or by-product of the workings of the brain, rather like the exhaust gas from a combustion engine. The emphasis in behaviour therapy was and is upon the measurement and treatment of observable problem behaviours or habits, such as compulsive hand-washing, or the extreme and 'irrational' fears which are often called phobias, all of which are held to be modifiable via the manipulation of their consequences, including the way that the afflicted person responds to their own anguish. Gradual exposure to the frightening situation coupled simultaneously with an effort to relax are the bread-and-butter of this approach – reflecting an ancient teaching that fears are best dealt with not through avoidance, but through confrontation.

Behavioural cures were fashioned in response to two perceived shortcomings of Freudian therapy: the lack of proof for its dynamic map of the mind, which had always been much more visible to convinced analysts and their patients than to sceptics; and the poor evidence for the effectiveness of analytic techniques. By contrast, behaviour therapy was seen as more scientific, because it followed from academic learning theory, rooted in experimental psychology, that is, the study of dogs, rats and pigeons and their responses to rewards and punishments offered in university labs. Behavioural healing also had a further advantage, for some, in its mechanistic view of the human organism – no need to mess about with nebulous things like feelings or hopes – and it seemed to make clear predictions about treatment outcome. It was also more amenable to testing by clinical trial, something that would become more important as the decades went by.

For the psychologists themselves, the behavioural remedies continued to offer a niche in which they could work alongside the psychiatric profession, and from which they could later challenge its dominance in the treatment of mental illness. These treatments flourished in the public health services, especially in relation to people with learning disabilities and those who could not afford to pay for psychoanalysis or other kinds of more labour-intensive talking therapy.[29]

But not all clinical psychologists were enthusiasts. Some, for instance, helped to establish the publicly funded Tavistock Clinic, a kind of national R&D centre for psychoanalytic ideas and their application to education, organisational management and child guidance. Others joined their psychiatrist colleagues in the pioneering of 'therapeutic communities', in which patients were given more say over the ward regime and were encouraged to work together in trying to understand and confront their individual psychological problems.[30] These communities were the forerunners of more radical experiments in rehabilitation that challenged the notion of mental illness, founded by psychiatrists such as R.D. Laing and his associates, at Kingsley Hall in London.

Perhaps the biggest change for the profession happened in the late 1960s, when it began to move out of the hospital and into community-based clinics, GP practices and adult learning disability services. From these new bridgeheads, the clinical psychologists declared themselves able to tackle a wide span of psychological problems for an expanded range of people, eventually including individuals diagnosed with what are usually seen as more severe and enduring problems such as schizophrenia, or personality disorder. These clinicians extended their repertoire of treatments to match demand, a story that continues to the present day, where they are involved in teaching, research and consultation. In the US and Europe, clinical psychologists work in an ever-expanding array of settings – including private hospitals, schools, businesses and non-profit agencies. In the UK, they are not licensed to prescribe psychiatric drugs, though some American clinicians can do so, pursuant upon an elective postgraduate training. In short, clinical psychologists offer talk rather than pills.

This post-war period also witnessed the flowering of the profession – or craft, as some would have it – of counselling. At the start, this was an offshoot of American clinical psychology where, in the 1940s, Carl Rogers had found that, rather than deep interpretation, a mixture of therapist warmth and concern seemed enough to help restore distressed people back to health.

Person-centred therapy emerged as part of what became known as the 'third force' in psychotherapy – a reaction to what many took to be the machine-like view of human beings, as passively determined, and in need of expert reprogramming, that underpinned both psychoanalysis and behaviourism. What was needed – or so it was argued – was an approach that acknowledged the essential freedom, emotional richness and potential of the fully self-directing human being. The humanist approach thus concentrated upon attaining health more than curing sickness.

The story of person-centred therapy also had a lot to do with the politics of the therapy world. Rogers had started out by applying psychoanalytic methods to his patients, only to become disenchanted with the length and stilted nature of the procedure. His own clinical experience had taught him that patients responded best to a warm, informal manner, in which the therapist sought to help the client to reflect upon their own thoughts and feelings as they expressed them, and with a minimum of interpretation or analysis by the therapist. He came to think that unhappiness had less to do with repression than with the lack of fit between each individual's own needs and values and the life that they were outwardly living. If so, then the client as much as the therapist was likely to be the expert in these matters: a radical departure, when contrasted with the behaviourist fascination with objective measurement of external actions on the one hand, and with psychoanalytic preoccupation with the unconscious, on the other.

All therapies must offer an account of how malaise comes about and Rogers held that our troubles begin when others require us to behave in artificial ways to gain respect or affection. We pay a high price for getting by in the world in this way. We lose much of our natural self-assurance, individuality and spontaneity. Rogers recommended that, as a first step toward healing, the therapist should provide the client with a safe and accepting relationship as an antidote to a constricted life. This relationship – based upon three core principles of the therapist providing unconditional positive regard (or warmth), empathy and genuineness – would encourage the client to acknowledge their feelings – thereby fostering their natural capacity for personal growth. The result: a more authentic and open-hearted individual, less prone to worrying how others might see them, and with an improved ability to solve problems and to live a more creative life into the bargain. So confident was Rogers that he proposed that political leaders should spend time in person-centred therapy groups as a means of tackling evils like the nuclear arms race, the Cold War, and the apartheid regime in South Africa. Rogerian therapy is certainly optimistic. Rogers' views have been modified by a minority of his later followers, who have taken pains to acknowledge the long-term damage to self-confidence that can result from the lifelong experience of emotional and physical abuse.[31] However, even these far-from-optimistic writers still retain their faith in the power of insight and therapist attention to heal the scars of deep-seated trauma and enable people to live in greater comfort, despite their socially noxious circumstances.

Together with the stripped-down and simplified Freudianism of the 'Self Psychologists', popular with urban and educated Americans, Rogers' ideas helped unleash a wave of counsellor schooling and employment that spread steadily across the western world in the following two decades, to culminate in an explosion in the field during the 1980s. Counselling came to be widely seen as *the* answer to almost every kind of personal and social problem: boredom, over-excitement, loneliness, low self-esteem, unattractiveness, rejection, workplace change and redundancy, marital infidelity or instability, divorce, addiction to alcohol and drugs (or exercise, shopping, sex, or pornography), educational failure, desire to change (or retain) one's sexual orientation, eating problems, disability, chronic disease and pain, assault and trauma (experienced directly or witnessed, even via watching TV news broadcasts), childlessness, parenthood, retirement, ageing, lack of interest in money, too much interest in money, youthful rebelliousness or conformity, bereavement, fear of death, or the desire to commit suicide. All of these and more have become targets for a talking treatment of one sort or another.

Throughout Western Europe and the USA, counsellors can be found in schools, colleges and universities and the personnel or 'human resources' departments of most large companies and government institutions. Counselling is certainly popular. In 2010, nearly one in five people in Britain were reported to have consulted a counsellor and almost half of the population to know someone who had done so.[32] At the time of writing, around half of all general medical practitioner surgeries in the UK employ one or more of these workers,[33] as do some NHS outpatient services and, increasingly, the Improving Access to Psychological Therapies (IAPT) scheme in England and Wales, a government-sponsored project intended to make psychological therapy available on demand to anyone who wants it. Enthusiasts see this growth as humanistic and medical advance. But there are also those who suggest that it can just as easily be seen as a shock absorber for social change, for the loneliness and loss of meaning that has gone with the decline of traditional religion and the shift to urban living.[34] The demand for counselling may also have something to do with the tightly rationed nature of general medicine, in which doctors have little time to listen to their patients' personal troubles.[35] A counsellor can hail from almost any academic and employment background, and will typically undertake professional accreditation (in the form of a diploma or postgraduate degree) in mid-life, as a 'second career'. The domain of the counsellor overlaps with that of the psychotherapist, whose practice is usually distinguished by its longer-term nature, by its focus upon the putative roots of current disturbance in early childhood, and by a greater accent upon academic credentials: many psychotherapists hold medical or other postgraduate degrees.

Another significant development has been the growth of Counselling Psychology in the US from the 1970s, and in Britain from the 1990s. As their name suggests, counselling psychologists claim special skills in building up warm and healing relationships with their clients, coupled to a scientific training through having a psychology degree. By tradition, counselling psychologists work with people suffering the milder anxieties and worries of ordinary life – as encountered in the fields of careers guidance, university student and couples counselling, for instance. With the overturning of traditional skills hierarchies in the British NHS,[36] and with the advent of doctoral level training in both Britain and the United States, counselling psychologists increasingly work in the same services as their clinical colleagues, and are claiming a similar range of expertise.

With some important exceptions (to be discussed below), few modern-day analysts, psychotherapists, or counsellors are so ingenuous as to talk about the 'cure' of their patients. They do, however, claim that the insights that therapy offers into our obscure motives and feelings will enable us to live more peaceably with ourselves, and to find more acceptable ways of meeting our otherwise hidden needs and motives: a cure by any other name.

Despite these gains for the talking therapy professions, biological psychiatry returned with redoubled force in the closing decades of the twentieth century. In part, this was because of the success of the previous criticisms of the 'anti-psychiatrists' like R.D. Laing and his supporters, who demanded a broader, interdisciplinary approach to mental health treatment and care. One unforeseen consequence was the creation of a conduit through which traditional psychiatry could make its return, in the guise of the biopsychosocial doctrine: the official rationale for almost every mental health service in the western world.[37] With what might be seen as stupefying obviousness, this principle holds that all cases of mental disturbance entail biological, psychological and social elements, both as causes and as consequences. In practice, many psychiatrists cleave as tightly as ever to the biomedical strand of this 'model' and view the other elements as also-rans, an attitude that undoubtedly helps to maintain their status as medical doctors, something that their peers in other fields of medicine have historically been loath to concede.[38] However, this narrow focus upon the faulty nervous system or mind of the individual sufferer is not confined to mental health professionals. For the last 30 years, it has captured the thinking and outlook of academic researchers, many of them having learned to avoid social perspectives on mental illness where once they would have embraced them. From the time of President Reagan and the 'decade of the brain' that followed, research grants for the study of the social causes (and remedies) of distress have been harder to come by and researchers have followed the money, in search of the answers afforded by biochemistry and brain scans.

Yet the rebirth of biomedical psychiatry has done little to halt the advance of the talking therapies that, if sheer variety means anything, are flourishing – with more than four hundred kinds at the start of the twenty-first century.[39] Even so, one type needs special mention: Cognitive Behavioural Therapy or 'CBT' – the practitioners of which claim to ameliorate mental disturbance in a precisely calibrated manner, just like any other medical remedy. CBT therapists attend upon people who have a wide range of diagnoses and this school is the market leader in most public health services today.

CBT was developed from the integration of behaviour therapy and cognitive therapy. In the long run, evaluations and case reports were unable to show that behavioural treatment could live up to all of the claims of its progenitors. By the late 1960s, even the supporters of behaviour therapy were beginning to acknowledge that it was not quite as effective as they had hoped. Patients did not always conform to the expectations of academic learning theory. Sometimes, they appeared to improve too quickly, before their new conditioning might have been supposed to have taken hold, or too slowly, implying that their distress was not amenable to straight-forward, mechanical procedures that worked well enough for dogs and pigeons, trapped in laboratory environments over which the researchers had complete rule. Patients' symptoms could fluctuate in strength or change unpredictably, while their beliefs and expectations seemed to have a bearing on treatment outcome, or at least upon the self-reported measurements by which it was evaluated.[40]

Finally, the behavioural approach proved unable to win the universal approval of its recipients and practitioners, many of whom came to view it as too mechanistic. Worse still, it denied the reality and value of subjective human experiences such as beliefs, memories and feelings, all of which were increasingly seen as both the essence of unhappiness and – in so far as therapists could claim to manipulate them directly – as central to its cure.[41]

The behavioural therapies – with their penchant for control over conversation – had always been the lot of the poor and the powerless, just as a wealthier clientele had chosen the more sophisticated treatments: a distinction upheld in the twenty-first century. With the rise of humanist therapy, many clients came to dislike what they saw as coldly impersonal treatments with little room for feelings and thoughts.[42] The ascent and triumph of cognitive psychology in the academic world also contributed to the sudden tarnishing of behaviourist ideas. It represented a new programme designed to indirectly (but objectively) map the hidden patterns of human thinking, memory and learning through careful measurement of the responses of individuals – usually undergraduate students – in carefully arranged experiments. The advantage lay in the objective recording of how long it took someone to recall a piece of information, to parse a sentence or to solve a particular type of problem, for example, and to thereby have some confidence about the outlines of how humans can think and make sense of the world around them, at least in the psychology labs. And there lay the rub. If much of this research has been attacked for its tendency to treat people like electrons, and for its triviality and limited relevance to daily life,[43] then its apparent success owed something to the appeal of abstract theoretical (especially mathematical) models, which promised to bring psychology closer to the envied science of physics. Its buoyancy also owed something to covert US military funding for research into the human–machine interface from the Second World War, and onward, into the 'Strategic Defense Initiative' of the 1980s.[44] The new outlook was welcomed, too, because of its harmony with the latest impressive technology, in the shape of mainframe computers. Its proponents 'sang the mind electric' as they tried to make thoughts and purposeful actions (if not, at the time, feelings) into respectable science, in the guise of 'information', handled by the nervous system.[45] The cumulative weight of all of these trends helped open the door to what is widely seen as the second, or 'cognitive' wave of behavioural therapy, which came to be linked, especially, with the work of two American psychiatrists, Aaron Beck and Albert Ellis. Both had originally trained as Freudian analysts, but were impressed when many patients seemed to improve faster when advised to challenge their unhelpful beliefs (though Beck had placed more emphasis upon the additional use of practical confidence-building exercises). From the outset, cognitive therapy was nothing if not practical, its aim to guide clients into developing more helpful or accurate ideas about themselves, their world and their future.[46]

Although the term 'CBT' was coined by Beck, it was popularised and the theory base expanded chiefly by clinical psychologists, faced with patients with complicated problems who seemed to respond best to a pragmatic mixture of therapeutic methods. The pressure of long waiting lists for therapy, combined with a respect for the scientific outlook of the behavioural tradition, encouraged these practitioners to take cognitive methods as a way of tackling the immediate symptoms of misery and to fuse them with behavioural techniques, designed to help patients to confront situations or tasks that they normally avoided. At the time, and ever since, few seem to have noticed the contradiction of blending a tradition that denied the potency of the mind with one that embraced it, as the fulcrum of happiness and distress.

Indeed, the 'cognitive' part of CBT is misleading. Neither Beck nor Ellis were influenced by contemporary 'cognitive science', but by ancient Stoic philosophy, as exemplified in the central tenet of this form of therapy, that 'there is nothing either good or bad, but thinking makes it so.'[47] This assumption is played out in the form of the Socratic dialogue, a systematic effort to help the client to identify and counteract their unhelpful ideas about themselves and their milieu, so as to make them feel better, as quickly as possible. The therapist works with the client to help them to set their own treatment goals and to guide and support the patient in attaining those goals. The supposition is that all of us are continually absorbing information about our environment and ourselves in a blend of perceptions, interpretations and recollections, and that these internal processes shape the way we think, feel and behave. A wide range of problems – from lingering misery to anxiety, panic, irrational fears (or phobias) and compulsive rituals – are all deemed to stem from our faulty and pessimistic thinking: about ourselves, others and the world around us.

In Beck's theory, early experience lays down the foundation for our thinking in the form of schemas – or general frameworks – that we use to understand the world. To the extent that we are usually unaware of them, these schemas represent a vestigial form of Freudian unconscious, and the biases in perception and judgement to which they give rise have more than a passing resemblance to the distortions and irrationalities of the unconscious mind, as identified by Freud. Once the schema is activated by an event, for instance – by a colleague's casual comment, that could be construed as a put-down – then it is said to give rise to negative automatic thoughts – such as 'I am a bad person', or 'nobody ever *really* likes me' – which then create emotional anguish, in turn leading to unhelpful conduct: in this example, perhaps ill-judged avoidance, or disproportionate anger.

The whole approach of CBT is geared toward giving the patient techniques that they can use to challenge false conclusions about themselves, leading to enhanced mood and more constructive actions. As a first step, the client may be asked to keep a thought record. This is a diary of their key impressions, ruminations and feelings, to be used as a basis for identifying underlying beliefs and then for collecting evidence for and against the latter, and with the ultimate goal of swapping them for more 'balanced' or 'realistic' appraisals. To this end, the client may be given homework assignments in which they might be required to tackle their negative thoughts directly, via affirmative (or 'realistic') self-talk, as well as indirectly, by placing themselves in situations that might refute their dark view of themselves – for example, by attending a party, and finding that, contrary to their pessimistic predictions, many guests are friendly and receptive.

CBT practitioners thus seek to modify thoughts, feelings, bodily states (such as fear versus calmness) and behaviours. In both practice and theory, however, it is the client's outlook that is viewed as fundamental to their ills, and to their cure.

For many clinicians and clients alike, CBT has a wide appeal, evident in its colonisation of almost every niche of professional counselling and guidance in the English-speaking world – from 'relationship work' to penal control. It is the therapy of choice for mental health workers and counsellors, health service managers, planners and trainers. There are many reasons for this success, including the large body of evidence accumulated in favour of this therapy (larger than for almost any other type), its skills-based and tactical nature, which lends it readily to standardised training manuals, and the wide range of techniques that can be chosen to suit each client and their problems. A further consideration is that CBT practitioners have been more willing than most of their competitors to view each client's distress in terms of a specific diagnosis or disorder, awaiting measurement by a rating scale designed for the purpose, such as, for example, the Beck Depression Inventory, or the 'BDI'. The approach therefore lends itself to quantification, making it attractive to health service managers, looking for treatments that reduce waiting lists, and can be equitably delivered with easily measured outcomes.[48] In Britain, CBT has become near-synonymous with the profession of clinical psychology, perhaps because it makes a good fit with the profession's preferred image of itself, as both applied scientist practitioner and service manager.[49]

Nevertheless, when you look close, it is hard to pin down just what exactly is 'CBT'. Currently, there are well over a dozen distinguishable varieties, committed to diverse portraits of the relationship between thought, feeling, behaviour and environment. Some practitioners acknowledge that CBT is not really a discrete single therapy, but a tool bag of ideas and techniques, some of them indistinguishable from something called 'interpersonal therapy', that is, from the provision of comfort, reflection and advice.[50] For some critics, the nebulous nature of CBT makes it closer to a tradition than to a scientifically coherent therapy.[51]

Few of these doubts have registered with the leading proponents of this therapy, who present their chosen method as the market leader in effectiveness, science and invention. CBT therapists have recently shown fresh enthusiasm for psychodynamic ideas about the importance of the transference of feelings between therapist and clients, and humanist ideas on the importance of therapist warmth, designed to deliver the techniques with greater acceptability and speed. The last decade has also seen efforts to weld cognitive and behavioural methods to the traditions of Buddhist meditation and of classical Stoicism. This constitutes the so-called 'third wave' of behavioural therapy, in which the emphasis has shifted away from the challenge of negative notions to one of acceptance and 'letting go'. New hybrid forms of treatment have thus emerged, under acronyms like 'MCBT', or 'Mindfulness-based Cognitive Behavioural Therapy'.[52]

As a symptom-focused treatment, CBT is well suited to the short-term regime which is all that most patients without private means can expect, whether in the world of managed care for the United States or in the British NHS, in the grip of its own market revolution. It would be surprising if the movement in health care toward 'evidence-based practice' and the standardisation and auditing of treatments had not been echoed in the procedures and theories of the talking cures. For all schools of therapy, there has been a shift toward demonstrating effectiveness through clinical trials, and for many, a renewed emphasis upon their technical aspects.[53] And there has been a parallel trend toward the hybridisation of approaches to create new variants, for example, cognitive narrative therapy.[54]

These changes, designed in part to make government-approved forms of therapeutic talk more accessible to the masses, also speak of CBT's wide appeal and of the enduring perception that, when troubled, it is 'good to talk'.[55] People with more serious and long-standing mental health problems are increasingly, and understandably, expressing their preference for human contact and conversation over the not-very-helpful drugs that psychiatrists prescribe.[56] And there is gathering disillusionment with the promise of designer pharmaceuticals, once heralded as the way to recast our entire personality, to make us 'better than well'.[57] Yet many of the leading schools of talking therapy promote their methods in a language that mirrors the over-confident assurances of psychiatrists and the pharmaceutical companies. More and more, psychological techniques are presented and packaged as fast cures for mental disorder.[58]

As should be clear by now, despite these commonalities, the world of therapy is riven by disagreement, for instance, about how much emphasis should be given to individuals' thoughts, versus feelings, actions, or even their situation.[59] And then there are the explanations that therapists provide for the nature and causes of their client's problems. Should these maps be shared at an early stage in therapy, as is done in CBT, for instance, or not disclosed until much later, or perhaps never, for the fear that such revelations might obstruct the client's self-exploration and discovery as it unfolds within therapy?[60] Perhaps the most heated debates are about what kind of therapy might work best for what kind of problem and client. Many CBT practitioners regard their approach as the most clinically effective (it is certainly the most researched). This view has been vigorously challenged by practitioners from other schools, some of them arguing that the clinical trial method – as used in medicine for the evaluation of drug and other treatments – is simply too crude a device to capture the subtleties and complexities of how talking therapy works.[61]

These are significant fissures. Yet the general rule has been for polite avoidance of these differences in the counsellor training literature and indeed in discussions at conferences, where instead there will sometimes be a nod to the need for more research, before the question of what kind of therapy works best for whom for what problem can be answered. There are many reasons for this avoidance. One of them must surely be the lack of agreement about what the aims of psychological therapy should be and how, if at all, its effects can be measured.[62] Whereas many, perhaps most, practitioners see it as a form of clinical treatment designed to reduce specific psychological symptoms, others view it as a form of open-ended enquiry that can lead in unpredictable directions, perhaps to a reassessment of the path that one's life has taken.[63] The extent of this disagreement can be gauged by the existence of a vigorous movement in the UK that opposes the idea of professional registration for all therapists (analogous to that required for doctors and dentists) because it will lead to a moribund practice that will quash spontaneity and creativity.[64]

These fundamental differences notwithstanding, there are at least two creeds upon which nearly every school of therapy has come to agree. First, there must be a warm and collaborative relationship between client and practitioner, as the vehicle that delivers the techniques, if not as *the technique* of change, in itself. Whether or not this consensus represents the advance of clinical knowledge, it certainly shows that the humanistic therapies have been successful at marketing their wares. Any sensible therapist 'listens' to their client, as do effective managers to employees or friends to each other. In the age of the customer, no psychological treatment can afford to ignore the client's desire to feel important and well served by the attentive professional at all times. The second consensus is that every kind of therapy must take its authority from an allegiance to a professional institution of some kind, confirming expertise in the mending of troubled minds. This is the most important claim of all, because it lends credibility to therapy as a companion to medicine, propped up by the authority of science and of a rigorous 'evidence-base'. Without these twin supports, talking therapies are simply conversations – something that everyone engages in, every day of their lives.

2
The Psychopathology of Everyday Life

Medicine, like all crusades, creates a new group of outsiders each time it makes a new diagnosis stick. Morality is as implicit in sickness as it is in crime or in sin.

Ivan Illich[1]

MEDICALISATION AND ITS DISCONTENTS

At the beginning of the twenty-first century, psychiatry remains the dominant mental health profession, whether in terms of pay, status, prestige, length of academic training, or legal power. It is the template against which the other professions – including the talking therapies – define themselves, in conformity or opposition. This chapter therefore presents an overview and critique of some of the main elements of the psychiatric outlook, as a foundation for the critical look at psychological therapies and techniques that follows in subsequent chapters.

In western culture and increasingly in other parts of the world, medicine is starting to make inroads into ethics, law and politics as another way of dealing with social problems. It has become normal for governments and clinicians to intrusively monitor citizens' health in the name of their own good, instructing or nudging people to maintain their own well-being.[2] This process, widely known as 'medicalisation', has two main consequences, as described by the social critic Ivan Illich in his seminal book, *Medical Nemesis*. First, in concentrating upon individual responsibility for health and illness, we lose sight of the bigger picture, of how pervasive problems like poverty can cause or exacerbate health problems. In disguising this reality, the health care system bolsters and protects those aspects of society that manufacture illness in the first place. Secondly, age-old aspects of the human condition, especially emotional and spiritual suffering, come to be seen as the province of professionals upon whom lay people come to depend in their efforts to understand and manage what they now take to be illness. Above all, medicalisation bestows a unique power to control people in the name of care, and this is no more evident than in the field of psychiatry.

Psychiatric surveys suggest that as many as one in four Americans will suffer from anxiety or depression severe enough to merit treatment during their lifetime,[3] and that Britain is not far behind.[4] In the US, the number of people so disabled by psychiatric problems that they qualify for some form of government assistance has more than doubled between 1987 and 2007. The same period has seen even more dramatic developments for children in the United States, who have suffered a 35-fold increase in mental disorder, which is now the leading childhood disability.[5] The World Health Organisation (WHO) has declared that by 2020, depressed mood will be the second most important health problem in poorer countries, and the most important in the wealthier nations, overtaking heart disease and cancer in lost productivity, diminished quality of life and in health and social care costs.[6] For those already diagnosed, where one psychiatric label used to suffice, increasing numbers are being affixed with two, three, or more labels; the scope is widened for still more treatments, some of them aimed at managing the side effects of the psychiatric drugs themselves.[7]

As we saw in Chapter 1, psychiatry and psychology have a long history of identifying deviant groups and of treating what now looks more like protest, anguish, or difference, as forms of biological and mental illness. Examples range from the unsavoury to the genocidal. Male doctors in the early nineteenth century diagnosed women who did not conform to the approved standards of femininity, as suffering from disordered or wandering wombs, later refining this 'sickness' to a derangement of brain and psyche. Such women (especially those pregnant outside of wedlock) were often subject to compulsory hospitalisation, sometimes followed up with surgical maiming.[8] In the nineteenth and for much of the twentieth century, people who we would now see as having intellectual impairments were widely viewed as the bearers of tainted hereditary bloodlines; the supposedly useless and ineducable objects of state supervision or private charity, they were consigned to grim institutions in their thousands, graded into categories according to the degree of their supposed pathology by means of newly minted scientific terms such as 'moron' and 'imbecile' – words that have since passed into common language as forms of personal insult. Together with the similar warehousing, sorting and maltreatment of the mad, the theories and practices that helped define people with learning disabilities and that deemed non-white 'races' to be inferior, laid the blueprint for the eugenic and racial extermination policies of the Nazis, in the 1930s and '40s.[9]

In the twenty-first, century, the two chief guides to psychiatric diagnosis are the *International Statistical Classification of Disease and Related Health Problems* (or the ICD), published by the WHO,[10] and the *Diagnostic and Statistical Manual of Mental Disorder* (or the DSM) published by the American Psychiatric Association (APA).[11] China has its own diagnostic system,[12] while the ICD is used most often for UN health policy making and for research that compares the rates of illness in different countries. The DSM, an American publication, is the more widely used for treatment and for all other kinds of investigation. It dates to the nineteenth century, when the US Census Department set out to tally the number of asylum inmates and the Association of Medical Superintendents (later to become the American Psychiatric Association) began to create a system for categorizing madness; the first formal data on the occurrence of these putative illnesses was gathered in 1921. By the mid-twentieth century, the collection of these statistics had become the responsibility of the National Institute of Mental Health, which supported the APA in their efforts to develop a new psychiatric classification scheme, published in 1952 as the DSM I, followed by a second revised version in 1968.[13] These early editions succeeded in doubling the total number of mental disorders to 182. They did not offer any single theory of cause, but they did underline the importance of conflicts and of poorly adaptive responses to problems in living, and thus bore the fingerprints of psychoanalytic ideas as well as those of early twentieth-century psychiatrists such as Adolf Meyer, who saw mental disturbance as the consequence of living in a disturbed world.[14]

The third edition of the DSM, published in 1980, inflated the number of disorders to 265, but dropped almost any discussion about origins. Instead, it offered lists of symptoms that could simply be counted to arrive at a given diagnosis. For instance, depression, the 'common cold of psychiatry', was (and is) defined by a set of five behavioural and mental symptoms that include loss of appetite, insomnia, lethargy, poor concentration and lowered mood. This focus upon flat description was a way of side-stepping criticisms of psychiatric medicine's scientific basis, which had been gathering for the previous decade.[15] These doubts came partly from critiques of institutional care, from civil rights activists angered at the coercive role of psychiatry in relation to black and poor citizens, and from detractors from within the mental health field itself, for example Thomas Szasz (himself a psychiatrist), who had argued incisively that mental illness was a myth. These issues found their expression in the debates around the diagnosis of homosexuality, reluctantly deleted in 1973, after a long struggle with gay and civil rights activists who had shown that there was no evidence to support the idea that their sexual preference was anything more than that.[16] In the same year, much to the profession's embarrassment, the social psychologist David Rosenhan had shown that psychiatrists and nurses in four different hospitals could not distinguish patients deemed genuinely mentally ill from those who had initially faked their symptoms, to gain admission.[17]

This third edition of the DSM strengthened the idea of psychiatry as a medical specialism. The symptom checklists were well suited to the requirements of a profession fighting off competition from psychologists and social workers and in need of a clear authority from which it could deal its strongest suit: drug prescription, an activity performed only by doctors at that time.[18] The DSM was and is that authority. It has grown stronger, and heavier, from a mere pamphlet in its first edition, to the most recent version at the time of writing – the DSM IV TR (or 'Text Revised') – which weighs nearly four pounds, and lists 374 maladies, each one assigned its own code number. In every incarnation, the DSM has been the child of committees that have drawn primarily upon the psychiatric profession.[19] In this age of the Internet, The DSM's fifth edition has its own website, which invites anyone to comment upon (and help create) future mental disorders.[20] The DSM remains at the centre of mental health care. Besides assessment, it governs treatment and its evaluation, financial reward, research and project funding, not just for psychiatrists, but for general practitioners, paediatricians and other specialist doctors, as well as nurses, social workers, occupational therapists, prison workers, psychologists and counsellors.[21] It is also a big seller, over a million copies having been purchased worldwide, and it accounts for more than one-fifth of the yearly income of the APA.[22]

THE SHAKY SCIENTIFIC BASIS OF PSYCHIATRIC DIAGNOSES AND TREATMENTS

To begin to get a sense of the problems that go with psychiatric diagnoses like these, it is best to start with the experience of the patient. If you are diagnosed with clinical depression, schizophrenia, anxiety, or bipolar disorder (to take some of the better-known psychiatric labels) and you then ask your clinician for the diagnostic test that confirms your malady you will be met with a blank look.

No x-ray, blood analysis, or brain scan can confirm the presence of any of the common varieties of mental illness. There are no physical signs, such as tumours, by means of which your mental disorder might be identified. This fact alone distinguishes psychiatric categories from almost every other kind of illness that doctors treat. In contrast to the diseases of physical medicine, anchored in the material world, the constructs of psychiatric illness have a free-floating nature. They are no more or less than someone else's judgement about the meaning of what the sufferer is saying and doing, of the extent to which it is 'normal' or 'abnormal'. This freedom has opened the way to a happy inventiveness on the part of psychiatrists, as demonstrated in the mandate for each official American Task Force assembled to overhaul the DSM. Any new (or old) psychiatric disorder has been included, as long as there is 'general agreement among clinicians, who would be expected to encounter the condition, that there are significant numbers of patients who have it and that its identification is important in [their] clinical work'.[23] In the annals of medicine, mental illnesses are unique in that they are created by committees, and are the 'only form of disease that can be caught by word of mouth'.[24]

There is another scientific problem with psychiatric diagnosis. In medicine, the validity of the physician's verdict rests upon the extent to which it specifies future symptoms, their duration, the best treatments and likely results. If medical diagnosis is an act of prediction, then psychiatric diagnoses might be compared to horoscopes. In the case of schizophrenia, for example, about one-third of patients will make a complete recovery, one-third will improve somewhat, and a final third might remain seriously disturbed for the rest of their lives, but the symptoms do not give a reliable prediction as to which of these groups any patient could fall into.[25]

Psychiatric treatments lead to outcomes that are vague and indeterminate as their non-specific modes of action might lead us to expect. 'Antidepressant' drugs can make people more sedated and indifferent to their problems but not, usually, more buoyant or optimistic. So-called 'antipsychotic' chemicals can blunt disturbing feelings, dim perception and slow down the body; in some people, they may even create agitation that can pass for boosted mood, but at best these drugs will suppress rather than erase the disturbing or unwanted beliefs and experiences that supposedly define psychotic 'illness'. For long-term users of anti-psychotics, there have also been terrible costs in brain-damaging side effects such as tremors, facial tics and other physical stigmata that have served to further isolate them from the rest of the population. Across the world, millions of people have been swept up in what the American journalist Robert Whitaker calls the largest unrecognised epidemic of medically caused illness in modern times.[26] Similar questions are being raised about the toxicity of the new generations of supposedly 'cleaner' anti-psychotics and antidepressants (the SSRIs), where the latter have been linked to aggression and suicide in a minority of patients.[27]

Psychiatrists, the popular press and lay people often talk about how these treatments restore a lost 'chemical imbalance' in the brain. But this is a theory and not a fact and there is little evidence for it. The three major classes of psychiatric drug – marketed to treat anxiety, psychosis and depression – were originally developed in the 1950s from anaesthetics, and infection and allergy treatments, which were accidentally found to pacify patients. The first major tranquilliser, Chlorpromazine, was soon promoted on the grounds that it achieved lobotomy by purely chemical means, a point that is rarely emphasised by the modern manufacturers of this type of drug.[28] When it was discovered that psychoactive agents alter the levels of neurotransmitters in the brain (as measured by their breakdown products in the patients' spinal fluid), then the theory grew that madness and misery occurred when the concentration of these chemicals in the nervous system went wrong. Because chlorpromazine lowered the amount of dopamine in the brain, it was claimed that schizophrenia came from having too much of this chemical messenger.[29] By contrast, because most antidepressants boost the brain's quantities of serotonin, depressed mood came to be seen as what happens when we don't have enough of this chemical.[30] However, correlation does not imply cause, and these patterns could occur just as easily if the drugs eased disturbance through another route, one that only accidentally affected the relevant neurotrans-mitters. To argue otherwise is to use the same dubious logic that would have us believe that headaches come from a lack of aspirin.

The evidence against the claim that these drugs change specific underlying disease processes diminishes steadily. For instance, there are indications that neurotransmitter levels are normal in people who go on to develop mental illness, while drugs that alter the levels of neurotransmitters in ways presumed to create psychological disturbance do not seem to have this effect.[31] A handful of psychiatrists have argued that withdrawal from psychiatric drugs might itself disrupt the brain's economy of neurotransmitters, leading to a biochemical rebound, often mistaken for mental illness, and met with more of the same doctoring that caused the problems in the first place. In the most recent of her many reviews of biochemical, pharmaceutical and genetic studies of mental disorder and its treatment, the British psychiatrist Joanna Moncrieff concludes that there is 'no evidence that any class of psychiatric drugs acts by reversing or partially reversing an underlying physical process that is responsible for producing symptoms'.[32] She is far from alone in her view.[33]

Amongst other things, recovery seems to have much more to do with the amount and quality of compassionate support given to the patient, both within the hospital and in the world beyond. In the 1980s, for example, the American psychiatrist Loren Mosher[34] tried to show that non-professional residential care with minimal (often zero) pharmaceutical treatment was a more helpful therapy for psychosis than the standard acute hospitalisation, followed by-drug based 'community rehabilitation'. Despite these encouraging results from the Soteria Project and its affiliates, the funding for Mosher's work dwindled, and by the 1990s had stalled altogether. The project was the victim of the indifference of the American Psychiatric Association, and its failure to encourage the relevant funding institutions to dig into their pockets, for what would have been small change by the usual standards of mental health project development.[35]

Two large-scale studies of 'schizophrenic' individuals, instigated by the World Health Organisation in 1969 and 1978 respectively,[36] showed that those living in poorer countries such as Nigeria or India had better mental functioning, fewer symptoms and better prospects of recovery than those who lived in wealthier Europe or in the United States – these advantages were still present 25 years on.[37] In fact, the US is one of the very worst countries in which to be mentally ill, especially if you happen to be poor.[38] At the time of writing, there is no consensus explanation for these differences. One account holds that less affluent countries make up for what they lack (in the latest drugs and psychotherapies) with agricultural and manual skill-based economies, cohesive communities and extended family networks: the bases for a modestly productive and valued role, in contrast to the segregation and enforced worthlessness that awaits so many long-term psychiatric patients in the West. This dramatic gap between rich and penniless countries may also reflect far lower usage of costly psychiatric drugs amongst the latter. This difference is significant in view of the growing evidence – intensely resisted by the psychiatric profession – that long-term drug treatment can interfere with a person's ability to think and to communicate with others and, as well as creating dependency, may *prolong* the experience of psychosis, in many instances.[39]

In addition to these problems of treatment, the act of psychiatric diagnosis is a far less reliable activity than in physical medicine. Despite decades of research efforts to improve the reliability of the checklists used in the DSM and the ICD, if two doctors are asked to categorise the illness of a disturbed person then they are less likely to agree when compared to any of their medical colleagues treating people with skin, kidney, or heart complaints, for instance.[40] Moreover, psychiatric symptoms do not reliably cluster together in the way that they do for physical illnesses; people present in unique ways that seem to combine the supposedly discrete symptoms of different kinds of malady – depression, for instance, is often entangled with anxiety.[41]

In the case of a disorder such as schizophrenia, these problems multiply, because there is a still larger pool of disparate symptoms from which the clinician can choose when making their judgement. 'Mrs Doyle' occasionally hears angelic voices commenting upon her looks and her moral probity. In her youth, they were frightening, but over the years she has reached an accommodation with them and they have transformed into an occasional distraction, embarrassment and (sometimes) a source of canny advice. 'Mr Miguna' believes that his thoughts can influence the content of television news programmes and the actions of friends and acquaintances. He is so frightened that he has stopped watching television, and has begun to shun all social contact. Once a dapper and punctilious man, it is all he can do to feed himself regularly, much less change his clothes. Day or night, he spends most of his time alone, sitting with the curtains closed and in darkness. 'Mr Jones', a carpenter by trade, has come to believe that he is the wealthy owner of a famous film studio. He will brook no arguments on this subject, even though his increasingly grandiloquent manner and rash behaviour have lost him his job, his marriage and most of his friends. Despite his sense of abandonment, he has to admit that he has never felt so confident and energized.

Because of their unusual experiences or conduct, all of the people in these fictional vignettes are troubled (or might trouble others) to varying degrees. But to a dispassionate observer, it is surely not evident that they all share a single underlying malady of mind or brain. The diagnoses discerned by psychiatrists are not objective facts, but networks of simplistic assumptions that fail to do justice to a complex and elusive reality. These categories are also based upon an error of logic, in which symptoms and diagnosis are used to support each other, like two drunks wandering along a street:

Q: How do we know that this patient is a schizophrenic?
A: Because she is hearing voices and they prevent her from being able to face her family and friends.
Q: Why is she hearing voices and unable to deal with her family and friends?
A: Because she is a schizophrenic.

It is possible to insert almost any psychiatric disorder into this bad syllogism.

FOUND OR INVENTED?

Products Create Markets – The Invention of Mental Illnesses

If psychiatric disorders had a firm basis in science, then we would expect them to bear little relationship to the interests of professionals, drug manufacturers and service users. But this is not the case.

The British psychiatrist David Healy has shown how diagnostic fashions in psychiatry follow marketing imperatives. In psychiatric hospital practice of the 1950s, depression was a relatively rare disorder and there was no concept of a specifically antidepressant drug as opposed to a general stimulant. When the antidepressant action of certain compounds was first proposed, drug companies were initially reluctant to develop and launch such products. In an unconscious alliance of interests, influential psychiatrists expanded and popularised the view of depression as a common biologically based disorder, amenable to chemical treatment and as yet frequently unrecognised. This concept had the dual benefit of vastly expanding both the market for psychiatric drugs and the operations of psychiatry beyond the asylum. From the 1980s, the research and promotional activities of drug companies transformed everyday 'bad nerves' to 'anxiety' and then into 'depression' in order to create a wider market for their new SSRI antidepressants, including the brand Prozac.[42] The impetus for these changes lay not with new discoveries, but with declining profits from sales of minor tranquillisers, such as benzodiazepines, which had begun to fall out of patent and out of favour with physicians and patients alike, who were troubled by the growing evidence of the addictiveness of these compounds.[43]

The pharmaceutical companies are among the most profitable industries on the planet.[44] The number of people treated for depression tripled in the decade after the inception of the antidepressant Prozac, and one in ten Americans above the age of six are now on antidepressants. In that same nation, the latest types of anti-psychotics, including Zyprexia, Risperdal and Seroquel, have quietly beaten cholesterol-reducing medicines as the best-selling class of medication.[45]

For 30 years, the pharmaceutical companies have overseen the publication of flawed and biased research trials that have downplayed or ignored the limitations of chemical cures for misery and madness.[46] The US Food and Drugs Administration (FDA) is supposed to oversee the testing and safety standards for all new medicines and foodstuffs. In the case of antidepressant pills, the FDA has allowed the drug companies to publish a small number of accounts of successful trials in the medical journals, and to withhold the dozens more that show these agents to be little more potent than sugar tablets.[47]

These industries have had a far-reaching effect on the outlook of psychiatry and allied mental health professions. This influence extends from the sponsorship of research journals and conferences (often featuring five-star accommodation in exotic locations for the biomedical psychiatrists), to the ghostwriting of research papers in the name of prominent clinicians and researchers,[48] to the financial leverage exerted upon academic institutions to dismiss (critical) scholars of whom the drug companies do not approve. Time and again, psychiatrists have been found to receive more payments from medical drug businesses than any other kind of speciality. The pharmaceutical industry offers patronage to the opinion leaders in the field. These prestigious individuals, in their lecturing, writing and research – and especially in their presence on the committees that create the DSM – help to mould the way that mental illness is viewed and treated. The fifth edition of the DSM was the first that required the clinician-authors to disclose their financial ties to the pharmaceutical companies, with over half of them admitting 'significant industry interests'.[49]

Other aspects of the commercial grip upon psychiatry are more insidious, but perhaps more potent. Marketing companies conduct regular surveys into what doctors desire from an antidepressant or an anti-psychotic. Clinical academics are recruited into opinion-leading focus groups for the same purpose. The average general practitioner or psychiatrist does not see that when drug companies provide free lunches, trinkets and trips to academic conferences, and lecture fees, then these incentives have the least potency in shaping their prescribing habits. In fact, it is *their own* opinions that are being mined to help shape each new drug brand, much as groups of high-street consumers are quizzed to help create a new brand of fizzy drink. When the 'actual differences between modern anti-depressants and modern anti-psychotics are minimal; the perceived differences come almost entirely from sophisticated consumer research aimed at understanding what physicians might swallow.'[50] Science and interest make uncomfortable bedfellows.

Then there is the process of 'disease mongering' – by which pharmaceutical companies seek to expand the market for a treatment by convincing people that they are sick and in need of medical help. This is achieved in part through commercially inspired 'disease-awareness' campaigns and by direct advertising to doctors and, in the US, to future consumers. Ideally, a new 'disease' will have fuzzy, general symptoms that cover a wide range of severity, from everyday twinges that few might see as a symptom of illness to serious distress.[51] New (and old) disorders and their treatments are also promoted by credulous journalists and advocacy groups: female sexual dysfunction and restless leg syndrome are among the more recent additions, but the same principle applies for older diseases.[52] In the US, the National Carers' Alliance (NCA) champions the idea that 'schizophrenia' is another biological illness, just like 'diabetes', and in need of continual management with prescribed drugs. The NCA has persuaded insurers and governments to follow their line of thinking, and like many similar organisations, it accepts funds from drug companies, whose profits increase when these groups lobby for what are claimed to be the latest and most effective therapies.[53]

Post traumatic Stress Disorder, or PTSD

By contrast, the rising popularity of other mental illnesses, such as PTSD, owes more to the activities of people afflicted with psychological problems and to changes in society as a whole. PTSD is the sole psychiatric diagnosis that acknowledges an environmental cause, in this case, rooted in exposure to a shocking event. The main features of PTSD include the unwanted reliving of the original disturbance in memory or dreams, coupled with an avoidance of all reminders of it, numbed feelings and an inability to relax.[54] Incorporated into the DSM III in 1980,[55] PTSD was the intended replacement for 'war neurosis' or 'battle fatigue', and designed to move the spotlight away from the soldier's personality and history as the putative root of their ills, and toward the horrors of war itself. In his account of the creation of PTSD, the American anthropologist Allen Young argues that these were essential requirements for returning disturbed veterans (from Vietnam), in need of both credibility and succour from a nation that had almost turned its back upon them. At first, their stories of atrocities and of what it meant to witness them were neither believed by their own Veteran's Administration, nor were the veterans the object of sympathy from a public disillusioned with the least popular war in living memory, and inclined to see these men as perpetrators, rather than victims.[56] As the revision of the DSM II moved apace in the late 1970s, a nucleus of psychiatrists, chaplains, psychologists and pensioned soldiers formed the Vietnam Veterans Group, to collect clinical data in aid of identifying a 'post-combat disorder'. Young suggests that they were successful in minting the new diagnosis, in part because it also met the needs of doctors and social workers whose waiting rooms were filling up with the casualties of Vietnam, and in part because the American media had highlighted a wave of violence, drug taking, anti-social acts and suicide amongst such men. This epidemic required an explanation and the new illness fitted the bill.

The PTSD category was intended to capture only extreme experiences. In recent years, however, mental health practitioners of all stripes have gathered a growing list of ordinary, if upsetting events under the PTSD umbrella, such as muggings, childbirth, verbal sexual harassment, or the alarm of bad (but incorrect) news, for example, a faulty medical diagnosis.[57] The claim that low-level but chronic threat can cue PTSD symptoms has led to the removal of the phrase 'outside the range of ordinary human experience' from the criteria for PTSD, in the DSM IV.[58]

Psychiatric diagnoses can also become plausible and popular because they reflect the changing economic and social climate, and those interests best served by the transformed conditions. New psychiatric illnesses are cultural weathervanes, faithfully swinging with the fashions in ideas of health and normality. For instance, the rise of the concept of depression seems to have closely tracked how unhappiness and sadness have become taboo in post-war western society. In the case of the diagnosis of PTSD, besides the interests of lawyers and patients seeking compensation, its popularity with patients and advocacy groups may also reveal yet another aspect of how notions of the self have changed in recent decades. There has been a drift from a more stoical acceptance of struggle matched with communal forms of aid, towards a focus upon the individual and their emotional fragility, their rights and grievances, and their need for restitution.[59]

From Restless Legs, to Social Phobia

Psychiatric categories creep steadily outwards, engulfing ever more forms of behaviour at their margins. The new DSM will make it easier to channel people into the status of mental illness via membership of so-called precursor illnesses (such as 'psychosis risk syndrome' or 'mild cognitive impairment'), or of a widened spectrum of potential madness and misery, including the 'schizophrenic spectrum disorder' and the 'obsessive compulsive disorder (OCD) spectrum'.[60] Conduct once seen as merely eccentric or different gradually becomes a medical oddity, in need of professional management. Take shyness, for example. As an object of concern, the trait of introversion was little discussed before the nineteenth century, when it was considered to be just another facet of one's character: lending strength in some instances and weakness in others. From the mid-twentieth century however, shyness has been increasingly viewed by the wider public and by educators and mental health professionals as an unhealthy state of being, a mark of failure in the race to be loud and proud. This changing view is encapsulated in the creation of relatively new diagnoses like social phobia, social anxiety disorder and avoidant personality disorder, respectively. Shy people often accept the dominant view of their condition and comply with moral pressure to overcome it – through drug therapy or CBT, or self-help books and websites. The sociologist Susie Scott has studied how people view shyness, through in-depth interviews with individuals who see themselves as socially awkward, and analyses of how 'the shy' are judged within popular culture and by the purveyors of psychological therapies and techniques, designed to cure them.

It is clear that widespread insecurities are driving the application of these and many other diagnoses, and that these apprehensions reflect a general fascination with celebrity, self-expression, talk and interviewing on the one hand, and the nature of work and social life in the twenty-first century, on the other. In comparison to our forebears, our contacts with other people are often passing and commercial, organised around our role in providing services as opposed to the production or repair of goods. Even labour-intensive industries have changed: for example, the shift from the sweated factory operative to the call-centre worker. The ethic

> ... of a '24 hour' society based upon flexible but long working hours, individual achievement and skills of teamwork and

communication almost by definition discriminates against those who are more reticent, and it is not surprising that they learn to evaluate their own conduct as problematic in relation to these values.[61]

The clinical and popular psychotherapies have had a hand in this process, because they have promoted the notion that we should be good, authentic communicators, and that they possess the techniques that can allow us to customise and upgrade our communication skills.

Autistic Spectrum Diagnoses, or ASD

Another group of people who are defined by their struggle to fit in with mainstream expectations of instant personableness and intimacy are those who are diagnosed with autistic spectrum disorder (ASD), especially at the 'higher-ability' end of this spectrum. Autistic individuals are said to have gaps in their ability to understand, empathise and communicate with others and to have extremely narrow interests, such as collecting old maps or knowing a great deal about one type of fossil, for instance. Such individuals are said to struggle in the day-to-day world, which they can experience as glaring, noisy and confusing. Autistic children are usually identified before age 7, because of their repetitive play, isolation from peers and arrested language development. By contrast, people diagnosed with 'high functioning autism' (or 'Asperger's syndrome') are defined by similar struggles with the demands of social life, but they will show essentially normal language development and intelligence. This syndrome has caught the imagination of the public. Celebrity CEOs like Bill Gates are said to carry these traits and there is a fashion for labelling famous historical figures such as Einstein and Newton as 'Aspies': an exercise that is impossible without detailed accounts from adults who knew that individual as a child.

Once again, however, there are large variations between clinicians in how they interpret the behaviours that might meet criteria for an ASD as opposed to schizophrenia, a learning disability, or OCD, for instance; this situation is complicated by the tendency for the signature behaviours to alter in children and younger people as they mature. A young person who is virtually mute and cannot take care of themselves, and an articulate, academically successful 14-year-old who struggles to connect with their peers can both end up sharing the ASD label. Accounts written by adults with Asperger's syndrome suggest that their lack of social grace can ease with time, as they learn to overcome it in their own individual way, through observation and practice and, above all, through finding a comfortable niche in the world – a process sometimes known as 'emergence'.[62]

Furthermore, there is no good evidence for any single brain deficit that might unite the people who attract an ASD label, although there is no shortage of hypotheses, which include defective coordination between the cerebral hemispheres, poor ability to shift attention and underactive mirror neurons. All have their champions and detractors. The most popular theory, advanced by the British psychologist Simon Baron-Cohen, is that people with Asperger's syndrome lack a discrete evolutionary neuropsychological 'module', that is, a piece of mental hardware that supports perceptive and nuanced communication in the rest of us. They are 'mind blind' – possessing a more extreme version of the ordinary 'male brain' which is set to analyse, rather than sympathise.[63]

Yet this notion seems paradoxical, in the light of the accepted view that 'autism' is a continuum of traits, varying to some extent even *within the same individual*, depending upon circumstance. This is the view of some people who carry the label, and of a perhaps large minority of clinicians and teachers who have worked closely with adults and children so described. For example, the educational psychologist Tom Billington shows that such children can be surprisingly insightful and perceptive – depending upon how secure they feel, and upon the thoughtfulness of the adults working with them.[64] Far from being unresponsive to others, they are 'hypersensitive to incoming stimuli from their environment. [T]heir feelings may often be of an intense and overwhelming nature – leading them to avoid interactions with others by a process of "shutting down" or shutting out.'[65]

Perhaps the most comprehensive critique of the autism spectrum diagnosis comes from the British psychiatrist, Sami Tamimi and his two colleagues, Neil Gardner and Brian McCabe, both of whom have been diagnosed with Asperger's syndrome.[66] They argue from clinical and personal experience, that labels like 'autism' and 'attention deficit hyperactivity disorder (ADHD)' can assume a life of their own, restricting not just the patient's expectations but everyone else's, too. Autism becomes *the* explanation for whatever the patient has done, or plans to do. On the one hand, this can mean that useful biological possibilities are overlooked, as when, for instance, undetected epilepsy might be blocking a child's participation in games and social life. On the other hand, the focus upon an autism diagnosis can displace situational accounts of personal problems, colluding with the tendency for modern institutions to view emotional literacy as the key to personal success.

Here, Tamimi joins Scott and other critics[67] in arguing that developmental diagnoses such as ASD can become a way of selecting and managing those who seem deficient in the face-to-face and emotional skills deemed necessary for the smooth functioning of neoliberal societies. Their argument is also compatible with the view that the focus upon emotional intelligence in the workplace – tacitly endorsed by the diagnosis of ASD, which offers a salutary warning about what the lack of social skills means – helps to subtly keep workers in line, where conflict, much less displays of open anger, has come to be seen as unhealthy, rather than a sometimes inevitable and even necessary part of public life.[68]

Recipients of the ASD label are sometimes strong advocates of this kind of view. Instead of being seen as tragic, they want acceptance of who they are, and of who they cannot be.[69] A good insight into this 'social rights' standpoint is provided by the satirical website: *The Institute for the Study of the Neurologically Typical*. Curated by the user activist organisation, Autistics Anonymous, it pokes fun at the perceived rigidity and narrow-mindedness ('the autism') of mental health professionals, through a new collection of diagnoses, like 'staff personality disorder', 'normal personality disorder', and of course, 'psychiatry disorder'.

The most prevalent of these is 'neurotypical syndrome', afflicting as many as 9,625 out of every 10,000 individuals. It is

> … a neurobiological disorder characterized by preoccupation with social concerns, delusions of superiority, and obsession with conformity. [Neurotypicals] assume that their experience of the world is either the only one, or the only correct one … [and they] find it difficult to be alone.

Worse still, they struggle to 'communicate directly, and have a much higher incidence of lying as compared to persons on the autistic spectrum'.[70]

Who is it, that needs to be put together again?

Attention Deficit Hyperactivity Disorder, or ADHD

Similar questions attend the diagnosis of ADHD, said to affect one in ten children in the UK, with 345,000 prescribed the drug Ritalin, prescribed to children as young as 18 months. In the

US, 10 per cent of boys under the age of 10 are taking a daily dose of stimulant medication and half a million are consuming anti-psychotic medication.[71] Like autism, ADHD is a collection of related symptoms that can be more accurately described as problems for anyone trying to care for a child: irritability, fidgeting, distractedness, impulsiveness, poor memory and 'babbling about nothing'. These are behaviours that could describe almost any healthy child. The diagnosis can bring relief to parents who do not have to see their son or daughter as shamefully wayward or to contemplate what might be going on inside their own family or their child's peer group to account for his or her difficulties.

A further aspect of this social critique of the developmental disorders concerns the strong gender bias that underpins them. Boys are diagnosed for problems like ASD and ADHD by a ratio of three to one in comparison with girls, and are even more likely to be given drug treatments. This is an almost exact inversion of the case for adults, where it is women who overwhelmingly present to mental health services for treatment of what are seen as 'mood disorders'.[72]

What is going on here? Tamimi, Gardner and McCabe argue that this pattern too reflects several interlocking social trends. One of these is a preoccupation with the vulnerability of girls and with the potential risks presented to them by unruly or aggressive boys. Another is that, in most western countries, beliefs about child rearing and education have shifted in the last generation toward an official 'gender-neutral' position. Girls and boys are often taught in much the same way, in the belief that they share common interests and incentives. But this regime may be ill suited to perhaps a large minority of boys who do not enjoy focusing upon or sharing their feelings, and are more attuned than girls for signs of trouble or excitement (leading them to be more easily seen as restless or distractable), and who appear to do better when elements of competition are introduced into their learning. Tammi and colleagues are clear that not all male children will share these traits to the same degree, and are agnostic about the extent to which evolutionary (as opposed to cultural) influences might be responsible, but they imply that both contribute. They suggest that this picture is further complicated by how the world outside of the school can make masculine development a tricky business. In some communities, for instance, there is a lack of reliable mature men to act as mentors for younger men and boys, just as there is a wide (indeed bewildering) choice of masculine identities available in the urbanised and wired twenty-first century, even while the main identity is also the most traditional, crystallising around toughness and control of self, and others.

If all of this adds up to confusion and unhappiness for many young men, and a rejection of 'feminine' ways of doing things, then the result is clear. Such boys become targets for medicalisation, as they struggle to fit the mould of a childhood that is studiously non-aligned with respect to sexual categories. It might be added that these more 'feminised' standards of modern education overlap in many ways with middle-class norms of conduct: that is, a careful regulation of anger and of emotional spontaneity in general – outside of 'therapeutic' or other tightly controlled situations – and a focus upon self-reflection and the verbalisation of feelings. Against these conventions and norms working-class and minority ethnic children are more likely to stand out as awkward.[73]

Of course, it has to be acknowledged that, for many, an ASD diagnosis has its uses. There is a large subset of people with an ASD diagnosis whose problems cannot be accounted for by social or psychological influences *alone*, and may indeed result from unidentified and poorly understood brain injury of some kind. These are usually people who have a severe or moderate learning disability. For those who are able to negotiate the current health and social care systems, acquisition of this label may open up pathways toward badly needed financial, material and personal assistance at school, college, or work. This can make life more bearable for families and can increase the odds of future success for everyone concerned. For most, the diagnosis may also be preferable to more pejorative labels like 'psychosis' or 'schizophrenia'.

And yet these therapeutic interventions can come at a price. Few of the drugs used to treat autism are licensed for dispensing to children, and *none* specifically for the condition itself. There is no evidence for long-term benefits, but for serious side effects, including strokes, and growth and learning impairment, it is indisputable.[74] While there are no medical treatments aimed specifically at ASD, the high rates of psychiatric drug prescription for people in this group is worrying, but cannot be altogether unwelcome to drug manufacturers, keen to market their wares.[75] The incentives for American parents to collude with the drugging of their children are even more acute. For many increasingly hard-pressed families, prescribed drug treatments are the passport to Supplemental Security Income (SSI) payments, predicated on the mental disability of their child. In the lexicon of American health care, mental disability, especially for poorer families, equates with drug treatment.[76]

Where then does all of this leave us? Critics of the autism concept who want to see it abolished may well be seen by those who have fought for improved services (usually parents) as cavalier and even callous, denying the suffering experienced by many. But this is not the case. In place of harmful drugs and erstwhile helpers who have become focused upon imparting narrow psychological or social skills-based 'solutions', the critics want to see better, more humane services for people relegated to the edges of a society that might also learn to become more tolerant.

The same kind of analysis applies to the presumptive disorder of schizophrenia. All societies seem to have had some notion of madness as inexplicable or bizarre conduct. However, the promotion of schizophrenia as a well-defined brain disease and as an explanation for troubling behaviour has only blocked understanding of the continuity between psychotic and ordinary experience, as well as empathy for people who suffer in this way. The biological view has also served to warrant the enormous profits of pharmaceutical companies for over 50 years and has aided the move toward greater restriction (and compulsory drugging) of people so diagnosed, under the guise of 'community-based treatment'. On a still wider plane, the acceptance of schizophrenia as a biological fact has helped to stifle debate about how severe mental distress reflects the extent of social inequalities and of poverty. This is a worrying development, given the growing suspicions that, 'evidence-based medicine' notwithstanding, the outcomes of modern psychiatric treatment may be worse than they were even half a century ago, at least as judged by exhaustive studies of psychiatric hospital admissions in North Wales, where, despite the decline in the number of long-stay patients, the rate of new admissions and suicides rose tenfold during the second half of the twentieth century.[77] In the western world, patients with severe mental health problems have the distinction of being the only group designated with a major illness, for whom life expectancy has declined.[78]

If Psychiatric Diagnoses are so Questionable, Then Why Do They Persist?

Surveys of lay people suggest that they view some diagnoses very negatively. Schizophrenia in particular is regarded as a serious and stigmatising disorder that implies dangerousness and unpredictability, marking a clear separation between the afflicted and everyone else. Other disorders, as we have seen, can be viewed in a more positive light as badges of suffering or difference and as legitimisation for support and care. By contrast to the mental health professionals, lay people seem more willing to ascribe the causes (if not always the cures) of some mental disorders – especially depression, addictions and anxiety problems – to harsh life circumstances and social pressure of all kinds.[79] It is only in recent years that mental health service users have been asked about their own views of psychiatric diagnosis and on the whole, they are more doubtful than anyone else. Though diagnoses are recognised as conferring access to much-needed services and disability benefits, they are also seen as stigmatising, stereotyping, a poor guide to the nature of their problems, and a fateful judgement upon their future: closing off the possibilities for non-medical forms of treatment and care.[80] Accounts of the lives of psychiatric patients trying to get by in their own communities bear out these observations, showing avoidance and rejection (which is sometimes violent) to be the norm.[81]

Many people remain willing to view intractable unhappiness, fear, or agitation as forms of disorder requiring expert management, and it is worth asking why. There can be little doubt that the interests of the mental health professions and of the pharmaceutical industry are of central importance, as they have spent decades in promoting and sustaining their ill-founded diagnostic system as the 'common sense' of our time.[82] Spurious medical language of this kind can also boost the morale of the professionals, because it incubates the shared belief that the treatments that they are trained to deliver represent genuine steps in the conquest of 'mental illness'.[83]

Yet the clinical and research evidence suggests that most of the disorders itemised in the DSM are best seen, not as organic brain illnesses, but as how most of us would respond to prolonged or intense loneliness, despair, deprivation, or mistreatment. The kinds of behaviour that are grouped under psychiatric headings are therefore not just reactions to harsh circumstances, they also represent the sufferer's efforts to control or parry the resulting emotional pain – through recourse to licit or illegal substances, or through apathy and withdrawal, compulsive rituals, self-harm, or violent rage.[84]

It is hard to square observations such as these with what leading clinicians such as the American psychiatrist Robert Spitzer have admitted about the third and fourth revisions of the DSM. Spitzer and his colleagues helped to create more than a hundred new mental illnesses, but without 'considering that many of these conditions might be normal reactions which are not really disorders'.[85]

Psychiatric diagnoses and treatments persist as the keystone for the medicalisation of social problems. In claiming to identify and treat objective bodily disease, mental health professionals have been able to reframe social ills such as poverty, economic insecurity and the widespread abuse of children and adults as medical issues, requiring expert management. The public has also conspired in this process, by demanding treatments for what might once have been seen as commonplace misery. In this way, hard questions are avoided, such as how we might better respond to people who are troubling and troubled, not to mention the wider issue of how to address the social inequalities and harms that cause distress in the first place.

At root, psychiatry is scientifically (and perhaps morally) bankrupt. In its current form, the product of a collusion – seldom conscious – between self-interest on the one hand, and the demands and rewards brokered by more distal economic and social powers, on the other. The resulting psychiatric map of the human mind does not seem to have enriched our understanding beyond what was known to the nineteenth-century 'mad doctors', and has led to a dead end, clinically speaking. The talking therapists have also drawn charts of their own, some of them, it must be said, far richer than anything achieved by biomedicine. But have these maps proved to be any more accurate than the psychiatric ones, especially when compared to what science is showing us about the working of the mind? It is to this question that we turn next.

3
The 'CEO of Self' ... ?

What our cognitive science has found out about the mind is mostly that we don't know how it works.

J. Fodor[1]

Since Descartes and Locke, western philosophers have assumed that we have direct and accurate access to our own mental experiences by a process of inward perception, much as our senses, and especially vision, allow us to register the external world.[2] Despite this idea having come under increasing attack during the last century, it is still widely believed by lay people that our own subjective experience is fairly reliable when we attend to it closely.[3] This notion is twinned with an equally hardy sibling – the belief that we are all the builders and managers of our own fates, each of us a kind of 'CEO of Self', in the apt words of the American politician, Herman Cain.[4] If cultural common sense of this kind is not just a way of seeing things, but 'the form and substance of our consciousness',[5] then it is no surprise that faith in the forces of insight and of self-determination (or 'willpower') nestle in the bosom of almost every kind of talk therapy and technique.

THE POWER OF INSIGHT WITHIN TALKING TREATMENT – WISDOM, OR MYOPIA?

It was Freud who first unsettled his clients (and most of the Victorian middle class) with the discovery of hitherto concealed motivations, said to underlie everyday conduct. In the end, these interpretations relied upon each client's presumed ability to accurately report on the images, words and feelings inside of their mind. In the twenty-first century, cognitive behavioural therapists assume that the client's more accessible thoughts (or 'cognitions') are open to scrutiny and challenge.[6] Some of these writers appeal to theories of consciousness that posit a physical workspace, or 'Cartesian theatre' within the brain, where these thoughts are espied, tagged and then processed into more benign versions.[7] This story of inward perception applies

51

even to schools that strive to break away from traditional ideas about the mind and its problems. For instance, narrative therapists deny the idea of hidden psychological depths and indeed the existence of a stable 'self' at all, and claim instead that we are the sum of the tales that we tell.[8] However, the ultimate test of the value of any story, therapeutic or otherwise, is how well it fits the beliefs and outlook of the client, which can only be established by what they say about their experiences. Even orthodox behavioural practitioners discuss the client's thoughts and feelings about their symptoms, seeking pointers for the behaviours that they will need to target later on. This reliance upon insight has become a two-way street, because therapists of most traditions increasingly claim a central place for their own intuitions about those seeking their help, as clues to their hidden problems and to treatment progress. Perhaps the ultimate testimony of the prized place held by self-awareness within the clinical field comes from practitioners who feel that it is possible for a client to 'benefit from therapy [even] when the therapist *says nothing*[,] because the client could develop some important insights merely by imagining the feedback from the therapist' – a feat that is surely worth the fees.[9] But not everyone who has studied mental phenomena has been this sanguine.

Over the years, more sceptically inclined philosophers and psychologists have noted the problems that arise when, in good faith, we try to accurately report upon what is going on inside of our heads. These difficulties include the subtle, intricate and fleeting nature of inner experience, the novelty of being asked to honestly and accurately share it with another, and the perhaps impossible task of distinguishing our inchoate impressions from the implicit images, metaphors and theories (both personal and cultural) in which we express them. For all of these reasons, the earliest forays into experimental psychology were riven by irresolvable conflicts – for example, about the reality or otherwise of imageless thought and the divisions between various emotions. This is enough to suggest the difficulty in giving a coherent and verifiable account of what happens, when we try to describe – and much less direct – our stream of thought.[10]

In recent years, the American philosopher Eric Schwitzgebel has made it his task to probe the limits of what we can confidently say about what happens inside of our minds from a first-person point of view. He notes, for instance, the poor evidence for any link between the strength of mental images that people report and their performance in tasks that might be presumed to rely upon such pictures in the mind's eye. Schwitzgebel also shows that people can display talents of which they are unaware and unable to describe, such as the ability to navigate via echoes when blindfolded, and that, historically, reports of dreaming in black-and-white versus colour seem to have shifted in line with the introduction of modern cinema and TV. These and many other demonstrable failings of our ability to talk with confidence about subjective experience are more than amusing. They imply that, contrary to the claims of most therapists, it is not our unique inner landscape, but the outside world that each of us knows best.[11]

Clearly, opinion on this issue is divided. How then to proceed? One way might be to use modern psychological methods, perhaps by taking a willing, intelligent and articulate person and, at random intervals of her day, ask her to record her immediate mental impressions without hindrance of reflection or analysis. Confusions or ambiguities in these recordings might be clarified, if necessary, by meeting regularly with the subject and then carefully (and neutrally) interviewing her about what she had observed. This is the method known as 'direct experience sampling' (or DES). It was used by Schwitzgebel together with his colleague, the psychologist Russell Hulbert and their trained volunteer, Melanie, who agreed to wear a beeper that periodically signalled her to stop whatever she was doing and attend as quickly as possible to her own stream of consciousness: a situation that corresponds to the forthright self-disclosure that features at some point in most talking therapies. The two researchers wrote a lively book about their DES project, entitled *Describing Inner Experience*, which captures some of their interviews with Melanie, and the wide-ranging debates that ensued between the authors.[12]

What is so fascinating about this account is how two intelligent and thoughtful individuals were unable to reach any consensus about the validity of Melanie's observations, or about the DES method itself. Although remaining an optimist about the chances for accurate self-awareness, provided scientific protocols are followed, Hulbert had to concede that Melanie's reports were sometimes contaminated by her memories and preconceptions, by practical contingencies and by a failure of words to map the subtleties of experience (as any poet might testify). Schwitzgebel remained unconvinced that something so elusive and unstable could be captured in this, or any other way. Above all, he doubted that Melanie herself was as sure about the nature of her inner experience as she at first appeared.

Recent studies of visual perception seem to be on Schwitzgebel's side. Take, for example, a long-running series of investigations into the phenomenon of 'change blindness'. These experiments show that when we look at a scene, the vast majority of us fail to notice rapid but gross alterations in what we are supposedly seeing; provided the change coincides with a break in our vigilance due to an eye blink or movement, or because of the brief concealment of the scene by a passing object. Up to a point, this is not surprising. In the film industry, specialists who are well paid to spot continuity errors have been known to miss them. Change blindness has been demonstrated in a wide range of situations, some of them as amusing as they are instructive, but with implications that stretch far beyond the lab walls. For instance, observers failed to realise that two characters depicted in conversation on a computer screen had just swapped their heads,[13] that a breakfast bowl in a freeze-frame scene had been removed, or that in a painting of a Parisian market scene, Notre Dame Cathedral had jumped abruptly to the right.[14] In a more life-like situation conducted on a university campus, over a third of individuals failed to notice when a lost and confused stranger clutching a map and in search of directions was surreptitiously replaced by an identically dressed substitute. The swap happened just as two workmen walked rudely between the stranger and the subject, carrying a large door that for an instant completely hid the lost visitor.[15]

A closely related phenomenon is that of so-called 'inattentional blindness', whereby an observer, intently focusing on the action in a given scene, can totally miss the sudden intrusion of an incongruous event or object, even if it is quite large, durable and 'obvious'.[16] In one of the more noteworthy examples, nearly half of all healthy and otherwise alert student volunteers, who were following a basketball game, did not realise that a person dressed in a large gorilla suit had sauntered into the middle and had then wandered off again.[17] Many more examples of these kinds of phenomena have been documented and we may often miss them in daily life because there is no one else around to check up on what we are seeing, and because, if we subsequently discover our error, we are inclined to smooth over the awkward cracks in our recollection of what happened. We try to make it seem to ourselves and then to others that we were more alert and consistent in our judgements than is really the case. Experimental psychology seems to be at last catching up with secrets known to generations of stage magicians.[18]

The implications of this research for our ability to probe what is going on inside of our minds are quite startling. Rather than building up a rich internal picture of the world around us, we instead track our surroundings through a splinter of conscious awareness. At any given point in time, our knowledge of what is outside this tiny fragment is rudimentary, but this ignorance remains invisible, just like the constant blind spot in our visual field, where the optic nerve opens into the retina of each eye. The gaps in the story are filled in by imagination and narrative: faithful to what is happening only to the extent necessary to help us achieve our aims.[19] Aside from casting further doubt over the general accuracy of self-reports (and their reliance upon prior beliefs and external prompting), these findings also raise a question mark over the psychological therapies that are supposed to rely upon the client's ability to boost their own mental images, intended to drive new thoughts, feelings and physiological states.

Of course, in talking treatment, it is the apprehension of moods and feelings that is particularly important; here, too, there are grounds to sometimes doubt the veracity of what we say to others and even to ourselves. In his discussion of what he calls 'affective ignorance', the philosopher Daniel Haybron argues that most of us have less ability to capture our feelings in words, or any other medium, than we might suppose.[20] Haybron is concerned with the elusive character of both positive and unpleasant feelings, which, all clinicians would surely agree, colour most aspects of our lives and are one of the main coins in which the success or failure of treatment is reckoned. Haybron wonders none the less whether many of us might remain habitually unaware of such feelings: not necessarily because we are trying to avoid them, but because they can form a low-key background illumination, too monotonous and dim to attract our attention. While Haybron's argument is largely analytical, he cites some supporting experimental evidence, for instance, showing that people can be surprisingly unaware of how their performance (and perhaps their long-term health) is being worn down by pervasive nuisance like noise, crowding and heat. It is certainly true that many people who work at call centres say that they get used to the cacophony and no longer recognise it, but it is equally the case that such environments can raise blood pressure and the circulation of adrenal hormones, associated with degenerative disease in humans.[21] These findings are complemented by other experiments, which suggest that our moods and our actions can be subtly shifted when we are exposed to emotive words or images, but seemingly without our conscious awareness.[22] All of which makes intuitive sense; most of us have probably had the experience of being the last to notice, unlike our friends and loved ones, that we are not as content as we claim, or that a new job or relationship has been taking a toll upon our well-being.

Haybron argues that the widespread use of quantitative mood assessment scales can distort the way that feelings are reported, as people try to cram a rich variety of elusive and complex experiences into the square multiple-choice frames of these clinical and diagnostic instruments. Perhaps the most serious of these problems fall under the heading of scale-norming, whereby individuals use widely varying subjective standards when asked to rate their own feelings against a supposedly shared metric. The problem here is that there is simply no reliable method for measuring feelings outside of the subjective reports given by each individual. And this problem not only affects the anchor points of measurement scales but the size of the units of measurement too – both within the same individual, and when they are compared with others. For instance, how can we be sure that my score of '6' on a 7-point anxiety scale is equivalent to yours? And am I really twice as anxious as someone else who scores a '3'? It is as if two builders were each making a house according to the same plan, but using their own surrealist 'soft ruler', each one a unique design from Salvador Dali. If neither of the builders were aware of this difference, then the two houses might end up looking very interesting – but they would certainly not be identical, or even comparable. Haybron notes that this fundamental problem is seldom addressed in the literature on mood and health, or, we might add, on psychotherapy practice and research – two fields in which, as we will see, the question of measurement is already a thorny one.

Our ability to verbalise our feelings, thoughts and mental images is not as reliable as we might have hoped, especially when we begin to reflect carefully about the matter. What then, about the extent of our insight into our motives? The question of *why* we say and do the things that we do is central to every form of talking treatment. Such stories may be compelling for therapist and client alike, but does this mean that they are also valid?

To look at how we explain our purposes, several scenarios available in the literature suggest the accounts that we give of the reasons for our decisions and actions are less reliable than we might suppose, even when we are trying to convince ourselves, let alone our therapist. In the case of clinical amnesia, for instance, patients who are asked about their past – obliterated by physical or emotional trauma – can easily invent false memories that are reassuring and convincing to listeners and to themselves. It has also been shown in laboratory experiments that synthetic recollections can be implanted during therapy, at the behest of a suggestive clinician; this phenomenon, controversially, may have led to miscarriages of justice, when vague or distant (and unsubstantiated) childhood recollections disclosed by adult patients in the consulting room have been transmuted into supposedly unquestionable legal evidence. In a more light-hearted vein, subjects who have previously undergone hypnosis will respond to a prearranged cue – such as flapping their arms in response to the word 'goose' – just as they had been instructed when they were in a trance, and will give a seemingly plausible explanation for their odd conduct, minus any reference to hypnosis. This seems to be because the true account of their odd behaviour is not accessible to them.[23]

The situations discussed above share the key properties that, when people are asked questions for which they cannot know the answer (although for different reasons in each case), their state of ignorance does not stop them from confidently tendering a reply, instead of saying that they do not know. Not only are these people unaware of what prompted their conduct in the first place, they have an additional blind spot about their own ignorance, which for them is a genuine 'unknown-unknown'. In creating plausible stories or 'confabulations' as they are called in the literature, these people are not lying to anyone, least of all to themselves.[24]

How far do these scenarios speak to daily life and especially to the process of psychological treatment? A series of social psychology experiments carried out in the last few decades offer signposts here, because people are forced to explain their actions in familiar situations that are nevertheless controlled by the researcher. Shoppers in an American mall were asked to choose a pair of stockings from an array of three; Nisbett and Wilson showed that these choices could be strongly influenced by the seemingly irrelevant detail of the sequence in which the items were viewed. Most participants selected the middle pair as the 'best' ones, justifying their selection by appeal to the superior quality of the item or to their own intuitive 'hunches'. When other shoppers were called upon to predict how people might behave in this situation, they showed exactly the same kind of general blind spot in their judgement, very few of them felt that people would choose items by their sequential order alone.[25] Nisbett and Wilson termed this general phenomenon as 'telling more than we can know'; it has since been demonstrated across a wide variety of day-to-day situations, for example, in relation to the reasons why people make public commitments to a charitable cause, or tolerate boredom or discomfort, including the pain of others.[26] Indeed, urban bystanders have been shown to be less willing to help a person in distress as the number of witnesses to the scene increases. The more people standing around watching someone lying prone on the pavement, the lower the odds that anyone will help. This result is as close to being a solid rule as social psychology ever gets. When queried, very few people involved in this kind of scenario seem to know that it is the numbers of fellow bystanders that is crucial:

> We asked this question every way we knew how: subtly, directly, tacitly, bluntly. Always we got the same answer. Subjects persistently claimed that their behaviour was not influenced by other people present. [But this] denial occurred in the face of evidence showing that the presence of others did inhibit helping.[27]

A MEETING WITH THE CHIEF EXECUTIVE OFFICER? ...
'WILLPOWER' IN TALKING TREATMENT

If talking treatments and techniques are wedded to a naïve belief in transparency, then they are just as committed to the notion of the autonomous self. From a broader cultural perspective, this should not be a surprise. In meritocratic societies, people frequently attribute their academic, vocational and financial success to their own inner determination to succeed, despite the overwhelming evidence to the contrary. For most of us, this kind of achievement depends above all upon having the right parents and social background, good health and luck.[28]

A similar story applies to how lay people seem to view the causes of physical health and illness. When invited to discuss these topics, British individuals of all social classes quickly mention ideas of self-responsibility and control, under the rubric of a 'holistic' view of health, in which mind and body blend: but always with the mind supervening the matter, and in a way that 'invites an assumption of guilt for illness which ... becomes one's own fault'.[29] Ironically, working-class interviewees are *least* likely to mention the social inequalities and environmental adversities known to make a fundamental contribution to their own degree of sickness and well-being. They are more inclined to react with disbelief when confronted with the evidence of documents such as *The Marmot Report*,[30] which spell out precisely this kind of relationship.

In the case of psychological problems, things are more ambiguous. Few of the seminal studies that relate psychological problems to life history and social circumstances have looked at the extent to which the afflicted individuals *believe* that their difficulties speak of their experiences. Certainly, the harmful nature of social circumstances rarely appears in the writings of psychological therapists. By contrast, surveys in the UK and elsewhere suggest that lay people from all backgrounds are more willing to place the blame for mental disturbance on worklessness, loneliness, abusive relationships, poor general health and material and financial hardship – in short, upon a cruel world. However, this welcome dose of realism is not quite what it seems. On the curative side of the balance sheet, the same emphasis upon individual effort returns, conceived as the struggle and responsibility to seek recreation, preserve friendships and, most important, to keep an optimistic attitude. Whether this outlook reflects the influence of health promotion messages in which the endeavour to maintain well-being has become a moral duty, or a pragmatic decision to make the best of things in the face of unyielding circumstances, it certainly sits well with the 'all in the mind' ethos of psychological therapy.

Most therapists aim to increase their client's sense of conscious control over themselves and their world. The construct of 'client motivation' is a kind of internal psychological dynamo, waiting to be rewound by an inspired reappraisal of options or hidden potentials; this notion has wide currency in health promotion, and in the treatment of addiction, depression, anxiety and low self-esteem.[31] In seeming defiance of their own analyses (which, when all is said and done, show that it is actions and habits rather than thoughts that are the bedrock of self-control), some psychologists have written popular works of self-help that boldly declare the reality of 'willpower', presented not just as a metaphor for how desirable behaviour or actions might be sustained, but as a kind of muscle behind the forehead, ready and waiting to be pumped up with the right dose of self-affirmation. Willpower thus operates at the level of changing one's subjective experience, and sometimes at the level of action as well.[32]

Blatant or subtle, the message is the same. The recipient of talking treatment is confirmed as an 'integrated, wilful, self motivated, choice making, bounded entity activated by some kind of inner force'.[33] We can choose to change ourselves, with a little help from outside, and for many, perhaps most approaches, it is a change of mind that comes first. As the British CBT therapist David Clark observes, 'all therapies work by altering dysfunctional cognitions, either directly or indirectly.'[34] CBT has always been among the leading examples of this outlook, its *raison d'être* that misery must result from an over-abundance of negative thoughts about self, world and future. However, the evidence for this claim is equivocal.

To show that disturbed thinking is the prime mover of distress, and that changed thoughts can change hearts, CBT researchers also need to show that disturbed thinking patterns are found more often in people who suffer from clinical problems, as opposed to people who do not. This key hypothesis is not always supported.[35] In the case of depression, for example, independent research suggests that people who are moderately depressed hold a more realistic view of their capabilities and of their ability to control their situation than do people who seem to be healthy.[36] By the standards of cognitive therapy – which began with the assumption that we are all in the business of testing our beliefs against reality and that we become disturbed to the extent that our ideas become unrealistic – such people are clearly functioning well. It might be said that for them 'reality' rather than cognition stands in need of adjustment.

Aaron Beck and other therapists have reacted to this finding first by acknowledging that some depressed people might be thinking logically (in fact 'more logically') after all, and secondly, by arguing that good mental health depends not always upon the realism of our thoughts, but sometimes, upon our talent for maintaining positive illusions. Whether or not this answer is an adroit development, or a post hoc fudge, is perhaps a matter of opinion. It certainly makes the theory more complex and vague in its predictions. This answer also brings Beck's teachings several steps closer to folk psychological notions of self-improvement (that is, 'look on the bright side of life'), and to prevalent self-help and popular culture, which holds self-regard synonymous with good fortune.

In the case of Beck's triad of gloomy beliefs about self, world and future (held to be the basis for depression),[37] there are people who show little sign of hosting this pattern of thinking, but who still meet all of the DSM criteria for a major depressive episode. They are, for instance, fatigued, restless, awake all hours, shedding weight and unable to find much pleasure in anything. They may be chronically overworking themselves, or have joined a religious movement or self-help cult, but in any case they declare their optimism, as they push onwards to the hoped-for recovery. Their condition is a direct refutation of Beck's claim.[38]

A further requirement in support of an 'all-in-the-mind' outlook is that it should be possible to show that the changes in cognitive patterns claimed to result from therapy will precede or at least keep pace with reported changes in the symptoms of emotional distress. Once again, the evidence is inconclusive. Most reported clinical improvement, for instance, seems to happen in the first few sessions of CBT, when therapists are getting to know their clients and before they deploy their mind-changing techniques.[39] Moreover, depressed patients with the least dysfunctional attitudes have been found to respond best to this approach. This is the reverse of what would be expected for a method that claims to work through the transmutation of misguided habits of thought.[40] Furthermore, it has been impossible to differentiate the cognitive effects of this therapy from other treatments, not so designed to remould the client's aberrant thinking style.[41]

A better test of the notion that it is change in conscious thoughts that drives clinical progress would be to study people who are undergoing therapy, to see what aspects seem to cause improvement. So-called 'treatment component analysis' studies seek to do just that, by splitting up the different therapeutic elements of CBT – for example, behavioural homework and cognitive restructuring – and then administering them separately to people in different groups, or to the same person, in a sequence.

In 2006, the clinical psychologists Richard Longmore and Michael Worrell reviewed all of the published studies of this type that they could find – 13 in total – in which nearly a thousand patients had been treated for a range of diagnoses from depression to generalised anxiety, as well as PTSD and OCD. The results were a surprise. Without exception, no matter what treatment components were involved, there were no signs that the cognitive part of therapy had had the most impact upon the profile of symptoms, either at the end of therapy, or at follow-up between one month and two years later. Indeed the segment of the therapy intended to modify thought was sometimes *less* effective than the section that focused upon changing what people *did*. In the treatment of depression, for example, behavioural activation – encouraging clients to make new friends or get a new job – was more helpful than trying to get them to rework their ideas about themselves. Several studies in this review also tracked the extent to which changes in the thought patterns of those receiving the different treatment elements might predict a subsequent lessening of their symptoms; in other words, the extent to which their conscious thoughts appeared to be in the driving seat of clinical improvement, as propounded by Beck and many others. Once again, Longmore and Worrel found little evidence to support this expectation.

As usual, the interpretation of these findings is not wholly straightforward. This time, because of the difficulty of assuring that the treatment elements were always kept entirely separate from each other, and (a rare admission) for want of measures sufficiently fine-grained to tap subtle changes in thinking and mood. Nevertheless, the overall analysis was consistent enough to be troubling: 'Taken together, these findings reveal a worrying lack of empirical support for some of the fundamental tenets of CBT.'[42]

Since their 2006 paper, similar results have continued to accumulate in the literature.[43] Beck and his colleagues have responded by asserting that CBT has always allowed that thoughts, moods, behaviours and bodily reactions can mutually influence each other, with a change in any one of them producing a shift in the others.[44] This view is more in line with what cognitive researchers like John Teasdale have been saying for 20 years,[45] and, while it seems like a step in the right direction on scientific and common-sense grounds, difficulties remain.

One of the most important of these is that CBT practitioners and researchers continue to make strong claims about the power of mind over matter because of a basic problem which afflicts virtually all the research in this field, namely the relentless focus upon the beliefs and emotions expressed by clients and research participants, with little attempt to compare these statements against the actual situations in which they live, and that might well have a profound effect upon how they feel.[46] This is rather like studying the patterns in one of those snowstorm-effect paperweights that need to be shaken to produce a blizzard, without reference to whether or not it had been shook a few seconds before.

Moreover, this school, in common with most of the others, holds that in the end, it is the client who possesses the inner strength to set themselves on course for a better life, via the diligent application of techniques. Whatever our mental and spiritual condition, there is a powerful (but perhaps slumbering) CEO inside of us, awaiting the therapist's call. But this notion, of a unitary conscious self as the ultimate decider behind all that we think, feel and do is questionable on logical grounds alone. If the self was the original fount of our actions, then, in trying to account for how such decisions are made, we would need another one sitting inside of it to explain *its* behaviour, and so on, in an infinite regress. The problem does not go away even when therapists adduce dynamic unconscious processes, such as the Freudian id and ego for instance, or the Cartesian theatre of the mind (the 'global workspace') favoured by the cognitive practitioners – because each of these retains its own mysterious agent-observer. British readers may recall the children's cartoon characters known as the Numskulls: a team of tiny humanoids, inhabiting the brain of a hapless middle-aged man, each of them responsible for pushing the buttons and pulling the levers that actuated his body in its daily round.[47] The traditional way out of such difficulties has been to assume that at some point, despite the myriad influences that constrain and shape us, the indwelling self somehow rises above to become an ultimate decider, completely free of prior causes or conditions: rather like God. The best that can be said of this notion is that it runs counter to everything known about the biological realm, not to mention the obvious weight of habit in human life. Free will is unnatural.

Though we all have the sense that we cause our actions, this feeling, compelling as it may be, is not necessarily a good foundation for grasping how the mind works, any more than the experience of seeing the sun circle around the horizon every day was a good basis for understanding the earth's place in the solar system.

The experimental psychologist who has probably done most to study the phenomenon of willpower is Daniel Wegner, at the Massachusetts Institute of Technology. The starting-point for his analysis is the psychological research that shows how our minds run at a mainly automatic level. Our immediate decisions and actions – as in driving along a familiar route, playing tennis, or making a snap judgement about a stranger – all are governed by processes of which we are usually unaware. In contrast, lay people (and many psychologists) have assumed that it is in more deliberate activities like playing chess, having a conversation, climbing a mountain, or working with a therapist to become more confident, that an inner agent or 'self' takes charge.

But even these forms of apparent conscious control are questioned by Wegner: when he considers a wide range of phenomena where people carry out purposeful actions but where 'the will' has appeared to break down, including hypnotically induced (and bizarre) conduct, automatic writing, dowsing, 'paranormal' communication, neurological syndromes that disconnect action from intention, and research which implies that the brain can prepare for voluntary movement before someone knows that they intend to act. With his colleagues, he has also conducted ingenious experiments, in which alert and healthy participants have been easily duped into the belief that they were, for example, steering a computer mouse shared with a confederate of the researcher, controlling the movement of someone else's arms (even when they knew that this was an illusion),[48] and boosting a basketball team's performance, via supposed 'mental influence'.[49] Absurd as some of these examples might seem in the light of cool reflection, many people came to believe in them, because they shared an habitual human tendency to assume that it is our conscious minds that cause things to happen, and this assumption is easily overextended.

For Wegner, this evidence points in one direction. In our daily lives, we use unspoken rules of thumb to decide whether or not it is our own thoughts that are causing our acts, which we then claim for ourselves *only* when they match what we are doing, when they happen just beforehand, and when we can see no contrary reasons to account for what we've done. Both our feelings of authorship *and* our actions are sustained by mechanisms outside of our ken 'When we look at ourselves, we perceive a simple and often astonishing apparent causal sequence (I thought of it and it happened!) when the real causal sequence underlying our behaviour is complex, multithreaded, and unknown to us as it happens.'[50]

Our conscious intention to change our behaviour, judgments, or feelings is not the cause of what follows, but is instead our best guess of what it will be. Wegner suggests that controlled, effortful activities, like restraining ourselves from lighting another cigarette, or spending an hour doing our cognitive therapy homework assignment, will feel as if they are strongly willed – the measure of our determination and grit – because we may have spent a lot of time pondering each activity (and perhaps in the grip of some emotional turmoil), before the intended outcome occurs. It is this agonised and prolonged 'preview' of the desired result that strengthens the impression that it was wrought by our conscious mind.

The basis of our existence is opposite to how we feel it to be. There is no single internal decider – 'some concentrated lump of mental specialness'[51] – pushing everything along and holding it all together. The self, as traditionally conceived (and as viewed in most psychotherapy) is an illusion. Rather than the source of our activities, it is more like a story, inscribed in our memory, line by line, every time that we have the experience of causing our actions, which we and everyone else then attribute to the little person sitting inside of our head. This view of consciousness, downgraded to a kind of afterthought, is shared by the philosopher Daniel Dennett,[52] and by the psychologists Sue Blackmore[53] and Guy Claxton,[54] who, in support of their views, draw upon classical Buddhist philosophy, as well as neuroscience.

Others are not so convinced. For instance, the Canadian cognitive scientist Merlin Donald argues that humans are quintessentially striving and goal directed, and that consciousness therefore remains the conductor of our activity in the world, even if it relies upon automatic mental processes to do most of the work. In our social lives, this labour can be very complex indeed, as Donald shows by the example of the artful heroine of Henry James's novel *The Bostonians*, as she weaves many layers of deception to attain her ultimate goals. Compelling as it may seem, however, this analysis begs the question of how far, from a more distant perspective, her performance would appear – not as her exclusive handiwork – but as a dynamic pattern that emerges from the interplay between her personal history, social milieu and nervous system; from this viewpoint, her conduct starts to look like inevitability, more than craft.[55]

Donald is also a critic of the kind of laboratory studies cited by Wegner, which cannot conclusively show that our feeling of control is an illusion – only that it can be fallible under certain unusual conditions. Strictly speaking, this is correct. It may be impossible to settle this question until we are able to map every aspect of brain function in a conscious subject, and then compare it to what they are doing and to what they are thinking, in real time. Such a day is far distant and may never arrive. In the meantime, the main weakness of this argument is that there are more situations in life that fit Wegner's theories than might be apparent, at first glimpse. Creativity and insight in the arts and sciences, not to mention mundane situations, often rely upon the harvesting of ideas that have grown, unbidden in the mind, long after the seed of a question has been planted.

More generally, 60 years of social psychology research has shown that we are only too ready to revise our memories of our attitudes and intentions to justify our actions.[56] It is as if the fox in Aesop's fable not only decides that it did not want the sour grapes in the first place, but that, in wandering near to the vineyard, it had never been planning to steal them, either. This unconscious smoothing over of the inconvenient contradictions in our narrative can happen for two main reasons. First, because the mismatch between our past intentions and present action is uncomfortable, and so we try to shrink our unease, by revising the truth in line with our preferred self-image as decisive, rational and consistent; and secondly, because we are not as transparent to ourselves as we like to believe, often having to guess our own reasons by watching our own conduct, which leaves the former a hostage to revision. These well-known processes are a requirement of the illusion of free will, which would be much harder to sustain if we could easily grasp the contradictions between what we said or did yesterday, and what we are up to today.[57]

A CEO, OR A COOPERATIVE?

The twin assumptions that drive the psychology industry and that have been examined in this chapter are dubious. Self-awareness (or introspection) is not a faculty available to the bidding of therapist or client. It is an action – built from the apprehension of inner speech and of feelings, from the observation of one's own conduct, and from memory, guesswork, the hints of others, and received ideas about how we should feel and think in a given situation. Likewise, there are few reasons to believe that we have a hidden faculty of willpower waiting to be engaged by anyone. If we might be no freer in an absolute sense than any other creature, then we are certainly more complicated and less predictable, precisely because of the many experiences and influences that have become part of who and what we are, and that lend us whatever passions, commitments and creativity we might have. Rather than being our own CEOs, we are more like an assemblage of voices – muttering, singing, or shouting of many things, some of which happened long ago, but few of them within the reach of the talking therapist. If such insights are sometimes surprising, then none of them are new. Perhaps the most interesting thing about the evidence discussed here is not that it exists, but that no one accorded with real authority in the field has ever bothered to take much notice of it.

4
Does Therapy Work?

Psychotherapy works. It works.

M.A. Hubble et al.[1]

... the mental health professions have made the egregious error of believing their own press releases.

R.A. Fancher[2]

It is no simple matter to make a clinical assessment of a talking treatment or technique. The earliest claims to effectiveness came from the single case studies of the psychoanalytic schools, but this approach was anecdotal, prone to bias and therefore unscientific. The original studies into psychotherapy effectiveness that focused upon recovery rates in groups of patients took place in the 1930s and 1940s, and suggested that about two-thirds of them improved and that one-third got worse after treatment – which was mainly with variants of psychoanalysis, the leading therapy of the day.[3] Psychotherapists everywhere drew comfort from this finding, until the behaviourist psychologist Hans Eysenck wrote a harsh critique in 1952. Studies of groups of 'neurotic' people (that is, suffering from anxiety or depression) who had received no talking therapy showed that similar proportions were cured or much improved within two years of the onset of their illness. He believed that this phenomenon of 'spontaneous remission' showed that most patients naturally returned to their normal level of psychological functioning after a period of time and that, as for many minor physical illnesses, their disturbances were 'self-limiting'.[4] This trend for milder forms of malaise to dwindle regardless has since been documented in a wide range of problems, and has been attributed to gains in emotional or material support, seasonal effects upon mood, escape from (or adjustment to) wearing circumstances, and the sufferer having learned to deal with their problems through personal experience.[5]

Even if Eysenck's original data and conclusions were later questioned,[6] the general issue of spontaneous recovery has continued to haunt the field, particularly in the era of managed care and evidence-based medicine. Over the last half-century, supporters of psychotherapy have followed the pattern of general medicine by trying to create better studies, in the form of randomised controlled clinical trials (RCTs). These are experiments, designed to test a new treatment in a situation that removes every alternative explanation for the clinical outcome. In a typical RCT, one group of individuals will receive the therapy in question, while another group will get either a different form of therapy that is well validated, or a credible placebo or sham treatment, intended to have all of the outward trappings of a curative method, but lacking the active ingredients. Some RCTs will also include a group of people who remain on a waiting list and who therefore do not receive any form of psychological intervention. In a properly run RCT, both clients and therapists should be randomly allocated to each of the relevant groups. Where a sham or placebo therapy is used, everyone – the researchers, the evaluators and the patients themselves – should be equally blind in respect of who is receiving it and who is getting the genuine article; the outcomes should be measured with yardsticks that are both reliable and valid, and by people who are as disinterested in the results as possible. Thousands of such trials have been done in the United States and Europe alone. The results have been generally positive but far from uniform.[7]

In search of a stronger case for talking treatment, researchers have turned to the technique of meta-analysis. The average findings of large numbers of RCTs are pooled and then examined together, in an 'efficient and maximally objective integrative summary of the primary studies', which makes the general trends much clearer, with the aim of settling the question of effectiveness once and for all.[8]

One of the first of these summaries, conducted in 1980 by Smith, Glass and Miller, drew upon 475 separate studies comparing treated and untreated groups, and concluded that the average treated client was likely to feel better than 85 per cent of those who stayed on a waiting list.[9] These findings were questioned for their over-generous and vague measures of outcome such as 'client satisfaction'.[10] However, further reassessments seemed to confirm the potency of psychological therapy, at least to the satisfaction of most practitioners within the field. Meta-analytic studies continue to be published, albeit with newer statistical methods that yield somewhat smaller effect sizes, about three-quarters of that found in the earlier studies.[11] Often, these investigations focus upon a specific group of patients such as elderly people, or individuals with drink problems, or upon a tighter range of interventions, such as psychodynamic treatment, computerised therapy, or group-based social skills training.[12]

Debate continues as to whether this meta-analytic literature shows that particular therapies, especially CBT, might be slightly more effective than others.[13] But the general message is the same: talking therapy is a reliable remedy for sadness, fear, worry and a host of other personal ills. It compares well with other psychiatric treatments such as antidepressants, that are themselves increasingly starting to look like placebo treatments.[14] Encouraged by these conclusions, many practitioners and researchers argue that there is no longer any need to study the clinical value of talking therapy per se, which is now an established fact, that justifies the use of standard treatment controls. The field has reached scientific maturity, and the focus should move instead to finding the therapeutic ingredients that are most suited to specific clinical problems and client groups, and in which particular settings – in other words, what works best, for whom.[15]

But how warranted is this confidence? The meta-analytic literature is a tower built from the many bricks of individual RCTs. In mainstream medical research, one of the main rationales for the creation of the RCT method was the growing realisation of the power of placebo influences, and because these present key problems in psychological research and feature so much in the discussion that follows, it is worthwhile taking a closer look at them.

THE PLACEBO EFFECT IN MEDICINE

The placebo effect refers to the successful treatment of a condition with an empty ritual or an inert substance (such as a salt or sugar pill) that, by the lights of current medical knowledge, can have no specific effect upon the malady in question. Placebo treatments have a long history in medicine. The sixteenth-century essayist Montaigne describes a fake but seemingly helpful enema therapy for kidney stones.[16] Up until the early twentieth century, doctors had little capacity to treat common diseases like cancer, pneumonia and tuberculosis and as they themselves sometimes perceived, most of their remedies were for comfort only, and some did more harm than good. Placebo effects show the impress of cultural beliefs; that mind and body are separate neither from each other, nor from powerful social influences.[17]

Clinical persuasion and patient faith (or credulity) still form a part of current medical treatments. For complaints that involve a large psychosomatic component, false but believable therapies can yield reports of improvement that approach those of active drugs. Gastric ulcers, rheumatoid arthritis and urinary incontinence, cough, mood changes, angina pectoris, hypertension and headache, nausea, the common cold, depression, asthma and chronic pain: all of these conditions and more can respond to dummy pills. Patients are also known to report 'side-effects from fake treatments, and which can manifest as skin rashes, stomach pains and changes in mental concentration and hearing sensitivity – the so-called "nocebo effect"'.[18]

In their in-depth discussion of the placebo influence as it relates to psychiatric interventions, the American psychologists Seymour Fisher and Roger Greenberg note that the scientific and advertising literature portrays the action of psychiatric drugs purely as a matter of chemistry.[19] There has been a concerted forgetting of the scientific literature of the 1950s and 1960s, which showed that what patients report about these agents is highly dependent upon their social background, their mental and physical state and upon where the drugs are dispensed, and by whom.[20]

For instance, the perceived enthusiasm and therapeutic conviction of the individual administering 'tranquillising' pills made of sugar and flour is important. A physician perceived to have a more senior status, or to have a warm, supportive attitude, can double or even triple the effectiveness of a placebo prescription, when compared with a more lowly or indifferent colleague. Similar rules apply to real drugs. Phobic and anxious patients do best with green pills and least with red. Patients can respond differently, depending upon whether or not they receive their tablets in ordinary outpatient clinics or in prestigious research settings, as individuals or as part of a group, and whether they had a chance to talk about how their bodies react to their medicine. Clients who wrongly believe that they are getting a diluted dose will respond accordingly, and not just for how anxious or calm they feel, but even for physical tests that measure their reaction time and strength of grip. Patients who believe (wrongly) that their clinician has been deceiving them, who think that they have been taking only a pretend capsule, will duly fail to report the normal subjective effects of a well-known tranquilliser such as phenobarbital. Researchers increasingly see that for any psychoactive substance, from alcohol to antidepressants, the line between what the person expects the drug to do and its 'actual' physiological and psychological effects is always blurred, and is more uncertain than was once believed.[21]

On the patient's side, the placebo reaction seems to reflect their hope that things will improve, and their openness toward the expectations of those who possess authority and expertise. Placebos work not just through the patient's openness to suggestion, but because they also serve their need for an experience that denies, justifies, or conceals important feelings. The placebo response confirms the reality of one's distress (if we respond to treatment then we must have been genuinely ill in the first place) and it can signify a desire to improve. The reaction is part of 'a general capacity to adapt, to capitalize on the potential provided by pretense and illusion, and to mobilize one's creative (self healing) powers'.[22] If reassurance and advice from an expert are a significant source of solace, then we are coming close, perhaps too close, to capturing the essence of psychotherapy itself.

PLACEBO EFFECTS IN THE TESTING (AND THE PRACTICE) OF PSYCHOLOGICAL TREATMENTS

One of the consistent rules of fake treatments in western culture is that the more impressive the technology, the stronger its placebo heft. Tablets with technical sounding names and boldly embossed packaging are more potent than their plainly wrapped equivalents, but they are not as powerful as imposing medical devices, gadgets and procedures – which can sway the doctor as much as the patient. In the United States, for instance, arthroscopy for diseased knees and a surgical therapy for angina were widely practiced, until placebo treatments involving anaesthesia and plausible (but superficial) surgical cuts showed that the genuine operations carried no added benefits.[23] In the realm of psychological treatment, this kind of placebo influence is almost certainly of importance for therapies such as CBT and some of its offshoots, such as EMDR (eye movement desensitisation and reprocessing – discussed later in this chapter): all of which use a technical vocabulary that implies a firm scientific grasp of the patient's problems, and a corresponding toolkit for fixing them.[24] Psychodynamic practitioners describe the arcane complexities of the transference relationship, the finely honed listening and interpretive skills that are required to reach the client's innermost world, and which can come only from lengthy training, and – for the purists – from personal analytic therapy.[25] This kind of jargon also bestows prestige and mystique and creates a sense of initiation and togetherness. If humanist practitioners are less inclined to deploy technical language, they instead demonstrate that they are seeking to build a relationship that is intense, and deep enough, to exceed most common-or-garden encounters between professionals and the people who pay for their services. Outside of the worlds of celebrity or of dictatorship, few of us can expect any listener to follow and scrutinise a monologue about ourselves with the care of an astronomer studying a new star.[26] All therapists share the normal human tendency for seeking information that confirms their pre-existing beliefs, and it is not surprising that after a few minutes of talking to their clients, they will rapidly find the mental constructs that they are looking for and exert more influence for doing so.

If we look at the therapeutic encounter itself, there are many other reasons why psychological treatment is likely to persuade. Thanks to the Internet, some clients might be better-informed consumers of talking treatment than was once the case.[27] However, the very term 'client' or 'service user' can be misleading, especially for poorer individuals who rely on public health care, who may have little knowledge of either the array of psychological therapies from which to choose, or control over what kind of therapist that they get.[28] In addition, poorer and working-class individuals are known to be generally more compliant in their dealings with middle-class health professionals.[29]

Even where the recipient is knowing and assertive, the therapist retains authority and influence. As experts, they have the most say over the nature and limits of the treatment, which typically occurs on their own territory, while the client is made vulnerable by their one-sided disclosure of secret worries and fears.[30] The consultation might happen in a medical outpatient or university setting, hinting at knowledge and proficiency, if not prestige, and in a consulting room perhaps lined with impressive professional certificates, books and journals (especially if the therapist is a senior practitioner, or working in private practice). Furthermore, few clients appear to see a clear difference between pop psychology – that is, the television world of Doctor Phil and Super Nanny with their confident diagnoses and quick cures – and its professional counterpart.[31] Together with the intimacy, emotional intensity and relatively prolonged duration of talking therapy, which can run from a handful to many dozens of sessions, these magical symbols and beliefs would be enough in themselves to ensure that psychological treatment is a potent form of persuasion.

The talking therapies also incarnate some of the central beliefs, or perhaps myths, of western culture. Most forms of psychotherapy, particularly the more mechanistic kinds such as CBT, reflect a widely shared belief that technology can solve our problems, in a society in which the chief value, purpose and goal is one of maximum efficiency and consumption, or happiness.[32] These expectations are mirrored in and authorised by the massive popularity of self-help publications, websites and television programmes promising techniques for curing everything from shyness to acne, and which closely resemble the methods used by qualified therapists and clinicians.[33]

Talking therapy also endorses the received view of the person as a

> ... bounded, unique, more or less integrated motivational and cognitive universe, a dynamic centre of awareness, emotion, judgment and action organized into a distinctive whole and set contrastively against other such wholes and against a social and natural background.[34]

According to the anthropologist Elizabeth Throop, this outlook (or perhaps 'inlook') is alien to most cultures across the world, in which feelings, actions and personal troubles are understood to be far more the gift of context – family, community, natural and supernatural – in which all are enmeshed.[35] The western preference for interior explanations owes something to religious ideas, the Judaeo-Christian belief in a soul, and its reinvention as mind–body dualism in the seventeenth century and onward into the Enlightenment.[36]

Indeed, many historians and critics believe that the ethos of modern talking treatments can be traced to religious (and especially Protestant) ideas of moral and personal improvement via self-scrutiny and affirmations to work harder upon one's personal goals.[37] The popular psychology movements that grew up from the close of the nineteenth century, reaching their apotheosis in the works of post-war writers like Dale Carnegie, who advocated positive thinking and self-promotion as the highway to well-being and competitive success in business and in social life.[38]

The main (often contradictory) goals of most therapies are to be happy, more self-aware, independent and fulfilled, and to make a better adjustment to the world – all through taking full responsibility for studying and manipulating one's feelings and actions. In this regard, and despite its focus on enjoyment rather than duty, twenty-first-century therapy still harbours religious undercurrents. It carries a heavy load of moral expectations. Prominent therapists and researchers such as Arthur Bohart and Karen Tallman[39] invoke the 'heroic client', as the chief architect of their own personal change, awaiting inspiration from the right therapist. Far from unburdening the recipient, this kind of outlook seems to do the exact opposite. As in the religious confessional, failure in therapy is seldom considered to be a failure of the method or philosophy itself (or even of the practitioner), but of the patient's unwillingness to be honest about themselves or to work hard enough upon the techniques.[40]

Almost every psychological therapy rests upon an implicit belief – literally, the 'faith of the counsellors'[41] – that whatever the client brings, *something* can be done to improve things. The concept of willpower remains central – often disguised in the language of motivation, desire, intentionality, or effort. Some early therapies explicitly embraced this idea: the German pre-Second World War psychoanalyst Otto Rank created 'will therapy', which lost kudos because of its association with Nazism.[42] But these ideas continue. 'Rational emotive therapy' emphasizes the need for clients to be forceful with themselves in practicing their new social skills and in rehearsing their desired, rational beliefs.[43] CBT practitioners chide their clients to keep challenging their negative thoughts. The self-actualising tendency – the desire for personal growth within Rogerian therapy – amounts, in the end, to an injunction that the client should be self-directing, even self-creating.[44] The American psychologist Roy Baumeister advocates a form of therapy explicitly designed to promote willpower, conceived as a kind of mental muscle that grows through the exercise of diligent habits.[45] It is but a short step from these notions to the belief that failure in therapy – that is, their wilful denial of the inner strength or discipline needed to overcome adversity – is shameful for the client.[46] Added to which, it seems that therapists' perceptions of their clients are often more disparaging than those of lay people, who, when accounting for clinical distress, are less inclined to reach for psychiatric diagnoses or to notions of stubborn resistance to the insights on offer from the expert.[47] In these circumstances, would it be very surprising then, if clients took action to pre-empt such harsh judgement?

The psychologist Anne Kelly thinks that this is precisely what happens. She has found evidence for what she calls a 'self-presentational view' of talking treatment.[48] By this, Kelly means that in the course of their therapy, many clients develop some diffidence toward their counsellor, because of the personal shortcomings that they have revealed. In compensation, she argues, each client strives to present themselves in a more favourable light. Kelly's focus is on the client's willingness to admit their previous culpable deeds and thoughts, and she takes it for granted that therapy is usually helpful. Nevertheless, her analysis clearly speaks to the possibility that this kind of fudging and silencing might extend to the client's willingness to say whether or not they are benefiting from their therapy: where both parties know that improvement is normal and expected. An admission of failure becomes a sign of personal inadequacy, and a source of guilty worry about earning the tacit disapproval of the healer. It seems reasonable to conclude that, in psychotherapy research studies, such admissions of disappointment might be avoided or denied by many clients: even – or perhaps especially – to themselves.

The key question, of course, is to what extent the claims for psychotherapy effectiveness might be distorted by such tendencies. As the American social worker and academic William Epstein points out, the scale of this problem becomes apparent when estimates of psychotherapy effect size are compared with what other investigators have discovered about so-called 'demand-characteristics', which were well understood by some researchers as long ago as the 1930s. These are the covert and unconscious cues given out by the researchers in psychology experiments into perception and memory for instance, and which encourage participants to report the kinds of results that the researchers desire.[49] Even lab rats running in mazes will change their performance in line with slight and unintentional differences in their handling by experimenters. In the case of humans, these directions are more subtle, and may include shifts in eye contact and gaze, voice timbre and pacing, and bodily posture. This capacity for covert communication to shape judgement and conduct (most notable in military organisations) can operate across a very wide range of situations. For instance, there is the 'Pygmalion effect', named after the myth of the king of Cyprus who carved a statue and brought it to life. When deceived into making a high estimate of the academic ability of particular students, teachers will teach these 'brighter' individuals with greater verve, leading to modest but significant increases in their academic performance.[50] Recent work in the American judicial system implies that a judge's beliefs about the guilt of trial defendants can be unwittingly conveyed to juries by the manner in which instructions are delivered, with consequences for sentencing.[51] In clinical medicine, a physician's tone of voice can predict their effectiveness in persuading patients to accept treatment, and their proneness to being sued.[52]

If these effects are powerful and reliable then, it also worth bearing in mind that, when they are measured, they can surpass the amount of change that is claimed for psychological therapy, which amounts to a warning sign that the standards of scientific investigation in this field need to be very high. But is this expectation borne out in practice?

THE LIMITATIONS OF THE PSYCHOTHERAPY OUTCOME LITERATURE

To begin with a caveat, the degree of reported benefits of psychotherapy in comparison to placebo controls is modest: across a wide range of outcome measures, no more than six to fourteen percentage points in the leading meta-analyses.[53] This slight margin might be acceptable, were it not for the many other sources of bias and distortion that overshadow the research.

For one thing, although the RCT method is widely seen as the gold standard of medical research, its adherents admit that it has some difficulties. RCT methods are not as objective and value free as supposed. It is hard – perhaps impossible – to provide an adequate placebo for any given psychotherapy that is under investigation, because a truly convincing sham treatment would amount to a new form of mind cure in its own right.[54] Some researchers have tried to answer this conundrum by creating what are known as dismantling and substitution designs, in which a group of patients receiving a specific therapy such as CBT are compared with another group in which key elements of this treatment have been left out or swapped for elements from a different therapy. These designs come closer to providing a genuine placebo in that the therapists are more likely to share a conviction in what they are doing because of its basis in a real treatment, and so might be that much more convincing for their clients, too.[55]

However, even these studies are questionable. CBT with the 'thought-changing' bits taken out is not really an empty placebo for the 'real' treatment, because even the rump-end behavioural techniques given to the placebo group might themselves be capable of inducing cognitive change. For instance, a shy individual venturing into situations that they had once avoided might experience some shift in their view of themselves as a more confident person than they had hitherto believed, at least for the period of their treatment. One attempt to get around these problems is the 'structural placebo'. This is a pretend therapy that mimics the established one (that is under test) in all outward essentials, including: the number and length of sessions, format, levels of therapist training, readiness to shape treatment to individual client requirements, and a willingness to focus on the problems that the client brings. The main drawback with a structural placebo is that it is still hard to be sure that the therapists providing it are fully blind to the fact that they are delivering a fake. This is because the relative lack of theoretical rationale and paucity of content might give the game away to all, with the exception of the most naïve. Structural placebos are seldom employed in psychotherapy research, because they are complicated and time-consuming to arrange. When they are used, then their effects have been indistinguishable from standard CBT, at least for the treatment of anxiety and depression.[56]

No given meta-analysis, founded upon research trials, can ever exceed the quality of the studies upon which it is based. Numerous flaws run through almost the whole of the psychotherapy outcome literature, to the extent that some academics and practitioners have admitted that it is hard to decide whether the current research can tell us whether psychotherapy or counselling are helpful or not.[57]

The field has long suffered from a bias toward the selective reporting and publication of studies that show only the desired results. Studies that are negative, inconclusive, or that run strongly against the expectations of the reviewers (who are usually themselves psychotherapists) are less likely to attain publication, and where they do, this process will take longer and they will rarely be mentioned in the academic and training literature. Because we do not see many of these negative or inconclusive investigations, we get an over-optimistic assessment.[58] This is only the beginning. Too often, there are serious inadequacies in the standards of scientific investigation. Many psychotherapy trials have included inadequate control groups, consisting only of individuals who remain on a waiting list or who receive a less credible form of pseudo-therapy, delivered with obviously limited commitment by the researchers or their colleagues.[59] Clients have been chosen from groups who are more likely to respond well to their treatment, such as university students, or on the basis of having less complex or intractable problems that fit a single psychiatric diagnosis, or, in some cases, for their 'psychological mindedness' – that is, their preference for describing their problems in the language of psychological therapy and their faith in its powers.[60]

Smith and colleagues' 1980 meta-analysis opened the gate to acceptance of these doubtful practices, which have since been widely replicated and indeed are often explicit, because researchers are interested in achieving a seemingly neat demonstration that a therapy works. It is easier to do this if the clients recruited have simpler problems and are not suffering from additional difficulties that complicate the picture. The studies that inform the large-scale and most widely cited meta-analyses are therefore demonstrations of efficacy: psychotherapy delivered under optimum conditions. This is very different to what happens in the typical outpatient clinic, where a third or more of clients will have multiple mental health diagnoses and a long history of personal difficulties, compounded by physical health problems and enduring environmental adversities, including abusive relationships, poverty and community breakdown.[61] Studies of clinical effectiveness in these more realistic settings give a better indication of how well the therapy works in routine daily practice.

Few critics seem to have been interested in posing the questions that are implied in the above discussion. Those that have, such as the philosopher Edwin Erwin, have argued that even as it continues to bloom, the psychotherapy field is in a state of scientific crisis, whether its supporters admit this or not.[62] Erwin's arguments were taken several stages further by the American social scientist William Epstein, who in the early 1990s examined some of the most cited literature on the effectiveness of talking treatment, and found all of it to be badly wanting on methodological grounds.[63] Fifteen years later, Epstein critically examined the best-quality research of the preceding decade, as featured in the field's top three journals: the *American Journal of Psychiatry*, the *Archives of General Psychiatry* and the *Journal of Consulting and Clinical Psychiatry*. A careful scrutiny of this evidence for psychodynamic, behavioural and cognitive behavioural therapy gave a similarly dispiriting picture.[64]

The most popular measurement instruments used by psychotherapy researchers were either unreliable – that is, unable to yield consistent counts of what they purported to measure, or of low validity – that is, unable to show that they were capturing the putative mental illness or behaviour for which they were designed. Some of them were deficient in both areas. Epstein also found methodological problems that were familiar from his previous assays: samples sizes that were perilously small, a failure to control for clients dropping out of the treatment or placebo groups (a pattern that can easily skew the results in favour of the treatment), and insufficient effort to ensure that recipients were randomly assigned to their groups. Studies were routinely analysed with statistical methods that concealed or downplayed large variations in client outcome, including the likelihood that some of the treated ones got worse.

Epstein has come to similar conclusions in a recent review of the literature on client 'empowerment' via psychological techniques.[65]

These were not the only concerns. One of the most fundamental was an over-reliance upon patient self-report. This has always been a questionable practice, given what is known about the influence of context and expectations upon what people will say to researchers; too often, researchers are the last people to see that they have been told what they want to hear.[66] Where it does not rely exclusively upon client report, the outcome research for talking treatment too often depends upon evaluations by therapists or by individuals associated with the institutions that support the practice, teaching and promotion of their work. It should be obvious that these are the very people who have the most to lose from any demonstration of the ineffectiveness of what they are judging.

These basic issues have been little discussed in the literature, which for the most part carries on as if experimental social psychology had never existed. Instead, the preference is for a credulous (and comfortable) acceptance of what clients and their relatives might say about their progress, in the absence of any third-party attempts to monitor the client's journey in the world outside of the consulting room. For this alone, there is little reason to believe that the claimed benefits of psychotherapy amount to more than placebo effects.

In his summary of the last half-century of this research literature, Epstein is damning: ' ... there has never been a scientifically credible study that attests to the effectiveness of any form of psychotherapy for any mental or emotional problem under any condition of treatment.'[67] The possibility that the talking remedies are the equivalent of pills made of sugar and flour is underscored by three other lines of evidence – the first of which is the relatively low impact of therapeutic methods as tools of change.

HOW IMPORTANT ARE THERAPISTS' TECHNIQUES?

In physical medicine, while the bedside manner of your doctor is far from irrelevant, what counts most is their mastery of the methods and tools of their trade. A warm-hearted physician who did not understand what pill to prescribe for your life-threatening illness could prove worse than useless.

In the psychotherapy field, things are different. The most well-regarded and cited summaries in the literature suggest that, rather than precise techniques, a range of so-called 'non-specific' factors account for at least 85 per cent of the apparent beneficial effects, however these outcomes are defined or measured.[68] The exact nature of these general influences varies somewhat from study to study, but they include the personal qualities of the therapist – that is, their warmth, respectfulness and ability to form a relationship (or 'alliance') with the client. But the front-runner seems to be what the client themselves bring to therapy: their desire for personal change and belief that it can be achieved, their trust and confidence in the therapist, their personal history and current circumstances.[69]

If client motivation for therapy is often cited as the most important of these, then it is seldom analysed any further, but there are good reasons for thinking that in part it reflects the impress of the client's social background, past and present. Little is known about how class status affects the experience of counselling or psychotherapy: a topic long ignored by therapy practitioners, teachers and researchers. Sociological studies of how lay people view health and illness suggest that blue-collar individuals are less inclined to value discussion of their personal ills with care professionals, because of greater deference and lack of trust, and because they have less reason to believe that talk will lead to substantive change. As far as research into psychotherapy itself is concerned, the evidence on this point is mixed. However, more studies seem to show that lower-class clients are most likely to drop out of therapy, and it is rare to find any study in which they gain more benefit than middle-class clients, whereas the reverse certainly occurs.[70]

Indeed, some researchers and clinicians, such as David Richards[71] and Anne Kearny,[72] have argued that the people who do best in psychological treatment are the ones known as 'YAVIS': 'young, attractive, verbal, intelligent and successful'. Originally coined by the American psychiatrist William Schofield, as a derisory comment on therapist preferences for well-heeled customers who seemed to benefit most from therapy but needed it least,[73] this term also describes the people who, historically, have been more likely to be included in clinical trials of talking treatments. The reasons for the YAVIS trend are a matter of dispute. To some extent, it may show that middle-class individuals are more inclined to share the values and outlook of therapeutic culture, especially the belief that it is useful to spend time exploring feelings and motives.[74] A further possibility is that such clients will also enjoy more of the personal, financial and social advantages that enable them to act upon whatever insights they might have garnered within the consulting room. This last possibility is suggested in a recent American study by Lydia Falconnier, a Social Work academic.[75] Falconnier looked at how therapy affected work performance as reported by lower- and middle-class patients who had been treated for depression either with CBT, interpersonal therapy, standard psychiatric care, or a placebo. This study, conducted under the aegis of the US National Institute of Mental Health during the 1980s, was one of the better ones. It boasted researchers without allegiance to the specific therapies being investigated, a large sample of over two hundred individuals and from a *relatively* wider range of economic backgrounds than usual (though it remained skewed toward the more educated and was deficient in black clients). This well-known investigation had already revealed the familiar pattern of *no difference* in outcome between the three bona fide treatments. Despite the information collected on each client's income and background, at the time social class held little interest for the researchers. However, Falconnier's subsequent analysis of the data showed that the lower-class clients did not gain nearly as much benefit in their ability to cope with their work as did the higher-status clients. This was an important result, because, aside from income, the ability to hold down (let alone enjoy) one's job is seen as crucial for good mental health by most Americans. She concluded that therapy for lower-class people should include some attempt to provide practical help with transport and child care, though she did not specify how a therapist might do this. Given what is known about the effects of social adversity upon mental health, the YAVIS trend may also be explained by the circumstance that better-off clients are less likely to be suffering from the more severe and entrenched forms of distress that resist therapeutic persuasion.

In contrast to client factors, professional knowledge and use of specific techniques routinely make a more modest contribution to the results: accounting for between 15 and 5 per cent of the outcome, at best. Moreover, those techniques and the theories that go with them seem to assume less importance as practitioners become more experienced. Over the years, therapists of widely divergent orientations seem to become more alike in how they guide and relate to their clients, and in their willingness to borrow methods and ideas from approaches outside of the ones in which they first trained.[76]

Perhaps more important than techniques is the *individual* who delivers the therapy. Only in recent years have a small group of researchers, such as the American psychologist Bruce Wampold, turned their attention to this phenomenon – sometimes described as the secret that everyone in the field knows, but is unwilling to acknowledge. Where researchers have tried to look for differences between therapists in effectiveness, then these differences account for the majority of the variance in outcome that is attributable to the practitioner – almost twice that attributed to the strength of the therapeutic relationship and far outstripping the importance of techniques. The reasons for this trend remain unclear. No one has been able to reliably show that plausible therapist attributes like gender, age, professional experience and qualifications are involved. Similarly irrelevant are the practitioner's use of clinical supervision, personal therapy or of an 'evidence-based' approach to their work, guided by the latest research and by the assiduous collection of outcome data from their clients.[77]

As in all areas of life, there is little doubt that some talking therapists are more charismatic and persuasive than are others. Geoffrey Masson's well-documented account of the abuse and exploitation of clients by some of the founding fathers of twentieth-century Anglo-American therapy suggests that such conduct could not have occurred, unless many patients were awestruck by their analyst to some degree.[78] In modern times, professionals are held perhaps in less esteem, but accounts written by contemporary clients suggest that they are still likely to accord their psychologist or counsellor a high degree of respect, and to fall in love with them on occasion.[79] This issue of charm and persuasion applies not just to individual therapists in their daily practice, but also to the teams of them who participate in clinical research trials, where the presence of charismatic leaders can potentially distort the results.[80]

In the more mundane world of daily practice, 70 years of research by humanistic therapists and others have generally shown that the therapists who do best are the ones who can demonstrate the most warmth, genuineness and attention to the thoughts and feelings of the client.[81] Exponents of the Rogerian school and integrative therapists such as Colin Feltham have argued that counsellors should be taught how to do these things more efficiently, perhaps even through an apprenticeship, rather than an exclusively academic training.[82] But if genuineness is expressed through each therapist's unique personality, then this seems to beg the question of whether anyone can be trained to 'genuinely care', and of whether most clients would be convinced by someone striving so hard to prove the point.

In line with the general verdict on the importance of non-specific effects that has been discussed so far, there is no solid evidence to suggest that the extent to which the therapist has set the client's problems in their given therapeutic model will result in any lessening of their symptoms or unhappiness. This is the conclusion of several well-conducted research studies into the value of 'clinical formulation', as it is often called.[83] This might not sound like a very significant problem for professional therapy; after all, it points in the familiar direction of a warm 'relationship' as the boat in which everything must float. But it is rather as if the client is being taken on a voyage in which the maps somehow don't count for much. Would anyone want to set foot on such a vessel? This rather discouraging finding led Chadwick and colleagues to the following reluctant (and rather understated) admission: 'at least some of the faith that therapists have in the potency of [clinical formulation] might be due to the impact it has for them personally.'[84] The British clinical psychologist Lucy Johnstone, an advocate of the idea of formulation, is honest enough to acknowledge the 'danger that [clinical formulation] is meeting our own emotional or intellectual needs and not those of the client'.[85] Other theorists perceive that techniques count mainly as symbols, but claim that they are useful precisely because of this ceremonial role, by means of which they can supposedly catalyse change in the client. Thus, therapeutic models and techniques

> … achieve their effects in large part … through the activation of and operation of placebo, hope, and expectancy. In fact, when a placebo or technically inert condition is offered in a manner that fosters positive expectations for improvement, it reliably produces effects almost as large as the bona fide treatment.[86]

Any fair assessment suggests that the theories and techniques of therapy represent little more than a comfort blanket for the practitioner and client alike, in the absence of which both of them might begin to lose faith. While faith can sometimes impel people into action, encouraging them to take up arms against their troubles, it is doubtful whether, in real life, it is enough to move mountains of the kind that lead the desperate and the deeply troubled to seek psychological therapy.

These types of findings have led one of the more thoughtful practitioners and observers of the counselling scene, Colin Feltham, to question whether talking treatment will ever deserve the appellation of being the coherent body of knowledge that it is made out to be. He asks just how is a psychotherapy system anything more than a

... mass of opinions, best guesses and selected experiences organized into one belief system among dozens of competing and conflicting others by partisan practitioners? It is more honest and accurate to say, I think, that psychotherapy systems resemble competing narratives.[87]

COMPARISONS OF AMATEUR AND PROFESSIONAL THERAPISTS

If it is difficult to show that theories or techniques are important to the outcome of talking treatment in the way that they matter in the field of medicine, then surely straightforward comparisons of amateur and professional therapists should settle the matter? There are vast numbers of professionally qualified therapists, many of them educated to postgraduate level. Health services, employers, schools and colleges must be doing something right in hiring trained professionals to administer psychological therapy – even if none of us quite know what it is, or how it works.

The first large-scale review to address this question was carried out by Durlak,[88] who collated the results of 42 separate studies that contrasted professionally trained therapists and counsellors with unschooled helpers. The professionals were a varied but eminently qualified bunch: psychologists, psychiatrists, social workers and nurses, all of them trained in psychotherapy or counselling to postgraduate level. By contrast, and depending upon the particular study, the amateurs were chosen for their reputation for being wise and helpful, or for being in a helping profession but for having received little or nothing in the way of training in talking therapy models and techniques. The results were a surprise. Apart from a single study, the non-qualified helpers were equal to or better than their trained counterparts. The irrelevancy of professional training was quickly echoed by Smith and Glass's famous 1980 meta-analysis of 475 studies of psychotherapy, which likewise showed that therapists' credentials and length of academic training were unrelated to outcome, a finding that was repeated in two other similar large-scale analyses during the same decade.[89]

Across the field, results like these have met with a mixture of dismissal and consternation. Going back to Durlak's original study, some academics and practitioners questioned his lack of discrimination in his choice of studies and of statistical methods.[90] In an attempt to answer these criticisms, Durlak's findings were re-examined with the use of more rigorous criteria that discarded some of the less reliable RCTs, but the results were much the same:

'clients who seek help from paraprofessionals are more likely to achieve resolution of their problems than those who consult professionals.'[91]

Not surprisingly, this statement met with some resistance and this review was re-examined in its own turn by another team of investigators, Berman and Norton, who winnowed out what they regarded as the strongest studies, based upon the best statistical analyses and careful design. The studies that favoured the untrained therapists were discarded most often from this second re-analysis.

The result still fell short of what might have been hoped, since the two groups came out as evenly matched. Even worse, there were no signs that the professionals were more competent in dealing with specific kinds of mental health problem, as might have been anticipated, given their previous experience and training. Berman and Norton wrapped up their findings within a rhetorical question: does training make a therapist more effective? 'On the basis of current evidence, we would have to concede that the answer is no.'[92]

In a similar vein, American research psychologist Robyn Dawes scrutinised a large range of studies that compared amateur or less-qualified psychotherapists with their more-esteemed brethren in relation to treatment, diagnosis and prediction of future mental disorder. He wrote about his findings in a landmark book, entitled *House of Cards: Psychology and Psychotherapy based on Myth.* While Dawes felt that his survey had shown that psychological treatment was helpful for most people, this was regardless of who delivered it. His main conclusion offered little consolation for the highly trained practitioner:

> Virtually all the research – and this book will reference more than three hundred empirical investigations and summaries of investigations – has found that these professional's claims to superior intuitive insight, understanding and skill as therapists are simply invalid.[93]

In contrast to these discouraging results, a more recent survey of studies focusing on the issue of academic training and therapist cure rates seems to give more succour to the professionals. In 1995, Stein and Lambert showed that postgraduate schooling in counselling or psychotherapy bestowed an advantage for rates of client satisfaction, therapy drop-out, and clinical outcome.[94] Despite the modest nature of this lead – about one-fifth of a standard deviation (which amounts to a small handful of percentage points of improvement) – this review is widely cited in the training literature as a clear and reassuring proof of the credibility of professional practice.[95] However, this optimism seems premature given the weight of the evidence discussed above, and secondly, that Stein and Lambert acknowledged that, in almost every study they examined, the amount of postgraduate schooling was confounded with another important characteristic that might have been expected to have a bearing upon their results: the extent of each therapist's prior practical experience of their trade.[96]

In fact, only two of the studies in their analysis were free of this problem: it may be no accident that these were the only studies that did not find in favour of the more qualified therapists.[97] One of these investigations, a relatively long-term scrutiny of postgraduate trainees in family treatment is particularly revealing. One hundred and seventy-six families were involved over a two-year period. These clients proved to be far less satisfied with mature trainees in the last year of their training than they were with the first-year rookies. For the original investigators, this unappealing result implied that students became colder and more rigid in their thinking, due to their growing need to get the techniques right if they were to pass their course. The authors assumed (or perhaps hoped) that after qualification, the trainees would develop a more confident and fluent integration of techniques with relaxed intuition, leading the way to superior performance. But there is an even more plausible (and damning) interpretation: that the most junior trainees were the most helpful because, unencumbered by meaningless psychological jargon and dubious theories and techniques, they had more room to listen to what their patients were actually saying, and were therefore more sensible, and humane.[98]

STUDIES OF PSYCHOLOGICAL THERAPY – ARTIFICIAL VERSUS REAL-LIFE SETTINGS

As noted above, many of the RCT studies cited in classical meta-analyses were performed in optimal circumstances upon clinically pure populations. In other words, they are studies with cherry-picked clients, in artificial environments, unrepresentative of how therapy works in the ordinary clinic. Here, many clients will have more than one psychiatric diagnosis and a range of complex and long-standing difficulties that are less amenable to therapeutic talk. Some of them will have been struggling for a long time with dependency upon alcohol or illegal substances, and suffering from physical ailments as well as from the effects of impoverishment, poor housing and community breakdown. Some of these clients will be malnourished, they may have been taking psychiatric drugs and other harmful substances for many years, with severe consequences for their general health and for their ability to hold a conversation, never mind develop insight into themselves.[99] In these circumstances, the clinicians are unlikely to be academically renowned experts, or at liberty to follow the treatment manuals designed for notional 'standardised clients'. Most likely, the practitioners will themselves be harried and poorly resourced in their work, perhaps having to see more clients per day than is good for anyone, and struggling to find a private and decently soundproof room in which to meet. These are often the norms of many public therapy services that are free at the point of delivery,[100] especially in the United States.[101]

Perhaps then it is no surprise that a consistent trend within psychotherapy outcome literature is that the better controlled the study, *and* the closer that it comes to real-life clinical settings, then the less positive the result.[102] One of the best examples of this kind of 'real-world' research design is the American multi-centre research trial, known as the 'Fort Bragg demonstration project'. The typical fragmentary care offered to troubled adolescents was compared to an 'integrated system' of mental health treatments – primarily talking therapy – delivered across a range of settings, from outpatient services to therapeutic foster homes, for a thousand children and their families in North Carolina, over a span of five years. One of the most carefully conducted studies of real-life family guidance and therapy ever undertaken, it boasted a huge client sample by the standards of the field.

The Fort Bragg project's findings were straightforward. There was no evidence of benefit in the symptoms or the lives of the recipients of the service, when compared with similar middle-class adolescents receiving ordinary (that is, hit or miss) mental health care.[103] A somewhat smaller 'replication study' carried out in nearby Stark County came to the same conclusion, but it also showed that troubled youngsters who got *no* psychiatric or psychological ministrations during the five years of the project were, at the end, as well adjusted as those who got plenty of both. Despite this resounding lack of evidence for success, most parents and children declared themselves highly satisfied with their treatment, which suggests, once again, that client contentment with psychological work bears little relation to what it actually achieves. Indeed, the leading researcher, Leonard Bickman, was rather less sanguine:

'these results should raise serious doubts about some current clinical beliefs.' In relation to psychological therapy, 'there is scant evidence of its effectiveness in real life settings.'[104]

IF THE RESEARCH IS INCONCLUSIVE AT BEST, THEN HOW HAVE THE TALKING THERAPY PROFESSIONALS REACTED?

One of the main responses of Anglo-American psychology to this research has been to ignore the flaws discussed in this chapter and to pretend that the evidence is a solid and reliable index of scientific progress. The instances of this phenomenon would fill many books, even a small library. But to take a few good examples, witness, for instance, many dozens of references in *The Depression Report*, written by the UK economist Richard Layard,[105] in collaboration with several psychiatric colleagues and the clinical psychologist David Clarke, from the Institute of Psychiatry. The literature cited in this document attests to the power and superior evidence base for CBT, as an exclusive cure for depression and anxiety, and for a host of other conditions. Yet Layard doesn't once mention any of the qualifications that surround this evidence base, of which many of the specialists whom he consulted must have been aware.

Francine Shapiro's most recent book on EMDR treatment for trauma and other problems, entitled *Getting Past your Past*, is another good instance of this practice. Often described by Shapiro,[106] the inventor of EMDR, and by its many psychologist and psychiatrist practitioners as a 'paradigm shift' in mental health care, EMDR is one of the most popular therapies in the field today. It works as follows: the client – who might be suffering from PTSD or from some other form of recurrent fear, anxiety, worry, or even from 'schizophrenia' – is asked to envisage whatever disturbs them, while visually tracking the therapist's finger as it sweeps from right to left in sets of 12 to 24 strokes. Alternatively, the therapist might rhythmically tap the client's arm or ask them to listen to a commercially available 'EMDR machine' that emits a steady stream of pinging sounds. Shapiro cites numerous studies supporting the effectiveness of EMDR. However, she fails to discuss the implications of the many studies which show, first, that EMDR is no better than any other therapy that seeks to encourage the patient to confront whatever is frightening them. She also fails to discuss the many challenges that sceptical neuropsychologists and others have made against her claims that EMDR works, uniquely, by helping the brain to effectively rewire itself, or 'reprocess' and 'reintegrate' 'trauma-related information'.[107]

Or take the renowned US psychologist Martin Seligman's endorsement of the American *Consumer Reports* magazine survey of 1994, which claimed to reveal the true extent of satisfaction evinced by American consumers of professionally delivered talking treatment. Seligman was both consultant to the survey organisers and the author of a widely cited article that praised its findings. Seligman concluded that, despite its methodological flaws, the *Consumer Reports* study gave good reasons to believe that psychological therapy is very helpful and satisfying, even for a majority of people with severe problems.[108] However, the flaws in the report are egregious. The response rate was tiny, even by normal community survey standards – only 1.6 per cent of the sample of 180,000 people said that they had actually attended therapy with a mental health professional. Worse still, the evaluation was a retrospective one and lacked a control group. This meant that it could not give a scientific answer to the most important question: whether the declared improvement was down to therapy, or to the healing effects of time, or to the well-known tendency for people to misremember exactly how they were feeling at the end or start of their treatment. Eysenck's spectre of 'spontaneous recovery' was hovering over the scene, an unwelcome (and ignored) guest. One corrective to these problems might have been to cite the rates of improvement found in the control groups used in the RCT and meta-analytic literature, discussed earlier, as a rough baseline for comparison. Seligman chose not to do this. Had he done so, it would have greatly reduced his estimates of the effectiveness of psychological treatment.

IF THE CRITICISMS OF TALKING THERAPY RESEARCH ARE DAUNTING, THEN WHERE DOES THIS LEAVE US?

Some commentators simply assume that not enough research has been done to give sensible answers to the many uncertainties about psychological therapy. This response prompts the question: how much more would be required? Literally thousands of such trials have been conducted in this field, over the last 50 years and more. Bear in mind that the efficacy of penicillin, for example, was settled without the benefit of an RCT, effectively in a single trial. Another common reaction is to argue that since the research outcomes for talking therapy are not conclusive, then the research itself must be inconclusive; this claim in fact represents a basic error of logic. Instead, the results are clear-cut in their failure to convincingly show that talking treatment works as a device for personal change.[109]

Another response is to try to dismiss the discomforting results reviewed above. According to Robyn Dawes, this takes three forms. First, therapists declare that the most critical studies have too many faults to be viable, while ignoring the key fact that they do not all share the same flaws, the one circumstance that would imply a systematic and perhaps fatal problem with this research. Secondly, they argue that once more rigorous studies are carried out, then therapy will be shown to be effective – what amounts to a statement of faith. Third, some have viewed these poor results as evidence for hidden interactions between therapists and the kinds of clients that they treat and the techniques that they use. Perhaps there are certain kinds of clients with certain kinds of problems that do better only with qualified therapists. If only we could uncover these combinations, so the thinking goes, then we would see that trained practitioners are obviously more helpful for this group. However, Dawes points out that if this is so, then it also implies that other kinds of client might do worse with qualified therapists. In which case, 'it would be extraordinarily important to discover who those clients are before employing professional therapists rather than paraprofessional ones. No such attempt has been made.'[110] And this area remains little researched at the start of the twenty-first century.[111]

Turning to the writings of Epstein, although he wrote a chapter for a book (published in Britain) that provided a platform for opposing sides in some of the key debates in the psychotherapy field,[112] this text was exceptional in the space that it gave to his observations. For instance, the latest edition of *The Handbook of Psychotherapy and Behaviour Change* (perhaps the most highly regarded and widely cited textbook in the field) cites him, without comment, as one of a number of critics of psychotherapy outcome research. More often, his work is simply ignored.[113]

One of the tiny handful of academic responses to Epstein's arguments can be found in a relatively recent edition of the *Journal of the Academy of Child and Adolescent Psychiatry* – one of the very few psychotherapy journals that bothered to review his most recent analysis of the evidence for talking therapy. In essence, Epstein is taken to task for demanding research standards that are impractically high. For instance, his belief that research on psychotherapy should be handled by non-practitioners is challenged: 'would we want research on cancer treatment handled by non-oncologists or trials of cardiac medication handled by non-cardiologists'[114] – but these analogies are false. Oncology is a proven science, with a high degree of consensus about the diagnosis, nature and treatment of the diseases with which it deals.

Epstein is also attacked for his failure to appreciate the potency of the placebo effect as a healing device that 'appears to do much good and may be the safest, most benign treatment available, more like a divine grace than a satanic deceit'.[115] This viewpoint is shared by a group of leading American researchers, Bruce Wampold being perhaps the best known, who endorse psychotherapy as an active placebo treatment, which can help the client to marshal their latent capacity to heal themselves.[116] This would be fine if we could be sure that the alleged improvements brought about by therapy, as found in the research, are more than just words. Since this is not the case, then this statement reads like an admission that the entire field is a form of snake oil. It also takes us very far away from the claims made by most therapists that it is their specialised techniques and knowledge that are the main ingredients of healing and the ultimate justification for their status and for their salaries. Could we really back graduate programmes of clinical and counselling training if all that was being offered was a mere placebo, and one that could presumably be dispensed by kindly, less highly qualified people and at a fraction of the cost?

Even those who accept the equivocal nature of the research have tended to do so in such a way that allows them to continue to support the idea that therapy is a valid and reliable way to bring about personal change, for example, David Pilgrim, a British clinical psychologist, and one of the most informed and incisive chroniclers of the psychotherapy scene. In his most recent review of the state of the art, science and effectiveness of the psychological therapies, Pilgrim argues that whatever potency they possess has little to do with technique and everything to do with the strength of the alliance between therapist and patient.[117] This viewpoint echoes the arguments of many humanistic and existentialist counsellors, who endorse the benefits of the informal elements of therapy that were at one time rejected by those who would have preferred it to be a strictly medical enterprise. Like the humanists, however, Pilgrim appears to assume that this therapeutic relationship has direct power to reach into the core of the client's psyche and remove or soothe their burdens. This conclusion is reached by way of an avoidance of the more hawkish critiques of Epstein and others, and thereby supports an over-generous interpretation of the outcome evidence for psychological therapy and of client assessments of its helpfulness. In the end, even Pilgrim finds himself unable to countenance the possibility that, too often, this occult method might be an illusion – the inevitable consequence of clients' shaping their judgements to conform to the story that they and their counsellor want to hear.

These manifold doubts come back full circle to the meta-analytic studies of psychotherapy effectiveness, discussed at the beginning of this chapter. Though presented as definitive and authoritative,[118] no meta-analysis can ever rise above the quality of the data upon which it depends. It is not enough to take a basketful of RCTs and insert them into an impersonal blending machine, hoping that something palatable will come out of the other end. In the psychotherapy field, the original analysis conducted by Smith and colleagues over 30 years ago set the standard for the acceptance of research trials of doubtful integrity. It was assumed that aggregated RCT data would cancel out the imperfections of each individual trial. However, this belief has always been questionable. In most fields of clinical investigation, it is more plausible to think that researchers will make the same mistakes in the same directions, because they tend to think alike and are looking for (and hoping to see) the same things.

The meta-analytic method is also suspect because the people who carry out the analyses rarely have a good practical knowledge of the realities of clinical research, which must be learned through hands-on experience, a process nearer to apprenticeship than to formal academic training. Without the benefit of this practice, it is impossible to judge the adequacy of the studies chosen for any given review. In the psychotherapy field, this criticism applies especially to the material cited in the US and UK government databases which provide the guidelines for all clinical procedures.[119] Furthermore, the meta-analytic method can only be considered relevant when the target group for the therapy is tightly and comprehensively defined, a rare achievement in this field, given the limitations of diagnostic testing and the tendency for researchers to ignore important biographical details when assessing their clients. Indeed, critics have argued that meta-analysis is altogether unsuited for the testing of hypotheses about particular therapies, and would be better employed in refining estimates of the level of health and illness in carefully chosen populations.[120]

IS TALKING THERAPY MERELY TALK?

In recent years, psychologists have been among the leading critics of drug company-sponsored research into the effectiveness of psychiatric medication. They have diligently exposed the methodological flaws that afflict the trialling of antidepressant and anti-psychotic agents: flaws that, apart from corporate sponsorship, are a direct mirror of those that afflict their own field. They have found it a lot harder to see the same problems on their own doorstep. By any reasonable scientific standard, the field of psychotherapy is in trouble. There is no consistent, good-quality evidence that any type of therapy can outperform a well-designed placebo, that any approach is reliably superior to another, or that any given set of curative ingredients outdo their competitors. Only one observation is upheld: that confident and emotionally warm professionals are more appreciated by their clients, and get better results, a statement that applies equally to politicians, salespeople and prostitutes.

5
'I'm not ill, I'm hurt ...' –
The Hidden Injuries of Inequality

From birth until I was the age of two, I was in the care of the Social Services, since then I have continued to be someone's patient, client or caseload. I have progressed through the socio-medico ranks from a child to a teenager, and now into my adulthood. During this time I have been 'treated' by an array of health care professionals, each of whom has tried to assist me with my problems in life. But let's not beat about the bush, what this means to you, the socially well adjusted, is that I am mentally ill, and, as I cannot cope with my daily life, I need medical help, or do I?

David Adam[1]

These words, from Scottish mental health service user David Adam, place him in the majority who attribute their torments not to damaged genes, or to a broken brain, but to the effects of a disordered world, which typically reserves its worst punishments for those with the least means. The aim of this chapter is to discuss the validity of this standpoint.

EVIDENCE FOR A SOCIAL GRADIENT IN HEALTH

At the start of the twenty-first century, for every measure of social and economic development and health that we can devise, the population of the UK is better off than at almost any other point in history. However, the benefits of these changes have not been equally shared. For example, if we take the official government categories of social class as defined by occupational role and income, people in the social class I live in on average live nearly seven years longer than people in class V, the lowest on the ladder. This is true even when allowing for the higher rates of perinatal mortality that afflict the least well-off.[2] When we compare certain regions of the UK, the contrasts in lifespan are even starker: 13.3 years of extra life for men living in Kensington, in the South-east, compared with their contemporaries residing in the most deprived areas of Glasgow.[3] If we look at the health of people in the western industrialised countries over time, then we can see that the decades from 1980 have witnessed a steady widening of the divide in mortality and well-being between rich and poor, with every sign that this trend is set to continue well into this century.[4]

EVIDENCE FOR A SOCIAL GRADIENT IN PSYCHOLOGICAL PROBLEMS

It is instructive to place this picture next to what is known (or believed) about the extent of psychological malaise in the general population, which at the present time appears to be widespread. Researchers have judged that each year, one-sixth of the working-age inhabitants of the UK experience enough fatigue, sleeplessness, irritability and worry to interfere with the demands of their daily lives, and that for a further sixth, such malaise is strong enough to merit treatment by a mental health professional.[5] Recent estimates suggest that over a million UK citizens are off work because of diagnosed mental disorder, at a cost of some £105 billion annually in treatment and health care, lost productivity and sickness benefits.[6] This is a lot of suffering, and the human costs are incalculable. The picture for many of the developed nations, including the United States, is comparable, or worse. It is projected that one in four adult Americans will suffer from a diagnosable mental disorder during their lifetime.[7] Across the world, psychological distress is the leading cause of disability in the young,[8] and for the US and Britain, in the middle aged, as well.[9] The reported incidence of these troubles seems to have increased over time. In the early twentieth century, for example, just 1 per cent of adult men in the United States said that they had experienced one episode of feeling very low or depressed by the age of 70. In the early twenty-first century, nearly a quarter of young people were so describing themselves.[10]

Mental suffering seems to be commonplace – but is there any evidence for a social gradient in such problems comparable to the one for physical illnesses? As Chapter 2 of this book showed, there are no physical tests for the vast majority of so-called 'mental disorders', which are therefore much more elusive and harder to diagnose than physical ailments. This is one reason why some psychologists[11] and psychiatrists,[12] reject the term 'mental illness' as a false medical label, concealing what could more accurately be seen as diverse forms of misery, fear, or confusion.

Notwithstanding debates over how to describe such suffering, its distribution tracks the shape of the social pyramid to a fair approximation. This is clearly revealed in the backgrounds of people who use mental health services, in case studies written by clinicians, and in community surveys, where large numbers of people answer questions about their health and their circumstances via the completion of questionnaires, and sometimes through additional clinical interviews.[13] This chapter will focus mainly upon this last approach. This is because both the very large numbers of people that are involved (sometimes several thousand), and the use of statistical methods for sifting the collected data, ensure that this method has an unmatched ability to map health trends within the population of interest. Community surveys come in two basic forms. First, the so-called cross-sectional variety focuses upon a representative sample or slice of the larger population at a single point in time. In Britain, examples include the General Household Survey and National Co-Morbidity Survey, which are conducted every five and seven years, respectively. Secondly, there are longitudinal or follow-up surveys that involve repeated assessments of the health of a selected sample from a population over a relatively long period, sometimes across decades. This approach allows researchers to build up a story of the changes in the health of the group over time, and to relate these changes to life events and sometimes to shifts in wider social conditions, thus getting closer to a reliable account of the likely causes of illness and health.

The majority of community surveys seek to identify social inequality through various kinds of status marker, such as occupation or educational attainment. Most of this research also seeks to tap into psychological disturbance through the use of questionnaires, derived from standard psychiatric diagnostic systems. The advantage of this approach is that it enables distress to be measured.

The most obvious indicator of social inequality is poverty. It was never the rich who filled the big asylums. In Europe and the US today, the poorer districts of cities and towns manifest the highest rates of distress, whether garnered from surveys or from studies of the rates of psychiatric inpatient admissions.[14] This should not be a surprise. Amongst other things, absolute impoverishment means malnutrition, inadequate health care and lack of shelter. More often associated with so-called 'underdeveloped' nations, this level of destitution is found amongst the substantial homeless population in the UK, the United States and in other western countries. Homeless people have short lives, compared to the mainstream population.[15] Psychiatric surveys of this group show that they have very high rates of mental illness as defined by standard psychiatric diagnostic criteria – more than three-quarters of them – according to some researchers,[16] and that violent assault is a 'normal' experience, especially for women.[17] The kinds of psychological problems suffered by the most downtrodden are also among the most severe, including alcohol and substance abuse, psychosis and the more controversial diagnosis of 'anti-social personality disorder'.[18]

However, most of the people who are deprived within wealthy societies are deprived in relative terms: they are lacking in the resources and amenities that nearly everyone would deem essential for participation in daily life. Numerous community surveys have shown that the prevalence and incidence of the most common mental disorders– anxiety and depression – are associated with measures of relative poverty: living on state benefits, in rented and insecure accommodation, feeling financial strain on a daily basis, and having no access to a car. Cross-nationally, mental health surveys find that mental disorders are two to three times as common among the poor as among the rich. They are more prevalent for people living in substandard or overcrowded housing, who have lower levels of education, or are unemployed.[19]

Many influences are at work here. In order to clarify the most important, researchers have turned to the device of meta-analysis, but perhaps with greater legitimacy than in the case of the evaluation of talking treatment (see the discussion in Chapter 4). Under the auspices of the British National Institute of Psychiatry, for example, Meltzer and colleagues combined the results of nine community studies of working-age adults from general household populations in the UK, North America, The Netherlands and Australia.[20] Eight of these investigations showed a clear link between one or more indices of lower social position and higher prevalence of the most common mental disorders, while no study revealed the opposite tendency. Contrary to expectations, occupational social class held the least consistent relationship with reported distress levels – showing a positive link only in three studies out of six that probed this question. On the other hand, educational attainment, unemployment, low income, and a lack of possessions all consistently raised the likelihood of mental health problems. People who had experienced two or more adverse life events, such as bereavement, also had a heightened risk of mental disorder. The best predictor of emotional disturbance was physical illness, which multiplied the odds of developing a disabling mental disorder by a factor of six. Overall, however, the findings were consistent with previous research, but they also reveal how hard it can be to make simple generalisations about social factors and unhappiness.

If there is a relationship between mental distress and social inequality, how can we account for it? The research literature offers three broad explanations: drift, artefact and social causation.

The notion of 'drift' suggests that the direction of cause might run from the individual to their social situation. Poor health might be the cause of one's lowly position on the social pyramid, instead of the other way around. Those who are prone to psychological difficulties might also be at greater risk of losing their income because of their inability to work, or to marshal what few financial and material resources they have. This theory also suggests that the evidence of greater distress in poor areas results from the inward migration of the indigent to less salubrious districts, in search of cheaper housing and the higher levels of 'social disintegration' that allegedly camouflage their odd behaviour.[21]

While this kind of movement undoubtedly occurs, it is far from being the whole story. For given areas of the UK and other countries, investigators have found strong links between key indicators of deprivation and psychiatric admissions, not just for psychotic disorders, but also for those labelled with less severe 'neurotic illnesses', in whom such downward migration would be unusual.[22] Population-based surveys which compare the reported mental health of individuals with area-based deprivation indices find a very close relationship between the two. The fit is tight enough to convince most investigators that it cannot be accounted for by drift alone.[23]

THE ADEQUACY OF GENETIC EXPLANATIONS OF MENTAL DISTURBANCE

Historically, proponents of the drift argument have viewed psychological disturbance largely as a matter of possessing the 'wrong genes', that predispose to misery or madness. This argument has a superficial plausibility. Studies of the pedigree of families with histories of madness, of the psychiatric problems of the adopted children of 'schizophrenic mothers', and of the mental health of identical versus fraternal twins: all seem to show that 'serious mental illnesses' are strongly heritable. However, this academic literature cannot withstand close scrutiny. The family studies are compromised by the fact that everyone shares the same home environment, which alone might account for the intergenerational transmission of personal troubles. The adoption studies likewise conceal serious flaws, including unreliable diagnostic measurement, bias in the selection of the key case reports, and a dependence upon adopted children who have been split too early from their carers – a circumstance that, in itself, can predispose to later psychological disturbance. These investigations are also hostage to the practice – widespread amongst adoptive agencies – of placing children in families that resemble their original family, and in ways that might contribute to the disorder in question.[24]

Twin studies rely upon the fact that identical siblings share all of their genes in common, whereas fraternal ones only share half of them. If the genetically alike twins can be shown to suffer more often from a given mental disorder, or to have more convergent personalities and histories – even when brought up separately, as the research appears to show – then a strong genetic influence is presumed. But these studies too, are compromised by biased sampling of twins who are especially alike, and by dubious assumptions, including the notion that pairs of identical and fraternal twins have similar environments (they do not, because most people respond more uniformly to the look-alike pairs), and that identical twins can collusively shape their family environment to their own, genetically driven, agenda. But this argument is based upon circular reasoning, since the *starting assumption* – that the twins' behaviour, temperament and personality are due to heredity – is based implicitly on the results of earlier, even more dubious, twin and family research. These studies of separated twins are also dogged by questions about the measurement and recording of personality traits, about whether the separation was genuine, and, most devastatingly – about the rigour of control for other, equally plausible explanations of the observed similarities in the identical siblings' lives, which might be otherwise explained by their shared age, gender and social backgrounds.[25]

There are further reasons to question the hereditarian argument. Surveys and clinical data suggest that, in the US and many other western countries, rates of depression have increased tenfold since the 1950s.[26] Some of this rise may be due to the lowering of the threshold at which mere unhappiness is deemed an illness,[27] but some of it is probably genuine, as implied in a growing burden of chronic illness and in levels of social inequality, reported loneliness,[28] and suicide – especially during periods of economic turmoil.[29] Also, as we have already seen in Chapter 2, the manifestation of mental disturbance changes with time and place. The symptoms of hysteria[30] and of catatonic schizophrenia,[31] for example, were once common in Europe and the US, but are seldom seen in the early twenty-first century. In the present era, for many East Asian people, enduring sadness or 'depression' is perhaps not so much about pessimistic thoughts, as about lingering aches and pains. The wide collection of symptoms that made up neurasthenia still flourish in China and Japan, where the diagnosis has been officially retained. And then there is the condition of *Dhat*, on the Indian subcontinent, in which men worry about the possible depletion of their semen, of *Koro* in South-east Asia, where they fret about the illusory retraction of their penis, and of *Latah*, in Malaysia, where middle-aged women – usually disenfranchised and impoverished – fall into an anxious and then trance-like state, from which they proceed to indiscriminate mimicry and foul language. No one has proposed that we should start looking for the genes that underlie this last group of so-called 'culture-bound syndromes', which so obviously represent publicly shared scripts for dealing with and communicating distress, and which imply that most of the contents of the DSM have a similar function.[32]

Furthermore, two decades of molecular research into the alleged genetic basis of abnormal behaviour or personality traits has failed to conclusively find any specific genes that could be responsible.[33] This is expected, because the levels of mood-shaping chemicals in the brain – to the extent that they are influenced by genes – are modulated by large numbers of these, which makes 'untenable the popular belief that a particular gene might have a specific effect on one type of behaviour or emotion'.[34] It is still possible that combinations of genes might contribute to the genesis or course of distress, via subtle influences upon emotional temperament. However, this contribution will only be one element in a mutual interlacing of personal biography, physical health, and social and cultural circumstances.[35] More pithily, we might say that 'a constitution which leads to one person being diagnosed as schizophrenic may, given a different life-history, be the basis of exceptional achievements.'[36]

Returning then to the concept of 'drift' as an explanation for the relationship between social rank and mental disorder, the genetic research discussed above does not appear to offer strong support. On the other hand, the artefact explanation suggests that the link between social position and mental health might reflect any of several kinds of bias: in the way in which people's social and economic position is measured, in the statistical techniques through which health effects are estimated, or in how people are encouraged to report their problems to researchers. It is well-documented that psychiatrists and other mental health workers often attribute more serious and pessimistic diagnoses to lower-class patients, irrespective of the objective severity of their symptoms.[37] However, this social patterning of misery still emerges where researchers and clinicians are trained to avoid such bias,[38] and there are plenty of good reasons to think that lower social rank might be more of a cause than a result of misery, or of the inability to organise one's life.

Impoverishment is soul sapping. It can mean exposure to a range of material and personal threats that come with living in substandard or slum dwellings. Aside from low pay, the poor are also more likely to be trapped in unregulated labour markets comprised of sweatshops, meagre piece-work rates, and abusive supervisors.[39] They are subjected more often to traumatic experiences such as accidents at work, in the home, or on the street, and to infections and other illnesses, as well as bereavement, job loss or insecure work, unsanitary and overcrowded housing, urban noise, and violent crime.[40] The children of the poor have few safe or pleasant places in which to play, and are more at risk of being run over by motorists.[41] This attractive package comes with lack of access to informal sources of financial aid, and higher costs for household durables, relative to income.[42] The less resources that people have, then the fewer pleasant events that they are likely to encounter by way of compensation for their travails, and the less chances for restorative calm, or rest.[43] Comparisons of the reporting of positive and negative life events by social class suggest that in any given period, poorer and working-class people are less inclined to report positive or uplifting events, such as having received a present, gone on holiday, or treated themselves to a new item of clothing.[44]

In her report for the UN on poverty and mental health, Lynn Freidli summarises a wide range of research conducted over the last 20 years into the consequences of poverty and material deprivation in wealthy western societies.[45] She notes that it is one thing to be broke in a society of producers and universal employment, and another to be a pauper in a world of consumers, in which identity and self-worth are defined as much by the monetised enjoyment of goods and services as by the work that people do. To be poor in this kind of world is to be instantly marked as less worthy of respect – both by oneself and by others.[46]

Follow-up studies which look at the effects of living in an impoverished area show that this can have an adverse effect upon reported levels of anxiety and low mood, especially for the least well off.[47] These effects seem to build up over time – resulting in more problems the longer that the person stays in an undesirable place.[48]

Deprivation and financial hardship also seem to influence mental health through increased risks of physical, emotional and sexual abuse – all of which are likely to traumatise and disturb.[49] Young girls and women are particularly in peril of such maltreatment.[50] Longitudinal surveys suggest that a pathogenic environment of this kind can strongly predispose to adult mental health problems. However, it is not clear whether these problems are *always* the direct outcome of early cruelties, or whether these are related to a third underlying but chronic influence – such as living in an emotionally chaotic family[51] – perhaps for a long time, before any child meets with outright aggression or predation.[52] While early abuse does not seem to account for all distress in adults, its contribution is beyond question, but is more likely to propel men 'outwards' into antisocial conduct and substance abuse, and to drag women 'inwards', toward depression and anxiety, as suggested in the disproportionate number of young men locked away in facilities for mentally disordered offenders.[53] In the West, women have a lifetime risk of developing major depression at least twice that for men; besides the effects of the harms described above, this also seems to reflect the undue weight of child and family care responsibilities, which can be suffocating for women with the least means.[54]

ETHNICITY, 'RACE' AND PERSONAL DISTRESS

Just as mental health status connects with lack of money and with gender, the same is true of 'race' and ethnicity. The use and ownership of these terms is hotly debated. 'Race' normally refers to physical differences between groups of people, most often skin colour, whereas ethnicity refers to a shared cultural, linguistic, or national identity. Given the wide genetic variation within, and overlap between, seemingly distinct human populations, the concept of 'race' has limited scientific value, and unsavoury political associations.[55] However, for many, it still says something about how they see themselves, and about how they are viewed by others. The research literature that relates ethnic and 'racial' background to mental well-being is multifaceted, sometimes contradictory, and laced with simplistic assumptions.[56] To attempt even a cursory overview of this material would be impossible in the limited space available here. Nevertheless, some helpful pointers can be found.

In Britain, the three groups most often studied and discussed in this context are probably the Asians, the Irish, and the African Caribbeans.[57]

Arguably, of any immigrant group, the very wide range of people from the Asian subcontinent have been subjected to more direct racism, both in ordinary daily life and from violent campaigns mounted by fascist organisations such as the British National Party (BNP).[58] However, Asians have long been under-represented in the mental health treatment system, which is a puzzle, if we assume that when people are treated badly, then they will start to feel bad. One answer to this conundrum is that within many such communities, there is considerable shame attached to admitting to a psychological problem. Further possible explanations include a tradition of tight-knit and supportive families that pre-empt the need for professional care, and a cultural preference for expressing distress via bodily symptoms – which are then 'misread' by western-trained doctors.[59] A fourth account blames the institutional racism of British mental health services, which, not surprisingly, has rendered them a service of last resort.[60]

In contrast, men and women of Irish origin are over-represented in *every* major psychiatric diagnostic category, and have among the highest suicide rates of any ethnic set.[61] Some of the explanations tendered for this state of affairs have hinged upon the unique demographic features of Irish rural life, and their downstream effect in the form of subsequent migration: amounting to large numbers of single (and potentially lonely) people settling in the UK, parenthood at a relatively late stage in the life cycle, and for the immigrants' offspring – higher odds of parental loss and bereavement during the first bloom of adulthood. Other writers have focused upon the guilt instilled by an all-pervasive Roman Catholic clericalism, and upon the self-doubt consequent upon child-rearing practices shaped by centuries of colonial conquest and linguistic and cultural suppression. Still others have noted the hostility of the host community in mainland Britain, and the perplexities that accompany an ambiguous (and historically despised) 'racial' and ethnic identity.[62]

Turning to the case of African-Caribbean people, over the years they too have featured too often in compulsory inpatient admissions and psychiatric drug treatment. Young black men, in particular, have been disproportionately labelled as 'schizophrenic' and 'dangerous', sometimes with disastrous consequences for the individuals concerned and for their communities.[63] Some psychiatrists view such treatment as a sensible answer to what they see as objectively higher rates of mental illness in this group. For others, culturally blinkered mental health professionals are too quick to misdiagnose acute religious and mystical delusions for the far weightier problem of 'schizophrenia'.[64] For the most critically minded, however, these patients are more distressed than ill. Their real problems lie not with inaccurate medical judgements, but with psychiatry itself – rooted in nineteenth-century eugenic thought and quietly poised to condemn black people especially as irrational, threatening and mad.[65]

What can we conclude from this brief sketch of the relationship between ethnicity and personal anguish? The sheer variety of these accounts underlines the complex relationship between any kind of distress and the situations in which it occurs, and does or does not achieve official recognition.[66] Indeed, context is all-important. How first-generation immigrants fare in their new home seems to follow both the social and economic conditions that they have left behind and the experience of migration itself, especially if it is impelled by trauma and marked by persecution.[67] Despite their unique geographical origins, all the groups discussed here have had to find their way in an (often) unwelcoming ex-colonial host country.[68] They have faced varying amounts of cruelty, including discrimination and racism – much of it subtle.[69] But when combined with other troubles such as poverty, and pressure to give up or deny one's original ethnic identity, it has amounted to an intolerable burden of torment and despair.[70]

'I WAS LOOKING FOR A JOB ... '

A recurring theme in the story so far is that in western culture, employment holds a central place in the lives of most people. Besides income, it confers purpose and status. Not surprisingly then, some researchers have argued that unemployment or even the fear that it might happen can be a key root of personal suffering. Surveys conducted from the 1930s to the present time show that unemployed people have worse physical and mental health than people of similar class who are working.[71] Those without paid employment are quicker to express dissatisfaction with their present life, as well as low self-confidence, loneliness, anxiety and depression. They are more likely to suffer from insomnia, alcohol and substance abuse, and to have a greater risk of suicide.[72] Furthermore, their depressed mental state makes it harder for them to find new work.[73] Job loss also seems to harm physical health, raising the odds of infectious and degenerative illnesses, and even of premature death.[74] These associations depend greatly upon the circumstances: leaving work voluntarily at age 35, because of an unexpected lottery win is rather different from forced redundancy, age 55, with dependents to care for and unpayable debts.

Unemployment is linked with depression and anxiety, particularly in men.[75] It can mean the feeling and reality of being branded as a shameful failure, and it brings the collapse of routines, rituals and social contacts – a loss of identity that amounts to a state of chronic unease and self-doubt. Without money, we have less scope for influencing our circumstances, or for planning a meaningful future.[76] Unemployment leads to strained family relationships, almost doubles the chances of divorce in the first year after job loss, and creates more suffering for children, who are looked down upon by their more fortunate peers. In the long term, all of these processes can add up to create an intergenerational cycle of ill health and premature mortality.[77]

'... AND THEN I FOUND A JOB ... '

However, work is far from always being a good thing. Jobs that are too demanding, boring, demeaning, or repetitive bring a greater risk of physical or psychological ills.[78] Low pay and insecure employment, or work in which the individual has little control over the content and pace of their duties, are as damaging for mental health as being unemployed. Even the announced threat of changes in workplace roles seems enough to induce anxiety and depression in many people.[79]

One of the best pieces of research to have spelled out the importance of these effects is the well-known Whitehall study. This is an ongoing longitudinal survey of the health, workplace roles and lifestyles of four occupational grades of middle-class civil servants in the Whitehall area of London, enlisting 17,000 participants. It has shown that those in the top administrative grade suffered the fewest deaths over a decade, while those at the other end of the gradient suffered a threefold higher mortality rate. This social gradient remained, *even* for the more health conscious who were non-smokers, exercised and took care of their physical condition: their risk of illness and early death dropped by no more than a third.[80]

These findings are doubly significant because, over the last 20 years or so, work for most people has become a harsher experience, as employers, in conforming to the demands of the international markets and to neoliberal economic doctrines, have in many cases sought to downsize the workforce and to demand ever more from those who remain, just as they have eroded pay, pension rights and conditions. For many employees, centralised surveillance and control by computer and audit have undermined whatever scope they might once have had to put their own stamp upon their job, much less imbue it with craftsmanship. Haunted by what the American sociologist Richard Sennett has called the 'spectre of uselessness', the new flexible (in truth, unstable and unpredictable) workplaces also favour a new kind of worker, who is directed toward short-term opportunities and willing to discount their past experience in favour of what managers and trainers tell them.[81]

It is little surprise that, since the 1990s, there has been an overall reduction in satisfaction with work and more reports of crippling anxiety and low mood, as British workers have taken increased time off for diagnosed mental health problems. Does this trend reveal an increase in psychological problems, or a disenfranchised workforce having to resort to the language of illness in order to express their grievances, or to temporarily escape the daily grind?[82] These explanations are much debated, and most likely both are involved. The increased suicide rates within some sectors – the British teaching profession, for instance, has experienced an 80 per cent increase in the last decade – suggests the presence of fundamental unhappiness.[83]

So far, this discussion has shown that a wide range of insults and demands can all bear down upon the individual to infect them with chronic insecurity and distress. Clearly, the pattern of influences and the reaction will be unique for each person. The nature and significance of environmental influence will change throughout the lifespan, in accordance with shifts in bodily power and social status, and the demands that a given society makes upon them. In childhood, secure attachment to parents and other caregivers will usually be most important, whereas for working-age adults, the need to reconcile conformity to the expectations of others with a desire for freedom and creativity is often the key conflict, at least in western cultures. For the old, physical health and social activity is usually foremost in maintaining good mental health. All of these dilemmas will be profoundly shaped by the economic and social circumstances of the individual.[84]

Indeed, the literature discussed so far has focused upon the effects of occupying a given situation or social strata, as defined by income, ethnicity, work, or gender. The implicit focus is upon the local causes of health problems, upon what it means to occupy a particular position or place within society, to have undergone a particular history. By contrast, a more recent research tradition takes a broader approach in seeking to show how the health of the individual is connected not just with their immediate social and occupational circles, but with the *degree* of inequality that obtains within the country or larger geographical region in which they live.

THE WIDER PICTURE: SEARCHING FOR THE 'CAUSES OF THE CAUSES' – THE INCOME INEQUALITIES HYPOTHESIS

Since the 1950s, the health divide between rich and poor has been widening in Britain, as noted for instance in the government-commissioned Black Report[85] (published in 1980) and its successors, which attributed this pattern mainly to material inequalities in housing, nutrition and health care. In laying the blame for poor health upon material deprivation, the Black Report was following the accepted wisdom of the epidemiological field. However, this is a perception that some researchers like Richard Wilkinson and Kate Pickett have come to question, most recently in their best-selling book *The Spirit Level*,[86] which promotes the so-called 'income inequalities' hypothesis of population health. They argue that once a country has gone through the phase in which most infectious and occupational diseases have been eliminated (the so-called 'epidemiological transition'), then improvements in medicine and material infrastructure count for little. The 'whole population can be more than twice as rich as any other country without being any healthier.'[87] For modern industrialised societies, the average health, well-being and longevity of the population is said to depend, not upon the level of absolute poverty, nor upon how dutifully people follow government recommendations for keeping themselves well, but upon the spread of wealth, and particularly the gap between the richest and the poorest.

Wilkinson and Pickett have applied their theory to a wide variety of health and social problems, including depression, drug and alcohol abuse, obesity, teenage pregnancy, general levels of paranoia and mistrust, violent crime and premature death. For instance, in the international rankings of illness and misery, the citizens of the Scandinavian countries and Japan appear, in general, to be healthier and longer-lived than their equivalents in Britain, the US and Portugal. It cannot be an accident, Wilkinson and Pickett aver, that the first group of countries enjoys a more equitable distribution of income, while the latter group is in the bottom league in this respect, with the biggest gulf between the haves and the have-nots. The size of this gap influences health indirectly by moving each society toward or away from a condition of social cohesion, in which norms and traditions of trust, sharing and cooperation are upheld. Historical patterns support this picture. From the 1940s, Americans and Britons have had access to a profusion of material goods and services of which their great-grandparents could only have dreamed. Yet, the authors argue, this abundance does not seem to have brought contentment, but rather family breakdown, addiction, crime, obesity, economic insecurity and increased suicide rates, together with heightened mutual suspicion and dwindling communal life.

How can intangibles like social cohesion and mutual trust (or the lack of them) affect mental and physical health? The proposed mechanisms are at once social, psychological and biological. Where everyone has enough shelter, food and medicine, then the main cause of the social gradient in health lies within our evolved, unconscious tendency to measure our own status against others: the greater the perceived difference in rank, then the heavier the unease. As income differentials increase, so we start to feel more competitive, and begin to eye one another with increasing wariness. Daily life becomes clouded with envy, distrust, shame, fear and anger, the discord self-perpetuating, because it undermines the bases for intimate and caring relationships. A life of chronic insecurity or perceived threat 'gets under the skin' via the release of cortisol, and other 'stress' hormones in the bloodstream. These chemicals cascade through our bodies when faced with situations that stir feelings of self-defence or flight, even if the pressures are purely symbolic threats to our self-confidence and status within our workplace or community. This lowers our ability to combat infection and to fend off heart disease, and other degenerative conditions.

Inequality is painful. For almost any income level, a fairer place is also a better place. One of the most interesting features of this theory is that all of these harms also find out the rich, who, in more unequal societies, have that much less freedom to enjoy their wealth in ease: 'even the millionaire suffers from a vague sense of guilt, like a dog eating a stolen leg of mutton.'[88] At the time of writing, these two authors can point to over two hundred different studies in support of their arguments, including government and academic community surveys, and official records from the World Health Organization and the US Census Bureau. And the public health implications are startling. A mere difference of 7 per cent in the share of income going to the bottom half of the population, it is claimed, would yield two extra years of life expectancy.[89]

HOW WELL DOES THE INCOME INEQUALITIES HYPOTHESIS HOLD UP, AS SCIENCE?

Two central assumptions of the income inequalities hypothesis are that most people are aware of their position on the social pyramid and that they perceive this situation to be unjust. But these are conjectures. In the 1960s, Runciman's well-known study of deprivation in Britain suggested that lowly people judged their social worth in relation to their family, friends, neighbours and workmates, but not in contrast to the lives of middle-class or elite groups who seemed out of reach, if not irrelevant.[90]

On the other hand, Runciman's work was conducted at a time when the average citizen was less exposed to images of material affluence and 'success' via the mass media, and when fewer still were enjoined to be entrepreneurs. Wilkinson's thesis certainly fits with other kinds of sociological evidence that people can *indeed* absorb negative messages about their class status, leading to what Richard Sennett and Jonathon Cobb called 'hidden injuries',[91] a largely unspoken but painful feeling of inferiority, revealed in more corrosive form, in Simon Charlesworth's in-depth interviews with working-class (often jobless) people living in Rotherham, Yorkshire, in the mid-1990s.[92]

Perhaps the key point is that, if the social world is experienced mainly as feelings (for good or ill), then sometimes people will be conscious of how it constrains or enables them, and sometimes not – depending, amongst other things, upon who is asking the questions, and how thoughtfully.[93] Unfortunately, this still does not settle the question of whether that world foments misery through the self conscious comparisons that people make between themselves and others, or through the frequency of unpleasant things, including punitive and disrespectful treatment and lack of control over personal circumstances, that more often befall people who are disadvantaged.

SPIRITS LEVELLED BY THE MATERIAL WORLD – PHYSICAL HARDSHIP AND CLASS CONFLICT

A group of so-called 'neo-material' scholars have argued that, for mental and physical well-being, social cohesion is far less important than the material and economic landscape in which all of us are embedded.[94] These researchers describe themselves as 'neo-materialist' because they emphasise the personal toll exerted by tangible adversities like job strain, damp housing, noisy streets, bad food, air pollution, exposure to crime (or the threat of crime, including physical or sexual assault), and inadequate transport and health care. The neo-materialists still accept that social relationships are central to health and illness. However, they argue that the most important of these relationships are tightly interwoven with the power structures of society and with the interests of some groups of people more than with others.

As we have seen, most investigations into the adverse effects of social inequality suggest that these outcomes speak to psychosocial variables, such as job role autonomy versus lack of control, as famously described in Marmot's 'Whitehall studies'. Neo-material critics, such as Charles Muntaner,[95] note that these studies show only part of the truth about what goes on between people at work and its possible import for health. This is because of an over-reliance upon the things that people say about their situation and about their mental condition – as measured via questionnaires and lay-administered diagnostic interviews – which seldom permit thoughtful dialogue, much less informed clinical judgement. In these circumstances, people can exaggerate their experience of social pressure of various kinds or of mental disorder. This is particularly so, in view of the extent to which there is a widely shared discourse about the pervasiveness and toxicity of psychological stress in the workplace, about the need for counselling and other forms of psychological treatment to help people to overcome it.[96]

And yet sociological research shows that our class location is not just about our material wealth, our position on the ascending steps of a temple adorned with progressively larger motorcars and houses: it is also about our freedom or otherwise from domination and exploitation, and about our access to things, relationships and practices that we value and that profoundly shape our own life chances, and our sense of self-worth.[97] The exercise of control and surveillance within the workplace and by state welfare bureaucracies is a very different matter for the rich, for the poor and for those in between. Even privacy is linked closely with financial status. The poorest share their minute living space with other families; those on a middling income anticipate little seclusion from passers by or neighbours, when the walls of their high-density dwellings are too thin to permit secrets about their most intimate moments and bodily frailties.[98] The privilege and discretion of the wealthy is built into their big houses; detached, dignified dwellings sheltered by tall hedges and set in broad roads and avenues that hold the world at bay, making it much less intrusive and threatening. It is surprising that so few mental health researchers have thought about how disorders like 'agoraphobia' can reflect the far more exposed social housing landscape in which so many people have to live.[99] Similar principles apply to health and finance. Most of us

> ... suffer our illnesses in public wards (or waiting on trolleys in corridors) and many have to answer detailed personal questions about income and spending when our old age pensions or benefits will not stretch to paying our bills ... [By contrast,] the financial affairs of the rich have always been shrouded in secrecy, or subject to 'commercial confidentiality'. The wages and benefits of the poor are everybody's business.[100]

If Wilkinson and Pickett are not blind to social rank, they are sometimes short-sighted, to the extent that they are focused upon what money allows people to buy, not upon what they have to *do* (or tolerate) in order to earn it in the first place. We can see the weakness of any reckoning of class that might characterize Bill Gates, for example, 'more by his capacity to buy a Leonardo da Vinci masterpiece than by his being a founder, director, and major shareholder of Microsoft'.[101]

The concept of social class is bound up with the production of goods and services, with the possession of the resources and tools needed to make them, and with the power to hire and fire and to decide who gets the most rewards. Owner, landlord, worker, or manager: all speak of the relationships that generate economic, political and cultural inequalities and that bring the issues of conflict and exploitation squarely onto centre stage. As already noted, over the last quarter of the twentieth century, there is plentiful evidence of decline in the quality of daily life for large swathes of the population, including white-collar employees suffering the kinds of workplace insecurities and indignities once restricted mainly to the labouring classes. Coercive control in the form of stringent targets, performance appraisal and increased monitoring and surveillance have become the norm, together with longer hours, contractual insecurity and the steady loss of pension rights.[102]

In this sphere of paid labour, it is difficult to separate the health effects of social position on the one hand, and of the degree of economic exploitation, on the other, although several sociological studies suggest that the latter might offer a more credible account of the genesis of mental health problems. For instance, in one recent cross-sectional survey conducted in Spain, supervisors were found to have higher rates of depression and anxiety than both upper-level managers and front-line employees. As Muntaner and colleagues observe, the income inequalities hypothesis would predict that supervisors – owing to their higher incomes and grade – should have felt lower rates of distress in comparison to front-line workers. This was not the case; the senior operatives were more troubled because they were in an uncomfortable middle-management position, combining accountability and powerlessness, compressed between the demands of upper management and a restive workforce.[103] A similar result came from the well-known Barcelona community survey, which explored the relationship between the self-perceived physical and mental health of over 6,000 adults in that city and – amongst other things – their employment status.[104] This study collected data on depression and anxiety levels via the use of standardised psychiatric questionnaires, together with information on tobacco dependency, eating habits and injuries. Against the received wisdom, it showed that health was poorer for *employers* than for the managers beneath them, and that supervisors fared worse than their subordinates.

In a later survey, Muntaner and colleagues explicitly looked for evidence of class exploitation by using questions that, in the context of the workplace, probed for the extent of the ownership of the means of production and also the extraction of labour effort in the form of managerial domination, poor wages and lack of increases in pay.[105] Once again, this study showed a relationship between employee misuse, their lack of power, and an increased likelihood of mental health problems.

Overall, this evidence points to the fact that while our position in a social hierarchy may influence our well-being, the tensions and struggles inbuilt into class relations are also important, even though they have long been ignored in most of the research literature on social inequalities and health, including most of that cited by the authors of *The Spirit Level*. Such observations offer a valuable refinement of and addition to Wilkinson and Pickett's arguments, suggesting that improvements in the health of the population depend not just upon a narrowing of income differences, but also upon more fundamental changes in workplace rights, and in the organisation of society.

CONCLUSIONS: SUFFERING IS SOCIAL

A growing body of evidence supports the contention that the main influence on people's mental health is their circumstances, past and present. Violent victimisation, harassment and discrimination are clearly damaging.[106] However, in many cases, teasing out the most likely causes remains a complex task, which often leaves us with as many questions as answers. For instance, when it comes to understanding the most important elements that define our position in a social hierarchy – prestige, conditions at work, material circumstances, or monetary wealth. All of these are relevant, but it is not clear if any one of them has universal pre-eminence. Furthermore, there is the thorny question of gender. Are women unhappier than men, or is it also that men often express their discontent more aggressively and at greater emotional cost to others – in the worst case, swapping the prison cell for the acute psychiatric admissions unit? Then there is the issue of health survey questionnaires based upon dubious diagnostic categories, designed to plumb the fitness of the population. Do these surveys add to our knowledge, or do they sometimes help to reinforce our prejudices about certain kinds of distress as illnesses, requiring treatment by professionals?

Still, the broad picture remains fairly clear. Physical health and material wealth, neglectful or abusive relationships, the values of the society in which we live: all of these intertwine to help shape or distort our biography, and especially the odds of toil, trouble and discomfort in our lives. It is possible that temperamental ('genetic') factors might make an indirect contribution to our susceptibility to some forms of unhappiness, although, as we have seen, the evidence for hereditary influences in this field has been hugely overstated; such effects, if demonstrated, would always be mediated by the environments in which some people must live. What is surer is that to the extent that we belong to a disdained, exploited group and especially if we are poor, then we are likely to face the worst aspects of life more often, more painfully, and with fewer joyful events to rebalance the scales. For many, the distress that is called 'mental illness' is likely, and for some, it is almost inevitable. If this is so, then how well have the talking therapies helped the distressed or confused get to grips with their predicament? This is the question that will concern the second half of this book.

Part II

Therapy in Society

6
Sweet Medicine – Talking Therapy as Control

Things happen ... that our own language grown more humane than our deeds, refuses to acknowledge.

Friedrich Engels[1]

The talking therapists claim to offer treatments that have a humanistic and rational basis in science, aimed at helping people gain mastery over their lives. It is no surprise that they are in demand, especially by mental health service users, fed up with diagnoses that conceal the personal and wider (social and political) meaning of their problems, and worn down by harmful or ineffective psychiatric drugs. The first part of this chapter will explore how psychological therapy can be just as effective in concealing the nature and significance of misery, and in suppressing critical thought about the world that gives rise to it: precisely because of the palatable and even seductive nature of this kind of treatment. The second part of this chapter will focus in more detail on selected examples of the misuse of psychological therapy and techniques – in the fields of education, offender rehabilitation, the management of victims of war and disaster, and the teaching of supposedly enlightened parenting techniques to those deemed inadequate by the authorities. This broad canvas will help to set the scene for the longer case study of the Improving Access to Psychological Therapies (or IAPT) service that follows, in Chapter 7.

THE ALLURE OF TALKING THERAPY

Besides a fondness for dubious techniques and the identification and treatment of entities that only the professionals can see, there is a further parallel between psychiatry and the practitioners of talking treatment: both of them hold up a mirror to our beliefs about human nature, madness and normality. A mirror that not only reflects, but distorts our image of what we are. In the 1970s and '80s, American cultural commentators such as Phillip Rieff[2] and Christopher Lasch[3] described what they called a 'culture of narcissism'. In their view, the decline of religion and traditional values, combined with a rootless urban existence and the lures of advertising and consumerism found their apotheosis in the popularity of psychotherapy and counselling, both as forms of treatment and as a new kind of moral injunction. Where traditional values had stressed self-discipline and fulfilment of obligations to others, psychotherapy and counselling, especially for more privileged fee-paying clients, focused upon the new duty: to attain personal satisfaction. The poor got behavioural therapy and – in more recent years – simplistic CBT therapies designed implicitly for the purpose of control.

These trends persist in the early twenty-first century. The American anthropologist Elizabeth Throop takes an even wider perspective on the problems with psychological therapy, drawing upon what is known about how people outside of the United States and Europe conceive of themselves, and their troubles. She observes that, when compared with other times and places, the US is almost unique in its focus upon the self as the supposed locus and cure of all unhappiness and strife. From the perspective of most other cultures and historical eras, this is an unrealistic, preposterous – even immoral – notion, of what it means to be human, and one that goes with astonishingly high rates of poverty, violence (including child murder), mental disturbance and infant death. The therapeutic ethos is a warrant not just for the selfish and pampered behaviour of well-off westerners, blind to their own privileges, but for their bad child-rearing practices, too. Parents and educators have abdicated their responsibility to provide moral guidance, seeking instead to befriend their children in the all-absorbing task of helping them to become more attuned to their feelings, and to improve their self-esteem. The result is young people who are far too preoccupied with their interior world and with the belief that self-expression is all; in the worst instances, they are close to autistic in their indifference to others. Throop argues that this trend is reflected in the increase in reported cases of 'narcissistic personality disorder', diagnosed most frequently in young men. The recent spate of massacres carried out by US high school students are not bizarre eruptions of mental illness or evidence of a chronic lack of self-regard, as the media and many expert psychologists would have it. Rather, they are the essential expression of adolescents who have been schooled to obsess about their feelings, stoked by cultural messages about the cleansing power of male violence and the responsibility of the individual to change their position in the world, should they be unhappy with their lot.[4]

Other recent critics, such as the British sociologist Frank Furedi[5] and the Canadian clinical psychologist Tana Dineen,[6] have focused upon what they see as the tendency for psychologists and policy makers to encourage a false sense of personal vulnerability. In Dineen's case, by overplaying the ability of therapists to diagnose and eradicate the signs of previous sexual and emotional abuse, and in Furedi's, by exaggerating the extent to which adults mistreat one another, and especially children. In a series of books commenting upon widespread anxieties and moral panics, and their relationship to child care and education policy in the UK during the last 30 years, Furedi has underlined the dangers of this kind of thinking. He shows that it has been adopted all too eagerly by governments that have lost their commitment to a wider political vision, and have instead sought narrow moral causes that appear open to quick, cheap and populist solutions.

The resulting 'therapy culture' has witnessed a growth in surveillance of personal health, family life and education by central government and their agencies. The citizen has been cast as emotionally fragile and confused, and in need, therefore, of guidance from wise experts who have a privileged hotline to the truth; their wisdom as emanating, not from particular moral or political standpoints (which can always be questioned by the layperson) but from supposedly inarguable 'research'.

Furedi fails to see that most therapies are sought out, not just because of their promise to ease pain and protect us from harm, whether imaginary or real, but because, in a commodified and over-managed world, they also appear to celebrate individual uniqueness and genuine emotion, and promise to increase our scope to make personal choices. These observations are the starting-point for the Israeli sociologist Eva Illouz's more subtle critique of the talking treatments,[7] which for her are not so much the authentic folk music of our inner lives, as the seductive theme tune of what she calls 'emotional capitalism'. This is her name for the process by which, in the course of the twentieth century, the seemingly distinct spheres of commerce and of intimate relationships came to reflect and then shape one another, like a newly formed double planetary system, revolving around their common centre of economic gravity. In line with the demands of the service economy, the workplace increasingly became a forum in which feelings were scrutinised and fine-tuned, in aid of better teamwork and of keeping customers happy. Outside of work, intimate relationships took on something of the business ethos, as the idea of emotional accounting and mutual exchange took hold: an 'I'm OK, you're OK' outlook. Emotional capitalism owes much to the teachings of the early American psychologists, who, as consultants to big business and the advertising industries, worked hard to transmute naked self-interest into the respectable cornerstone of daily existence. It also owes something to the 1960s boom in psychological therapy and specifically feminist versions of it, which demanded emotional parity between the genders.

Illouz argues that, far from turning personal and family life into a refuge, much less solving the problems that some feminists sought to address, this therapeutic regime has created new, and perhaps unrealistic standards by which our relationships are judged, as we are taught to nervously itemise, hoard and bargain for our most cherished feelings. Like other critics such as Deborah Cameron[8] and Lucy Johnstone,[9] Illouz maintains that the widespread use of therapeutic jargon and techniques for 'better relating' has made it harder for many people to use their own intuitions, to see how their feelings arise from what is going on in front of their noses.[10] In the belief that they are more self-aware and sensitive, highly educated professionals have in fact adopted new conventions and styles of conversation, one of the main purposes of which is to distinguish them from the lower orders, who are less willing to dress their feelings in psychological argot and indulge in pious self-reflection. For Illouz, there is no easy way out of this impasse, because for the middle classes (and those who aspire to join them), the therapeutic outlook and its language have become all pervasive, their mastery essential to success in education, work, love and play.

HAPPY DAYS – THERAPEUTIC SCHOOLING

The notion of self-esteem is central to contemporary professional psychotherapy and self-help, because it is widely seen as the basis of personal happiness. The concept of self-esteem might appear to be less open to misuse than is the idea of stress, because interventions to improve it sometimes involve an effort to change the person's environment, as well as their internal psychological world. This is certainly the case for the British education system, awash with policies intended to enhance self-awareness, personal well-being and the 'soft outcomes' of learning. In the UK, perhaps the best publicised strategy for delivering these things to pupils is the one known as Social and Emotional Aspects of Learning (SEAL), or 'emotional literacy' by another name. Issued by the Department for Education and Skills, it covers positive self-concept, self-protection, making relationships, resisting pressure, stress management and negotiation.[11]

The therapeutic outlook that informs this way of teaching runs across the whole spectrum of British education, from primary schools to FE colleges to universities.[12] It inculcates practices like 'circle time' in which students and staff (in their own separate groups) are encouraged to sit together in order to disclose their private feelings and thoughts to their colleagues in the interests of bonding, team building and in order to prevent conflicts and bullying. In both Britain and the US, there has been a focus upon raising student self-esteem by means of a simplification of the curriculum, which has made it harder for students to fail in their academic or vocational work. Teachers and lecturers have been encouraged to deploy more 'positive strokes' to their charges, while simultaneously playing down their own pedagogic expertise and exaggerating their experiences of academic vulnerability. This way of thinking comes straight out of the principles and practices of specialist support for a minority of struggling or damaged children, now extended to the majority. From its inception, the trend toward 'therapeutic schooling' was welcomed by many progressive educators, who were understandably disenchanted with target-driven education, and with the emphasis on the teaching of skills deemed 'relevant to the marketplace'. One example of this approach is the use of neuro-linguistic programming (NLP) by the British CfBT Educational Trust, which specialises in 'fast-track teacher training'. Tyro teachers continually reward the children via the subtle modulation of the words used for feedback about work standards, so as not to harm the self-confidence of their charges.[13]

What is wrong with the curative culture? For those of us who had to sit through endless rote learning at the behest of 'teachers' who felt that they were still in the army, all of this should come as a welcome change. Unfortunately, in practice it has amounted to the exchange of one set of dubious assumptions for another. Self-esteem and confidence have become *the* foundation of meaningful learning, instead of valuable by-products of good teaching where students achieve something tangible, and important. The worship of self-regard ignores the consistent failure of researchers to find any convincing causal relationship between satisfaction with oneself and academic or any other kind of performance in the real world. Careful observations of what people do (as opposed to what they *say* in paper-and-pencil personality tests) suggest that where efforts to raise self-esteem enjoy any success at all, they boost the odds of narcissistic and callous conduct.[14] To some degree, the virtues of direct speaking have been undermined. Children and young people, less naïve than adults suppose, can often see through the prettified language and realise that in the end, failure is failure, whether in the classroom, or in the world of work/unemployment, when they find that their qualifications are inflated and useless.[15]

These attempts to enhance the personal satisfaction of students – part of a wider campaign to increase emotional literacy in schools – strengthen the idea that emotional and interpersonal skills are decisive in the teaching environment. Public attention is thus drawn away from evidence that the quality of teaching accounts for only 5 or 10 per cent of the variance in academic performance for state schools. The rest depends upon the social background and health of the pupils. In Britain, as in so many other countries, better education standards are achieved best of all by taking families out of poverty.[16] Therapeutic education also runs against the grain of objective intellectual inquiry and the acquisition of knowledge, because it views the emotional skills associated with learning as more important than the subject content, even in the field of higher education.[17]

REFUGEES AND THERAPY

In the last 20 years, international aid agencies, NGOs, military establishments and western donor governments have come to offer afflicted populations not just sanctuary, foodstuffs and medicine, but counselling. Traumatised individuals and populations may be shown how to understand their responses through the lens of diagnoses like PTSD so that they can find the symptoms in themselves and others, and seek the guidance of a psychologist or other suitably qualified helper.[18] The guiding assumption is that calamity equals widespread mental trauma and PTSD. In fact, careful observations of people unfortunate enough to meet with natural calamity or to become refugees, show that this rarely hobbles their ability to get on with their daily lives.[19] Even when caught up in extreme hardship and threat, people continue to be active. Indeed, anthropologists and other social and medical researchers have questioned the universality of PTSD as yet another American export, not unlike Coca-Cola, or Nike trainers.[20]

The British academic Vanessa Pupavac believes that long acquaintance with hardship can in some circumstances build mutual aid, strengthening communities and individuals, whose refusal

of therapy is too often viewed by NGO workers
a denial of psychological disturbance. Pupavac ar
trauma counsellors who are the most vulnerable to
the horrors that they witness or hear of, second-hand,
foreigners, they have few real friends to whom they can tur.
recent research suggests that trauma counselling or 'de. .g'
after disturbing experiences can make people worse, because it
undermines their own ways of managing their problems and can
prevent them from seeking advice and succour from within their
own community.[21]

The propensity to treat war and its consequences as a kind
of mental illness may have even wider consequences. Florence
Nightingale, the founder of the nursing profession, forcefully
opposed the creation of the Red Cross, because she felt that its
existence would sanitise warfare, making it more likely in the long
run.[22] In the modern era, western psychological approaches to victim
relief and conflict management abet a compliant mass media in
the job of steering policy makers away from a willingness to think
about (much less tackle) the upstream economic and political origins
of conflict.

'SENTENCED TO COUNSELLING' – CBT IN THE PENAL SYSTEM

In western countries, crime rates – both officially reported and
unofficial – rose dramatically from the 1960s through to the late
'90s. Crime indices in the UK, however, have declined considerably
in the last ten years. Yet fear of crime remains high, along with a
widespread perception amongst both the public and policy makers
that previous governments have failed to tackle this problem. For
the generation that followed the Second World War, penal policy
operated under the banner of rehabilitation, founded upon the twin
pillars of community-based solutions to crime and an attempt to
redress the circumstances of the individual offender, seen as at
least contributing to their misdeeds. Prison was viewed as a last
resort, and probation officers sought to help former lawbreakers
back into civil life through a casework approach, which aimed to
improve their work skills and their economic and social prospects,
amongst other things. Since the 1980s, by contrast, the UK, Canada
and the United States have been in the grip of what the American
academic David Garland calls 'the culture of control'; a response to
the social and economic uncertainties of the period, this is above all
a politically driven outlook. It downgrades the views of academics

who pointed to social conditions as important causes of crime), and replaces them with a populist language of retribution, protection and victimhood. The appearance of managing crime in the eyes of the public comes to outweigh any other consideration, including the commitment to a 'just, socially engineered solution' to this perennial problem.[23]

In consequence, there has been a shift toward greater numbers of people being imprisoned and for longer custodial sentences. Prison populations in the UK and the US are at an all-time high. In addition, there has been a blurring of the line between custody and freedom. More and more offenders are given sentences that entail time spent under supervision on both sides of the prison wall. The probation profession has lost much of its former social work ethos. Overloaded with the bureaucratic demands of meeting service delivery targets, it has been reduced to administration, risk assessment and the enforcement of community-based sentences in which lawbreakers must accept responsibility for their deeds, but without much of a counterbalancing effort to help them to move away from the circumstances that encouraged their offending.[24]

In June 1998, the Home Office published Probation Circular 35/1998, entitled *Effective Practice Initiative: National Implementation Plan for the Supervision of Offenders*. The document was the starting-gun for what came to be known as the 'What Works' initiative, a search for practical and 'evidence-based' tools for reducing crime, as measured by the collection of outcome statistics from the penal services. 'What Works' has opened the door for a small army of clinical and forensic psychologists, now deeply embedded in the correctional system. Their main jobs are to design and test risk-assessment protocols for use by probation and custodial workers, and to incubate and monitor programmes that draw upon cognitive and behavioural techniques, intended to deter criminals from further transgression.[25] The consequences have been described as 'the biggest experiment in social engineering that this country has ever seen'.[26]

Offenders are shown how to monitor and replace their habitual defective cognitions with more 'rational', 'accurate', or 'helpful' ones, by keeping weekly diaries of their thoughts, learning how to imagine themselves behaving more honourably and getting involved in role-plays that teach them how to overcome temptation. Because this training usually happens in a group format, self-disclosure is taken to be a particularly powerful switch for behavioural change, analogous to what happens in religious conversion. Official confidence in the programme has been large. In the words of one high-profile chief probation officer responsible for overseeing the early phase of the UK programme, offenders will not reform themselves just because they have been told to, 'but because we have managed to profoundly change the way they think',[27] which implies an almost Pygmalion-like personality conversion.

At first sight, this kind of reprogramming does appear to be modestly effective, when applied to a wide range of criminal conduct, including violence against persons and property, robbery, sexual assault and dangerous driving. Data from Canada and the US, largely in the form of meta-analyses, suggests that offenders who undergo 'What Works' educational programmes commit fresh crimes less often – somewhere between 5 and 10 per cent – when compared with people who receive custodial sentences. Some officials in the probation and police services claimed that reductions in reconviction rates of 25 per cent and above were feasible.

Yet the scientific flaws are many. In the UK, the 'What Works' programme was set up on the strength of several small-scale and inadequately controlled and randomised pilot studies, before proper evidence was available for its effectiveness – a reversal of the proper procedure for an 'evidence-based' endeavour of the kind which this proclaims itself to be. According to some observers, this initiative has been organised in a climate of almost evangelical fervour, in which managers discouraged the open expression of doubt as 'unprofessional'.

For instance, the outcome measurement period is far too short – six months on average, which is not long enough to establish whether an offender has really changed their ways. The outcomes of these programmes are measured in reconviction rather than re-offending rates, an important distinction, given that, first, only 5 per cent or less of crimes ever result in prosecution and secondly, that these programmes do not make use of properly randomised samples of trainees. There is a two-stage selection process for the 'What Works' courses. In the UK, probation officers will recommend those that they deem suitable and then magistrates will make their own decision as to whether or not to follow their suggestions. Home Office guidance directs probation officers to seek out the keenest individuals for the programme – that is, people who express an interest in reforming themselves and atoning for their offences and who declare themselves ready and willing to attend the weekly sessions.[28] Like born-again Christian prisoners who say that they have suddenly seen the error of their ways, these people are the very individuals whose 'thinking skills' and self-control are least likely to be at fault.

It is surely not implausible that this group might also include people who are better at telling criminal justice officials what they want to hear and perhaps, having more wit for avoiding apprehension for any subsequent crimes committed. This self-selection process undermines any scientific comparison of the reconviction rates of offenders on accredited CBT schemes and those sentenced to a different fate. The Home Office and the Probation Service acknowledge that because random allocation is not possible, then the best yardstick is to compare the reconviction rate of 'What Works' graduates with their theoretical predicted reconviction rate. The prediction was that a 5 per cent reduction would emerge here, but the actual results in the most carefully controlled studies suggest that there is scant improvement in the groups who have completed these programmes. In many of them, especially of course those conducted outside of prison, the dropout rates are very high, with up to three-quarters no longer attending at the close of a 20-week course, in the worst cases. Even the authors of some of the key reports on 'What Works' recognise that the benefits are short-lived, that most of the studies are unsound, and that the more reliable ones yield the least impressive results.[29]

Few insiders are prepared to speak out about the shortcomings of the system. One of 'What Works' most vocal critics, an ex-probation officer and magistrate, is David Fraser,[30] who has publicly expressed some of the doubts that seem to be widely shared amongst his colleagues. Fraser has challenged two chief probation officers and a chief constable to produce tangible evidence in support of the glib and grandiose claims that they have made about the success rates for this programme. In all cases, he says that he met with denial, obfuscation, or silence.

It is the policy makers and the managers who have proved the most credulous. In sharp contrast, a Home Office study, published in 1997, at the very inception of the programme, was more sober and reliable. It observed that there was no good evidence that 'cognitive behavioural approaches, or indeed any other type of approach, routinely produce major reductions in re-offending amongst mixed populations of offenders'.[31] Subsequent investigations, although conducted by individuals sympathetic to the 'What Works' outlook, confirmed this picture, in that the techniques are still seen as 'promising' rather than effective. Crime rates in the UK were declining before the introduction of 'What Works' and there is no evidence that regional variations in its introduction have been reflected in local crime rates. Canada, the home of 'What Works', continues to experience high levels of crime.[32]

Studies of people who re-offend have not always been in agreement about the reasons why some people are more likely to do so than others, but those most at risk of recidivism are poor young men (especially if they are black) with few educational qualifications, lack of employment, a history of abuse, and the absence of a peer group or community conducive to a better way of life. Painstaking research into people who abandon a life of wrongdoing suggests that cognitive change of the kind envisaged by 'What Works' usually occurs after the fact, and is often irrelevant:

> Our main point is that many of the desisters did not seek to make good – they simply desisted with little if any cognitive reflection on the matter … The majority of men we interviewed desisted from crime largely because they were able to capitalize on key structural and situational circumstances … .[33]

Circumstances count. Rates of offending, especially for the poor and for violent crime and theft – the ones that most concern the public – strongly mirror the extent of poverty and of social and economic inequality.[34] It is no accident that young black men are over-represented in the British and American prison population and probation services. On an immediate level, people commit crimes because of callous disposition, bad judgement and opportunity. But from a wider perspective, offending and mistrust of the police and the criminal justice system are far more likely when, for instance, people are targeted for stop-and-search procedures because of their skin colour,[35] and when they are poorly housed and impoverished because of discrimination and because of cuts in benefits and services, and when their prospects for stable remunerative employment all but vanish – within a society that values material wealth above all. These factors have long been associated with crime,[36] and – together with a widely shared recognition that the country had been beggared by an elite who had filled their own pockets and escaped all punishment – were identified as central to the riots that gripped England in the summer of 2011.[37] Against this morass of material influences, the power of 'new cognitions' as taught by earnest correction service workers must look pretty thin. An excessive focus upon individual responsibility for crime makes it harder to see, let alone think about, these broader social harms.

'IF IT'S NOT TRUE, THEN IT OUGHT TO BE' – HEALTH PSYCHOLOGY, AND THE NUDGE TO WELL-BEING

For the common illnesses, medical practice shifted dramatically during the course of the twentieth century: from the giving of bedside comfort, laudanum and little else, to biomedical treatments that worked, more often than not. But as doctors became more expert and impersonal, so their patients grew more knowledgeable, mistrustful and demanding.[38] It was into this widening breach that the profession of health psychology made its entry, a late arrival of the 1970s. Its practitioners presented themselves as sympathetic listeners allied to medicine, and as scientifically trained guides to improved physical and mental well-being. In pursuit of these aims, health psychologists have sought, for example, to help the obese to lose weight, the emotionally disturbed to get more rest or to take more exercise, and those suffering from debilitating illness or intractable pain to cope better. In recent years, they have worked with those who endure an indistinct array of discomforts, usually diagnosed as chronic fatigue syndrome (CFS). Less often, they have tried to prevent illness within communities through educational campaigns, and, for the more adventurous practitioners, through attempts to create political change.[39]

As far as the theme of social control is concerned, there are a number of questions that can be asked about health psychology. One of them concerns the paucity of published criticism of what appears in the professional journals, which is low, even by the pallid standards of the talking therapy field. This is key, because most health psychologists, working in clinics, concentrate upon changing the conduct of individuals and not the social systems that surround them. If the psychologists' methods are not as effective as supposed, then some patients are being encouraged to assume an unnecessary burden of responsibility for their ills.

The American academic James Coyne and colleagues carefully scrutinised a 'classic study' that had seemed to show that psychotherapy promotes the survival of cancer patients, and that had passed into a guiding myth within the field of health psychology and in the public eye. Coyne and colleagues showed, however, that the result was owed, not to the power of mind over matter, but to a flawed experimental design. Their systematic review of the wider research literature within this area, they found that

> … no clinical trial had ever improved the median survival time of women with metastic breast cancer. Furthermore, no trial in

which survival was chosen as the primary outcome ahead of time ever demonstrated a survival effect for patients with any type of cancer.[40]

Coyne and his colleagues then turned their attention to four published meta-analyses of psycho-social treatments for cancer patients.[41] These analyses, too, had created a stir, because they seemed to show that the treated patients had better overall health and were less likely to die from their illness. Alas, the supposed benefits turned out to be artefacts of the kinds discussed in Chapter 4, but with the additional twist that the patients who had psychological therapy often received better medical attention; enough to account for their improved survival.

Scepticism is the hallmark of science and of clinical medicine; were these findings then greeted with sober curiosity by the researchers' peers?

The president of Coyne's university received two letters complaining about his work and one demanding his suspension, and an academic reviewer of the above paper complained bitterly that its authors had 'assumed the role of "Supreme Judges" of the work of others'. Perhaps it is not surprising then, that Coyne believes that the whole field is beholden to the implicit belief *that if something is not true, then it ought to be.*

What then about other areas of health psychology practice, such as helping people to lose weight? For morbid obesity, and for other medical conditions, such as arthritis or high blood pressure, weight loss has an obvious utility. However, health psychologists have more ambitious goals:

> ... if current trends continue, 60 per cent of men, 50 per cent of women and 25 per cent of children in the UK will be obese by 2050 ... [Moreover, a] wide range of serious co-morbid conditions are associated with being obese, such as hypertension, diabetes, coronary heart disease (CHD) and stroke. In addition, obesity will adversely affect an individual's quality of life both directly but more importantly through the higher risk and incidence of disease. The cost burden imposed on the NHS as a consequence of obesity has been estimated at £479.4 million ... .[42]

These statements – the official view of the British Psychological Society – are alarming, but are they justified? The assumption that fatness is automatically bad for health may have been overstated, perhaps in part, because it is too easy to calculate someone's body mass index (BMI) as a supposed scientific measure of corpulence, based upon height and weight. However, the BMI is a crude snapshot of build. Fatness depends not just upon body size, but also upon the distribution of adipose tissue and its ratio to muscle. Contrary to the pronouncements of governments and health promotion experts on both sides of the Atlantic, nearly half a century of international research, most of it using more careful assessments of bodily mass, suggests that it is only people classified as either 'morbidly obese' (with a BMI of over 40), or as underweight (and with a BMI of less than 18.5), who show clear evidence of ill health because of their weight. Indeed, a well-regarded American study revealed overweight men to have *lower* mortality than their ideal weight counterparts.[43] And this result is not unusual. What appears to be a good-quality meta-analysis, published in the *Lancet* in 2012, compared rates of cardiovascular disease with the BMI measures for nearly a quarter of a million people, across a decade. The risk of heart attack did not increase when fat was concentrated around the waist, in flat negation of previous wisdom on this subject, and neither did BMI scores predict the likelihood of heart disease, once allowance had been made for blood pressure, cholesterol levels and diabetes history.[44] Whether or not these findings hold up in the long run, they point to a general flaw in the literature cited by anti-obesity campaigners: its failure to distinguish the effects of body size from the many other things that are more surely known to influence mortality and morbidity – nutrition, exercise, and the long-term harmful effects of cyclical or 'yo-yo' dieting, and of commercial 'slimming drugs'. In the US and Britain alike, the health risks linked with increasing weight are small, when compared with those associated with being poor, male, or black. In fact, there is a good overlap between the demography of race, class and fatness – especially in the United States.

In western culture, fat people get more than their share of condescension and disdain. In Britain, some hospitals have refused surgical procedures to such patients, on the dubious grounds that the health risks associated with their weight discount the benefits.[45] Politicians moralise about the duty of the poorest citizens to stay healthy and trim; as if they had plenty of scope for pleasant and accessible recreation, local shops from which to buy the approved healthier foods at an affordable price, and few of the worries that goad people to overfill their stomachs with starchy, comforting food.[46] Most fat people know how they are seen and some of them are frequently demoralised.[47] Too often, health psychologists have added to their woes, by joining their medical colleagues in promoting the twin myths that size is destiny and that there are reliable behavioural and counselling techniques for reducing weight. The reality is that the vast majority of people who complete any kind of weight loss programme will return within two years or less to their starting-point, or will end up heavier than when they began.[48]

These are not the only problems with the health psychology field. It may be the only therapy specialism that has the potential to impede medical progress in regard to problems like CFS, irritable bowel syndrome, non-specific back pain, and other difficult-to-verify diagnoses, which also resemble psychiatric ones in their capaciousness. For doctors, these labels are convenient round holes into which to consign the square pegs of patients with obdurate but vague and difficult-to-treat problems. Such patients can then be dealt with by ancillary professionals, such as health psychologists, who are paid to listen exhaustively to their complaints, and to cast them as the presumed outward expressions of hidden psychological troubles. The neuroscientist Michael Myslobodsky suggests that overworked or 'psychologically minded' physicians no longer bother to carefully think about or research their patients' symptoms, which might be speaking of unrecognised physiological disorders.[49] If this sounds strange, consider that stomach ulcers were for many years wrongly assumed to be the wages of anxiety. Closer attention to the clinical and epidemiological evidence might have prompted a faster search for bacterial causes, and for an effective cure.

As far as health psychologists themselves are concerned, Myslobodsky, referring primarily to the American scene, notes their fondness for alternative, holistic and complementary 'mind-body' healing techniques, which, even when combined with more familiar behavioural methods, for instance, cannot add up to a coherent body of knowledge or practice. He argues that their ambitions have exceeded their reach, and that they have ended up trying to tackle too wide a range of health problems of dubious provenance, with a wide array of therapeutic tools of unproven effectiveness.

As for all forms of therapy, a further issue for this field is to what extent people are persuaded to conform to the psychologist's (or the doctor's) idea of how they should be. CBT-based pain management techniques, for instance, can still leave some patients struggling to understand and communicate what they are going through. Some health psychologists have tried to bridge this gap with narrative therapy, converting the person's illness experience into a story, intended to confer dignity and meaning upon their anguish. But this manoeuvre can be a more subtle denial of the wretchedness of the sick person's predicament. A key aspect of suffering resides in its arbitrary, unjust, or even meaningless nature, particularly where bodily affliction and pain hold sway. Such experiences are mostly about feelings beyond mere utterance, and can be fully acknowledged only through acts of care and practical comfort, through 'the hand stretched out, the cover pulled over'.[50]

To be sure, some practitioners have developed useful insights into how health services might become less patronising, but they have also revealed the limitations of individual health psychology. Noting with alarm the declining effectiveness of health promotion campaigns directed at risky, unprotected sex, and indeed the sometimes perverse effects of these campaigns, the researcher Michelle Crossley asks why it might be that some gay British men reject condom use.[51] Her interviews suggest that, for those who already see themselves as stigmatised, then the additional burdens of low income, poor education and loneliness soon overcome their resolve to guard their health with these prophylactic measures. The information and counselling provided by health psychologists at a personal level cannot be enough. The social and economic causes of powerlessness also need to be addressed, and these are things that few psychologists can alter. Similar conclusions can be drawn from the sociologist Hillary Graham's 1998 study of single mothers who smoked, and who were dependent upon welfare benefits.[52] For the most part they were well aware of the harmfulness of their habit, but they persisted, because smoking helped them to stay calm and focused in the face of exhaustion and of acute domestic pressure. In the years since, the endurance of high rates of smoking amongst the poor (despite incessant anti-smoking health promotion campaigns and official smoking bans in most public places throughout Britain), have vindicated both Graham's arguments, and the cautionary words of American health psychologist Marshall H. Becker, from nearly 30 years ago. He warned of a need to be 'explicit about what we can and cannot do. The domain of personal health over which the individual has direct control is very small when compared to heredity, culture, environment, and chance.'[53]

Finally, no discussion of the use of psychological methods in pursuit of well-being can avoid the concept of 'nudging', as promoted by recent governments in Britain and the US. Conceived by the Chicago-based economist Richard Thaler, this is a distillation of a diverse body of research in the fields of social psychology and behavioural economics, which seemed to show that people's choices could be subtly channelled by the situation in which they found themselves, though they remained, in principle, free to do whatever they wanted.[54] Perhaps the most familiar application is the life-size image of a housefly, etched into airport urinals: intended to improve the customers' aim and reduce the toilet-cleaning bills. Thaler was invited to apply this kind of thinking to government health and social policy in the UK and the US, where citizens might be nudged towards desirable decisions about things like nutrition, alcohol consumption and smoking. The nudges exerted their leverage via penalties, such as taxation for products and lifestyles that are officially deemed unhealthy, and through rewards for conduct deemed to be desirable – for example, by paying pregnant women with supermarket vouchers, in return for their continued abstinence from smoking.

The New Labour Prime Minister Tony Blair had shown an early interest in the idea, and as early as 2004 his Strategy Unit recommended a 'fat tax' upon unhealthy foods.[55] The subsequent Coalition government has set up a Cabinet office – the Behavioural Insight Team – or so-called 'nudge unit' – that will use behavioural economics to persuade citizens to choose what is best for themselves, and for society. The unit has been briefed with the task of prompting people to make improved decisions about their health and lifestyle via financial incentives.[56] The British Psychological Society and many other commentators have enthused about the potential for 'nudge' to improve the welfare of the population. What could be wrong with this brand of 'paternalistic liberalism', as its supporters describe it? Quite a lot, as it happens. To begin with, many of the policies are based on questionable premises, for instance, that both being fat and drinking moderate amounts of alcohol are bad for health. In fact, many studies suggest it is the teetotalers who die soonest, and that people with a moderate intake, defined as one to three drinks per day, have the lowest mortality of all. Research into the effects of alcohol and tobacco advertising consistently fail to demonstrate that they raise the consumption (as opposed perhaps, to brand choice) of anyone. Likewise, the assumption that the banning of smoking in public places will foster further decline in the habit is not well supported – in many cases, habitual smokers just light up their cigarettes elsewhere.[57] If we want people to stop smoking, then the policies that seem to have the most influence are those that give people more economic security *and* possibilities in their lives – the elimination of poverty, opportunities for social mobility, improvements in education and steps toward gender equality.[58] Besides ignoring this kind of evidence, the disquieting aspect of these nudge policies is that the values of the politicians and their supporters – a moralizing dislike of what, in particular, working-class people like to do – are enough to banish all caution and doubt, and to make inconvenient scientific evidence invisible. The whole approach betrays disrespect for the intelligence of the citizen that ill befits governments that call themselves democratic.

BETTER PARENTING THROUGH PSYCHOLOGY?

There is a long history of wealthier people denigrating the poor for their immoral habits. Nowhere is this is more apparent than in recent British and American policy on child rearing. This is part of an international movement, whereby inadequate parenting has come to be seen as the epicentre of the worst social ills, transmitting disadvantage, illiteracy, crime and bad behaviour straight to the next generation. In the UK, prominent commentators blamed bad child-rearing practices for the riots of 2011 and any other forms of civil disorder that they could think of. It is nothing so gross as money or material advantage, but personal responsibility and parenting, which uphold the social order. In the early years of the twenty-first century, Bill Clinton was extolling the virtues of families sitting down together for dinner as the answer to all these social ills, and the Bush administration carried on the theme: assigning the child caretaker the job of solving the problem of social deprivation, by following expert advice on engaging their kids in the use of language and in the joy of reading.[59]

Where state support traditionally meant direct help – that is, material and cash benefits – it has been replaced by parenting classes. This situation reflects what the sociologist Frank Furedi has called the 'creeping professionalization' of child rearing; for example, in the UK, the National Family and Parenting Institute has been created as a 'centre for excellence' and expert advice on bringing up children. Historically, this line of thought owes much to the work of post-war clinicians, like John Bowlby (who highlighted that healthy child development depended upon good emotional attachment to the 'primary caregiver'), and to laboratory psychologists who believed that the subtlest of exchanges could be broken down into a set of behavioural and cognitive competencies.[60] More recently, neuropsychologists have been promoting the idea that the first three or five years of life (depending on the author) are crucial for brain development, a critical window in which children learn the social and thinking skills required for adulthood. Should they miss out, because of the negligence or laziness of their caregivers, then their brains will not develop properly – condemning them to a criminal or poverty-stricken trajectory in later life. In order to prevent future tragedy, the experts, in publications with titles like *Parenting Matters*,[61] advocate child-rearing lessons on a mass scale, especially for the feckless and the poor. British Prime Minister David Cameron is an enthusiastic advocate of such programmes. In 2012, the Conservative-Liberal Democrat coalition government[62] launched a £5 million scheme called 'Can Parent', which gave the mothers and fathers of children under age 5 a £100 voucher to be redeemed against lessons on parenting from independent organisations like the National Childcare Trust.[63]

One problem with this outlook is that it relies upon what might be called the 'neuromyth', that is, the idea that, as far as brain development is concerned, parents must get things right in the first three years of their offspring's life, else all will be lost. But this notion, often implicit, is based upon a tendentious reading of the scientific literature on the effects of childhood deprivation – in which false parallels are drawn between, for instance, the development of children raised in Dickensian East European orphanages, and that of British youngsters brought up in certain British households, in which everyone watches too much television. In the words of Stuart Derbyshire, a psychologist highly critical of what he calls 'neuromythmaking':

> Politicians, scientists and commentators who claim that neuroscience demonstrates early intervention will prevent antisocial behaviour, crime, educational failure and poverty and will improve physical and mental health are ... being dishonest ... At best, we know that children who are severely deprived struggle in the immediate years after deprivation but they demonstrate considerable catch up.[64]

A further problem with this way of thinking is that the people who teach the parenting techniques have been trained and advised, in many cases, by psychologists, who have forgotten that it is more than the want of parenting skills that leads people into troubled lives, and that relationships between people are not diagrams, but living realities – inseparable both from the unique individuals involved, *and* from the situation in which everything happens. In nurturing children, as in so much else, a key part of this context is social class, as the British sociologist Val Gillies and her colleagues have shown, in their extensive interviews of privileged and poor parents.[65]

Middle-class mothers and fathers are able to use the idea of their child's specialness, passionately upheld, to justify the educational and vocational advantages that go with their family status. They do not need coaching in 'parenting skills': they have a good knowledge of the educational and assessment system and can call upon formal and informal contacts for advice, influence and support. They can afford private tutors to boost their children's performance on entrance examinations and they are able to consult experts who will reframe middling or low academic ability as a vague developmental disorder such as dyslexia, or mild autism. On the whole, better-off parents have more leisure to devote to their children and the relatively pleasant and interesting nature of their work leaves them with reserves of energy for dialogue and helping with homework. Poorer mothers and fathers sometimes hold more than one job to keep their household afloat and this, together with the drudgery of their work, shrinks the time and energy for leisurely family discussions. Even when squeezed for time as busy professionals, the more solvent parents can afford nannies and other helpers to spread the load.

Bitter experience of failure has taught the underprivileged parents to be less worried about their children's academic performance, since they are seen by many teachers and social care professionals as troublesome and inferior. Perhaps it is no surprise that these parents believe that they must teach their children to survive by fitting in and not to standing out from the crowd. Some of them valued personability, good behaviour and helpfulness but in general, Gillies finds that these parents take a firmer line in child rearing. Often this is because they have fewer hours or energy to spend in negotiation, but also because they see themselves as readying their children for survival in a harsh and unstable world, where 'emotional intelligence' will have little place. If poorer parents look more favourably upon the purchase of costly trainers and computer games as rewards for their children, this is not because they are trying to buy affection and avoid conversation. They are only too aware that, in a consumerist world, such goods can compensate for the material and social advantages that they can never attain, while also encouraging their youngsters to stay off the crime-ridden streets and to avoid the allure of local adolescent gangs.

If Gillies' analysis is correct then, for most families, especially the hard-up ones, we wouldn't expect parenting instruction programmes to make much difference to anything, and so it proves. It has been impossible to find good evidence that this training can reliably change how adults behave toward their offspring in daily life, and still less that it can yield lasting psychological (or any other) benefits.[66] It might be that parents with significant learning disabilities or serious disturbance can gain from professional advice about the practicalities of infant and child care, but this group represents a minority of the recipients of current programmes in the UK. Even here, the most effective help is likely to be of the practical hands-on variety, placing warmth and solidarity above instruction – qualities that are in short supply for such parents (and especially mothers), targeted for surveillance by the welfare agencies.[67]

It is all the more troubling then, that since the first wave of the early twenty-first-century economic recession, parenting advice 'services' in the UK and other countries have been generously funded, just as desperately needed practical help has been withdrawn.[68] In the era of austerity-inspired cuts in public services, the most vulnerable parents struggle to feed their children and to find decent housing, or, when suffering domestic violence, to enter the refuges with them, because the shelters are threatened with closure for want of cash.[69]

CONCLUSIONS: A SPOONFUL OF SUGAR?

In their love of vague diagnoses and hidden vulnerabilities, psychologists and psychiatrists have helped to narrow down the number of ways in which it is acceptable to be human. As an old saying has it, 'the more laws the more crimes';[70] that is, the more ways there are to describe illness, the greater the scope for feeling that we must be lacking, as we start to police ourselves and each other for signs of backsliding. The therapeutic outlook allows the more prosperous sections of society to put the yoke of responsibility for social problems (like impoverishment) straight upon the necks of the poor, the prime targets for parenting training, and many of the other interventions that we have considered here. The implication is that they deserve what they get, because they are supposedly deficient 'in character, in integrity, in impulse control, when in reality what they are lacking is money'.[71] This kind of nonsense is promoted by people who should know better, including social work educators, community leaders and a good many academic researchers, and is probably the most harmful effect of psychological therapy. It entices people into believing that they are inadequate or substandard rather than downtrodden, trapped, or damaged, and it denies them a language with which they might begin to grasp their predicament, let alone change it.

No conscious conspiracy is needed. The therapeutic tale that places both the client's misery and the capacity to heal it more or less inside of their head is, in part, a kind of optical illusion, caused by two individuals meeting in a room to discuss the personal problems of one of them. When it comes to understanding the roots of distress, the subjective experiences of both parties loom misleadingly large. Add the ingredients of professional interest and political expediency, and there is little incentive to probe beyond the conventional scripts that popular culture provides for our woes, which so often boil down to individual defect, illness, or irresponsibility. If they could think and talk, two goldfish swimming around in their bowl might find a great deal to say about the fascinating details of their small world. They would need to look much further afield to understand what ultimately sustained their well-being, or threatened it.

7
Theory Into Practice – The Programme for Improving Access to Psychological Therapies (IAPT)

... machines eat people and steal jobs, the human hand is indistinguishable from other tools, and the workers, who imitate machines, do not get sick, they rust.

E. Galeano[1]

This chapter examines the British government's programme called 'Improving Access to Psychological Therapies' or IAPT, as an example of the mass application of psychological techniques – in this case, available on demand, free at the point of delivery, and aimed at both improving national well-being, and at reducing the number of depressed and unemployed people in need of government financial support.

Inaugurated in 2006, by the end of its first three years of operation, IAPT had recruited and trained its own workforce of 3,600 therapists administered by ten local 'Pathfinder Centres', each based in one of the Strategic Health Authorities of England. These IAPT workers are officially grouped into two broad categories: first, the Psychological Well Being Practitioners, schooled to deliver basic mental health and self-management advice – primarily via telephone, the Internet, or through group work, and secondly, the more highly trained High Intensity Therapists – who focus largely upon traditional one-to-one therapy. Both types of IAPT workers are equipped to deliver these treatments in accordance with a set manual, and to assess each client's well-being and employment status each time they meet, using a range of questionnaires. The scheme runs alongside, and will eventually supplant, most of the existing therapy services within the NHS and the voluntary sector, in England and Wales. By 2011, the programme had done well, having delivered talking treatment (mainly CBT) to 400,000 individuals, with a recovery rate of 40 per cent, and with nearly 14,000 of these clients having been 'moved off' sick pay or other state benefits – mainly into training, or employment.[2] This was an industrial and cost-effective approach to therapy that would have quickened the heart of Henry Ford himself.

IAPT – A BRIEF PRIMER

If every brainchild has a parent, then in the case of IAPT we must begin with the British economist and 'happiness czar', Lord Richard Layard. As director of the Centre for Economic Performance (CEP) at the London School of Economics, Layard had been invited by the former New Labour administration, to come up with ideas for modernising and improving the NHS's adult mental health services.[3] Over several years, this New Labour peer charted the anatomy of what was to come through a series of talks and publications – first, under the aegis of the Sainsbury Centre for Mental Health, and then of the CEP, culminating in the policy proposals featured in *The Depression Report*.[4] This report was issued with the national *Observer* newspaper, and signed by an elite metropolitan group consisting mainly of psychiatrists and NHS CEOs, including Layard himself, whose thinking had been infused by recent academic and applied research into 'happiness psychology', especially the work of the conservative academic and writer Martin Seligman.[5] A former chair of the American Psychological Association and adviser to the US military, Seligman's experiments on 'learned helplessness' – on the emotional breaking of laboratory dogs via random electric shock – had informed the Bush administration's torture programme at Guantánamo Bay.[6] In more pleasing terrain, the research into 'happiness' carried out by Seligman and his colleagues had seemed to show that personal well-being was about more than mere money, personal temperament, or circumstance.

For Layard, two main lessons seemed to flow from this seemingly radical insight. On the one hand, the mental health of the population could be significantly improved through a range of 'upstream' antipoverty and child-care measures, fuelled by redistributive taxation; a suggestion that owed most to the kind of epidemiological research discussed in Chapter 5 of this book. On the other hand, the secrets of well-being, once thought to be elusive, had now been distilled by experts and could be packaged into a set of psychological competencies. It was a short step from here to the idea of boosting the national contentment quotient through individual psychological interventions.

There was a good *clinical* rationale for all of this, because the psychologists had at last come up with an effective, scientifically proven mental health practice in the shape of CBT, a treatment capable of addressing any kind of personal and social problem, if only the government could muster the political will required for mass prescription. Layard had confessed his ignorance about mental health matters from the beginning, but he had benefited from reading the productions of the National Institute for Clinical Excellence (NICE), in which the guidelines for psychological therapy were tilted heavily in favour of this form of therapy. He had also gained in wisdom from the advice of a small group of clinical psychologists and psychiatrists from the University of Oxford and the Institute of Psychiatry.[7]

The New Labour government had made it clear that efficiency, cost effectiveness and indeed profitability were key considerations for any kind of health resource.[8] And Layard's speeches and writings – including *The Depression Report* – marshalled strong economic as well as 'scientific' and 'clinical' arguments for the creation of a new kind of mass talking therapy service.

The financial case therefore looked to the statistics that showed emotional disturbance to be both common and costly – afflicting one in six of the population, according to some estimates. Layard indicated that over 1 million people in Britain were living on Incapacity Benefit (IB) due to a mental health problem, at an annual cost to the Exchequer of 18 billion pounds in treatment and care, and of 12 billion pounds in lost economic output – or 2 percent of GDP. Indeed, there were more people drawing IB than unemployed people on Jobseeker's Allowance.'[9] It was therefore obvious that 'we desperately need a better NHS, delivering more help and understanding to patients. But for many patients, work is a major route to recovery. And as taxpayers who pay for Invalidity Benefits, we can all say amen to this.'[10] Clearly, any treatment service that could make inroads into these problems would be well worth the price. It was then a happy coincidence that there was little difference between the cost to the exchequer of a month's Incapacity Benefit, and the average regimen of CBT – about £750. As *The Depression Report* enthused, '[I]f the person works just a month more as a result of the treatment, [then] the treatment pays for itself.'[11] The savings accrued when the long-term depressed and unemployed re-entered the labour market would allow the entire scheme to fund itself, sparing the public purse many millions of pounds in disability benefit payments into the bargain. In seeking to appeal to his paymasters, Layard had clearly set his sights as much on the cash, as on the cognitions.

As a direct response by the Department of Health to Layard's proposals, the first incarnation of IAPT took place in 2007, in the form of two 'demonstration sites' – one based at Doncaster in Yorkshire, and the other at Newham, in London. From the outset, the character of the programme cleaved to the commercial service-sector approach to health care, favoured by New Labour. Both of these projects and all subsequent IAPT teams have worked according to what is known as a 'hub and spoke model', in which 'quality control' and 'service development' come from managers at the centre. Their decisions are based upon NHS and central government directives and upon a 'minimum data set' collected from all clients as they pass through the service. This information is gathered in every therapy session in the form of answers to a set of standard questions intended to measure each participant's mental health, well-being and work status.[12]

The two pilot schemes have set the mould for all subsequent IAPT services. A call centre serves as the first point of contact for most customers, giving on to successive layers of increasingly personalised and value-added services, in which therapy is dispensed at mounting levels of 'intensity', according to the principles of 'stepped care'. For example, low-intensity treatment at steps 1 to 3 focuses mostly upon 'self-management', or what might be better called 'self-service'. The worried individual is offered reassurance and guidance from an IAPT operative over the phone or the Internet, together with access to an online interactive 'CBT therapy package' – such as *Beating the Blues©*, or *Fear Fighter©*. If necessary, this can be stepped up to a handful of encounters with a 'low intensity well-being advisor', perhaps in conjunction with a 'course' of ten weekly sessions of 'psycho-educational group work'.[13]

If the client's problems are too severe for these basic remedies, then they might qualify for 'high intensity treatment' in the guise of up to twelve or more sessions of individual CBT, or, perhaps, psychodynamically tinged 'interpersonal therapy', in both cases, dispensed by a more thoroughly trained 'high intensity' therapist. Escalation of the client's problems into crisis might take them out of the service, towards in-patient care. Clients can thus move up the IAPT stairway in line with their state of mind, although the aim is to convey them out of the system as soon as they show enough improvement. This graded approach was presented by the advocates of IAPT as a brand new idea in mental health services, the equivalent of the smoothly efficient department-store escalators that deliver customers to their chosen floors. In truth, however, stepped care is a formalisation of the wearily familiar care pathways that have always been trodden both by the worried well, and by those in the early stages of more intense anguish.

So much for the blueprints, what then of the actual performance of these IAPT projects? Officially, both of the pilots and their descendants have been a big success, as measured by the numbers of people referred, treated, improved and satisfied. At Doncaster, for instance, over one seven-month interval, a total of 2,347 patients were treated, and while three-quarters of this number said that they were moderately depressed at the start, less than a quarter of them claimed that they were still down in the dumps at the end. This much celebrated result was achieved almost entirely through the application of guided self-help manuals, as opposed to more intensive individual therapy. Patient satisfaction rates were even more impressive, running at close to 100 per cent.[14] Dr Alan Cohen, national primary care lead for the IAPT programme was jubilant:

> We have made psychological therapies practical and available to primary care patients, which is fantastic. The finding that 49% of patients no longer have a clinical diagnosis after treatment is the sort you see in randomised controlled trials. To be able to duplicate that in practice is extraordinary.[15]

The original plan had called for the IAPT demonstration sites to fully prove themselves before funds could be released to support further expansion. But as if to confirm the axiom of cognitive therapy – that good cheer can create its own kind of fortune – approval for Stage 3 was granted by the Department of Health (DoH) in 2007, well before the outcome data from Doncaster and Newham had been fully reaped, let alone analysed.[16] The British news media were for the most part jubilant. Here is BBC correspondent Mark Easton's report on the first wave of results from the eleven IAPT Pathway Centres: 'Look at the "before and after" table below. The proportion of patients exhibiting severe depression is halved. The moderate categories have been reduced by three-quarters. The proportion of patients with no depression or anxiety has increased ten-fold.'[17] A star performance indeed – and in 2008 the Doncaster pilot duly went on to 'scoop' a national Health and Social Care Award for the category of 'breakthrough ideas' for 'the improvement of frontline services'.[18]

Impressed by the good results, the Conservative-Liberal Democrat Coalition government that replaced New Labour in 2010 pledged an additional £400 million to the scheme, in 2011. Continued growth for the following three years thus assured, the DoH set its sights upon new patient groups: children and adolescents, older people, and those suffering from long-term physical problems and medically unexplained conditions. All of these constituencies accounted for a large slice of state health and welfare agency budgets.[19]

Supporters say that the IAPT is the biggest improvement in mental health services since the introduction of community care. Even many of its critics hold that the scheme will redress years of chronic underfunding in mental health services, in a 'bold attempt to expand psychological therapies and to link that expansion to the use of effective therapies'.[20] For anyone with a longer memory, the idea that psychotherapy might in all seriousness be used by a national government to boost happiness and employment is a surprise. It was not long ago that psychological therapists were struggling to find the smallest scrap of convincing evidence in support of what they do.[21]

GOOD CLINICAL SCIENCE, OR GOOD PUBLIC RELATIONS?

As we have seen, the IAPT started out as two 'demonstration projects' – billed as attempts to rigorously show that large-scale graded treatment with CBT could successfully alleviate the most common forms of psychological distress. It was expected that the scientific principles of the IAPT and stepped care, once established, would make a compelling case for the subsequent 'unrolling' of a full-scale national programme. If we ignore the far-from-minor problem that in this case, the conclusions preceded the results, we do not have to look hard to see that the IAPT project bears scant resemblance to a meaningful experiment. In clinical medicine, this means, above all, an effort to keep constant all of the variables that might influence patient improvement, apart from the treatment of interest. As we saw in Chapter 4, this also means that certain minimal conditions must be met. Both the disorder and the therapy should be well specified, so that other clinicians and researchers can understand what illness has been tackled and with what degree of success. The measures used to select the participants and to describe the outcomes must be reliable and accurate. The participants must be drawn randomly from the broader group of sufferers, in order to ensure that the findings of the study are representative and can be more widely applied to those with the disorder under investigation.

There should be adequate placebo and waiting list control groups, with adequate blinding on both sides if patient and clinician are not to be unduly influenced by their own beliefs about the treatment. The data should therefore be collected by outside parties, with a minimal stake in the outcome.[22]

These are the basic ABCs of careful psychotherapy research. Aside from the use of client samples that are truly huge by normal psychotherapy research standards, not one of these criteria have been met by the IAPT scheme, either in its 'experimental' pilot forms, or in the proposals for the full-blown national scheme.

For instance, if we begin with the diagnosis of mild to moderate depression – the main form of illness which the programme is intended to address – this one, in common with most other psychiatric categories, is sorely lacking in validity.[23] As Chapter 2 showed, this diagnosis tells us little about the history, causes, or nature of the sufferer's problems as they see them, and still less about what kinds of help might be of most use to them and over what time-scale. Two individuals, each labelled as 'depressed', can show entirely divergent symptoms, so that it is not clear that they are in fact suffering from the same putative disease at all.[24] This psychiatric category also lacks reliability, in the sense that it often overlaps and is confused with other problems such as anxiety, obsessional states and even with psychosis, where the distress is severe.[25]

This kind of muddle was reflected in the comprehensive version of the UK government's clinical guidelines for the treatment of depression, as set by NICE, and current at the time when the IAPT pilots were conceived and initiated:

> … the most significant limitation [with the evidence base for therapies designed to combat depression] is with the concept of depression itself. The view of the Guideline Development Group was that it is too broad and heterogeneous a category, and has limited validity as a basis of effective treatment plans … In part, these limitations arise from the problems associated with the randomised control trial methodology for all interventions.[26]

And yet, for the IAPT, the selection of clients and the outcomes of clinical treatment were (and are) framed first, in terms of each person's depression or anxiety scores, as measured by one of two clinical 'instruments' – the Patient Health Questionnaire (PHQ)[27] and the Generalised Anxiety Disorder Assessment (GAD).[28]

If these uncertainties were invisible to the architects of the IAPT, they were echoed in the conflicting official statements about who exactly would constitute the main targets of the new service. Richards and Suckling stated that the demonstration phases of the project would be tailored toward those who were suffering from 'mild to moderate depression and anxiety': the group, according to them, most likely to benefit from short-term CBT. Whereas the Centre for Economic Performance seemed to think that this early phase would be geared to treating people with 'crippling depression and chronic anxiety'.[29] At the heart of the programme lay a muddle, which suggested that the psychologists had been overselling their wares, that Layard and the British government had been too credulous, or both.[30]

From a scientific standpoint, a further difficulty with the sampling of clients is that there has been no attempt to randomly select them from the very large group of people in the general population who might meet the criteria for depression. Instead, most of the people who enter the gates of the IAPT have been referred by themselves, or by their GP or other health and social care professional – and on the basis of expressed symptoms and presumably of their willingness to engage with psychological treatment. This is fine, if we are interested in this better-motivated group. But if the claim is that the IAPT can help all comers, then it is worth wondering what might happen at a later stage, when more seriously distressed or less motivated people might begin to enter the system. It is doubtful that any form of demoralisation that can be solved by reading a set of self-help booklets, by following a computerised recipe, or even by sitting through a handful of 50-minute sessions of focused conversation can be all that serious to begin with.

The specification of treatment is similarly nebulous, when we look behind the bright illustrations in the brochures, websites, and PowerPoint presentations through which the scheme has been marketed. The shape and content of most therapeutic conversations seem to be preordained in the numerous decision trees and colourful flow charts of the official IAPT treatment manual – which claims to lead clinician and client from the dark basement of negative automatic thoughts to the daylit atrium of positive coping strategies and personal change. In practice, the manuals to which the IAPT workers must turn in search of a wide choice of micro-interventions (and still wider choice of combinations) belie the claim that the scheme offers well-defined treatments. Rather, it is possible to receive elements of lifestyle advice, cognitive therapy, 'psychoeducation', interpersonal therapy and counselling. Just what was it, exactly, that was being tested in the original demonstration projects, and in the subsequent 'roll out'?[31]

For many critics, 'CBT' is a kind of shorthand for what pragmatic and advice-minded clinicians have found to 'work' for their clients, but without having bothered to worry much about what was actually happening, beneath the surface.[32] It is certainly the most pragmatic version of CBT that runs throughout the guidelines that the IAPT workers must follow, like the letters in a stick of seaside rock. Complex as these treatment diagrams may be, they none the less omit almost everything that is important about the actual practice of therapy as a human encounter, which should allow scope for exploring ambiguity and for posing difficult ethical and sometimes political questions about the grounds of one's unhappiness.[33]

A further problem with this focus upon CBT is that the architects of the IAPT programme proclaim that their favourite school of treatment is the most desirable because it has the firmest evidence base and is therefore, by a leap of logic, the most effective. We have looked at this question earlier on in this book, and these arguments will not be rehearsed here. But it is worth recalling that none of these claims are as solid as they appear.[34]

Even the comprehensive version of the NICE guidelines were ambivalent when it came to the question of CBT and the treatment of mild-to-moderate depression, where there exist

> ... significant limitations to the current evidence base ... These include very limited data on both long-term outcomes for most, if not all, interventions ... In part, these limitations arise from the problems associated with the randomized controlled trial methodology for all interventions ... .[35]

In sum, the architects of the IAPT have used CBT to lend the scheme a superficial authority.

We have already noted the fundamental importance of placebo controls in clinical research or in 'demonstration projects' of any sort. One of the most obvious drawbacks with the IAPT programme has been the complete lack of control groups of any kind. Instead, outcomes are derived from a comparison of each client's score at initial assessment with their attainment at the end of treatment. This method is unsatisfactory, because without a genuine control group, there is no way to exclude a host of highly plausible alternative explanations for whatever improvements are observed. What we are talking about here are of course placebo factors, and for the IAPT these are numerous.

At the most obvious, perhaps, there is the knowledge (shared most probably by just about every therapist and perhaps by large numbers of clients) that the treatments are taking place within a widely publicised flagship health scheme; a circumstance that, in itself, should carry potent expectations of cure. At their first clinical assessment, poorer clients who are on the verge of starting their therapy will have every reason to exaggerate the severity of their problems, because of an entirely justified belief that the declared severity of their ills will affect their future eligibility for much-needed benefit payments. Many others might be tempted to similarly exaggerate, in the hope that overstating their health needs might lead to more intense, prolonged, or effective treatment. Even a frank placebo conversation would give the illusion of clinical effectiveness here, because the client would have less reason to talk up their unhappiness as their (bogus) treatment progressed.

The IAPT enterprise seems to have enjoyed a moderate success in recruiting clients who are economically and socially marginalised.[36] Nevertheless, it is worth bearing in mind that when it comes to disclosing their feelings about their health problems and their lives, people from such backgrounds are at their most cagey and superficially compliant when talking to middle-class health or social care professionals, of the kind employed by this scheme.[37]

There are many other features built into the IAPT programme that seem almost calculated to increase the likelihood of the participants' exaggerating the supposed benefits of their treatment. The DoH refers constantly to 'performance indicators' as a demonstration of the success of the programme. These are, in fact, targets that each therapy team are required to meet – both in supposed cure rates and in the number of people levered out of the roster for sickness and unemployment benefits. All of the IAPT posts entail a relatively good salary by British public health service standards and for psychology graduates, and represent a doorway into the health and social care professions. Indeed, social workers, nurses and clinical psychologists are themselves rushing forward to become high-intensity therapists. At the time of writing, competition for these jobs is sharp. It is likely to become sharper as the economic recession deepens, as the Coalition government continues to cut back on all public services, and as the supply of new vacancies within them dry up.

When it comes to the issue of vested interests in the outcome of treatment, then the combined weight of these circumstances are substantial, which in turn prompts the question of just how autonomous and critical could the average IAPT therapist afford to be? We can judge the scope for independent thought by one simple observation: as part of their routine data collection for each therapy session, they are required to ask each client about their employment status.[38] Because we live in a society in which to be of working age and jobless is to be seen as faintly disreputable, then this is not a neutral question. The fact that it is asked every time implies that, for large numbers of indigent and workless recipients, the therapeutic encounter will be navigating across a subtle undercurrent of shame; raising the odds of compliance and suggestibility.

These are not the only issues of assessment for the IAPT. A more subtle – but no less damaging – objection, resides in the repeated use of the same measurement scales at every stage of the scheme. As all pub quiz fans will observe, the repeated use of the same questions is not a good way of finding out what people really believe or know. Clinical researchers have shown that the recurrent use of a psychiatric symptom scale will routinely lead to a fall in client symptom scores, even in the absence of *any form* of psychological therapy.[39] The familiarity that comes with frequent use seems to give the sufferer a strong hint as to the 'correct' answers to which they should aspire: both as a good patient and as a responsible, health-conscious citizen, dutifully following the professional's advice and expectations.

Meanwhile, the practitioner is employed to achieve targets for client improvement and disengagement from state benefits, and their job and future career as therapists depend upon their performance. In the practice of CBT, as in many other psychological therapies, hopes of betterment, openly conveyed by the practitioner, are presumed to contribute directly to client improvement via the strengthening of the therapeutic bond, task commitment and positive thinking.[40] Is it conceivable that a therapist in this situation is not going to communicate the expectation of 'cure' to each hapless client? Far distant from the idea that psychotherapy might be a form of solidarity with the patient, against a cruel world, this set-up also violates every sensible rule for the disinterested collection of information – even at the level of a 'consumer satisfaction survey' conducted in a local supermarket.

ANOTHER NICE MESS ... ?

Beyond these questions, however, we also need to see the limitations of the NICE evidence base itself, and the recommendations to which they give rise, notwithstanding that government ministers, NHS managers and clinicians will often refer to these documents in tones that suggest absolute – even biblical – authority. For here, as elsewhere, it is worth remembering that the dictionary defines a 'guideline' as a form of advice and not as a commandment.[41]

NICE takes meta-analytic studies as among the highest standards of evidence. But there are significant limitations in the meta-analytic approach, to the extent that some researchers and clinicians believe that most meta-analyses have little scientific or clinical value. This is because of their reliance upon the results of disparate studies that, upon careful examination, often turn out to draw upon ill-assorted populations and to use procedures that are similar only when judged by their external appearance. A meta-analytic summary only begins to approach usefulness when each study that goes into it has been carefully sifted for possible flaws, gaps and inconsistencies in both measurement and in design. As we have seen in Chapter 4, these issues are sharpened in the field of psychotherapy research, because the influences exerted by clients, therapists, treatments and the settings in which they meet can mutually entangle one another in ways that are hard to foresee.[42] The professional and social backgrounds of the participants, their personal characteristics and their commitment to the type of therapy that is under consideration are just some of the decisive factors that are completely absent from the clinical research trials and meta-analyses cited in the NICE guidelines in this field.[43]

A RESTRICTED MENU

If the chief therapy for the Improving Access project is CBT, then there are also questions about its suitability for all. Psychotropic chemicals produce happier results in some people than in others, and this is no less true of talking treatments.[44] Given the chance, clients and practitioners will choose therapies on the basis of their personal characteristics and outlook, and will report more success with the brand that best suits them.[45] When mental health service users are asked for their views about Cognitive Behavioural Therapy, then they can be more sceptical than the people who dispense it.[46] In the light of considerations like these, the abundance of CBT (and not much else) within the IAPT scheme has been compared to a bizarre café that has numerous options on the menu but where in fact almost every item turns out to be a variant on Spam.[47]

But this is more than an issue of personal preference, it is also about the extent to which therapy speaks to the conditions of people's lives. The CBT research literature has paid scant attention to minority participants and to how well the assumptions and methods of the approach fit their cultural background, circumstances and experiences.[48] In the some of the best-known training literature, including that for the IAPT programme itself, terms like 'race', 'racism' and 'feminism', let alone 'social inequality', or 'exploitation' either make no appearance, or are elided into the bland social-policy speak of 'cultural competency' and 'service user inclusion',[49] notwithstanding that the IAPT has underperformed in recruiting minority clients and is intended to serve all communities throughout England – in places like Wandsworth, South London, it has started to come to mosques and temples.[50]

Another general concern lies with the reliance upon diagnostic schedules to measure results – a method not exclusive to CBT, but one that its proponents have certainly pioneered, and that is integral to its practice. Over the years, some of the more thoughtful therapists have noted that the people who appear to do best in short-term treatment – as measured by their ticking of a symptom checklist – are often the ones whose problems are well concealed. For them, the appearance of superficial cheerfulness has long become a habit, concealing deep-rooted inner torments, and almost guaranteeing that it will take them a long time to build the trust needed for sharing their real troubles.[51] How likely is this kind of dialogue, in a setting in which workers are carrying caseloads (80 in the case of a low-intensity worker)[52] that are far beyond what more experienced psychotherapists would wish to handle? It is not necessary to believe that psychotherapy can offer an eventual cure, to see that the target-driven environment of the IAPT project will provide little room to give suffering its real due,[53] even supposing that the practitioner – whatever their 'intensity' – were interested in doing so in the first place.

The question then becomes not just whether the professional was helpful, but whether they were doing harm. Studies of the recipient's experience of therapy suggest that when treatment is rushed, then what from the therapist's viewpoint seems like efficiency starts to look more like indifference, from where the client is sitting.[54]

THE PUBLIC FACE OF THE IAPT

As any good storyteller or politician knows, what is left out of the tale can be more important than what is retained. This precept is no more evident than when considering how the IAPT has been presented to the public, following the pilot projects in Doncaster and Newham. A well-publicised report on the first year of full operation, or 'roll out' of 34 IAPT sites, from October 2008, was widely seen as demonstrating that 'NHS psychological therapists enable four in 10 [clients] to recover', in the words of *Therapy Today* magazine.[55] This appears to be an impressive success rate, based upon the referral of over 130,000 people across the scheme over a two-year period. But the devil is in the details. A closer look at the North East Public Health Observatory report,[56] shows that only just over half of the people referred even attended for their first assessment. These constitute the study group, of which about half again were judged to have formally completed their contact with the service. Of this smaller subgroup, only a third had successfully finished their treatment; the rest had terminated their engagement because they were judged unsuitable, or had dropped out, refused further therapy outright, or because it was stopped for reasons unknown. The remaining half of the study group were deemed to be still 'in contact' with the service. This could mean a lot of things, but most of all it implied that they had not yet completed their treatment. The overall conclusion, however, was plain. The widely trumpeted success – 'four out of ten recovered' – applied only to the 12,000-or-so people who had actually finished their therapy: exactly 9 *per cent* of those who were originally assessed. This is not a dramatically successful cure rate.

This picture is even worse than it looks. Of the remaining group, deemed by the researchers to be still in treatment, the therapist and service evaluation consultant Barry McInnes asks a very pertinent question:

> Is it credible that 47 per cent of those referred are really still in the system, or has contact with them been lost and their cases simply not closed? In my experience of services of this type, over the course of a year no more than 10 per cent of cases are likely to remain open.

Confidence is not increased, when we learn that in excess of a third of all clients dropped out of the scheme after their first therapy session, and that the figures quoted above are averages, derived from many different sites, one of which, for example, had outcome data for only 2 *per cent* of its clients.[57]

HELPFUL AND BENIGN?

If there are strong doubts about the scientific integrity of the whole IAPT enterprise, then what about its political role? Is this somehow more sensible and benign? It is worth recalling that it was not a liberal politician, but Margaret Thatcher, who was the first British prime minister to introduce counselling services for people who had lost their jobs because of 'economic restructuring'.[58] If we take the issue of re-employment for many of the programme's clients and the resulting savings in benefit payments, then the question must be asked: what kinds of jobs are the people who are 'cured' likely to find? Even with the help of JobCentre advisers, the moderately depressed or anxious are not likely to be an attractive proposition to many employers in a period of recession, assuming, of course, that such employers will be found in sufficient numbers in the first place. The majority of IB claimants are concentrated in the economically battered industrial heartlands of England and Wales, areas in which decently paid employment is even harder to come by than in the relatively prosperous South.[59] At the time of writing, there are no large-scale schemes of the kind that would be required to create the necessary jobs in the areas where they are needed. In these circumstances, few people are likely to find the gainful employment that they need. When they do manage it, they are likely, out of desperation, to take up work that is neither financially rewarding nor personally fulfilling; this might, in the end, reinforce the mental health problems that prompted them to seek treatment to begin with.[60] Conversely, those unable to find work but who are no longer entitled to IB will face impoverishment and insecurity when forced to rely on the even more meagre payments of the 'Job Seekers Allowance' to which they will be entitled.[61]

WELL DONE, OR HALF BAKED?

From the point of view of someone suffering from mental health problems and from that of society at large, the IAPT may still have its good points. Individual psychological therapy is not without its comforts, short-lived though they may be. For the isolated and lonely – the real constituency of the 'moderately depressed' – the IAPT scheme offers temporary respite in the person of a cheerful, optimistic and most likely young therapist. In some instances, IAPT practitioners may be able to refer the downcast and the miserable on to local, community-based agencies that are designed to address these problems of indifference and abandonment in one form or another. The project may also help a portion of those who are facing financial, housing, or employment problems to better cope with their burdens, in virtue of the extra advice and support that they might receive. However, even these modest indicators may need revision, in light of the evisceration of frontline health and social care services set to occur during the next few years. It is doubtful that voluntary organisations will have enough resources or timeliness to step in to the breach. For the neediest citizens, there will be no 'big society', waiting to pick up the pieces of their lives.[62]

Britain is not the only country to have taken this route – Sweden has likewise deployed CBT as one of the main planks of its mental health care system, having spent 2 billion Swedish krona to enable people to train in and then deliver this form of therapy. The Swedish authorities had started to worry at what they saw as the high numbers of people leaving the workforce and claiming benefits and early pensions, all because of their mental health problems. CBT was seen, by the Swedish National Board of Health and Welfare, as the best (evidence-based), way to reverse these trends, and all funding for alternative psychological therapies was stopped.[63] So far, so like the IAPT. According to the internationally known psychotherapy researcher Scott Millar, *Socionomen*, the main journal for Swedish social workers, produced an authoritative report upon the national government's assessment of its own project. Rather than the expected improvements in mass mental health, however, the widespread application of Cognitive Behavioural Therapy

> … had no effect whatsoever on the outcome of people disabled by depression and anxiety. [A] significant number of people who were not disabled at the time they were treated … became disabled, costing the government an additional one billion Swedish crowns. Finally, nearly a quarter of those who started treatment dropped out, costing an additional 340 million!

The CBT monopoly was officially ended in the summer of 2012.[64] The Swedes too, it seemed, could tire of a diet of Spam.

This chapter began with happiness and has ended with, if not its opposite, then perhaps with its cold twin: the unwelcome truth, which is still less welcome if you wish to believe that long-standing social and political troubles, or for that matter, people, can be repaired with talking therapy. Are there any other lessons that can be distilled about the value of and prospects for the IAPT service, if it continues to unfold in its current form? Sometimes, a longer, historical view can help to make things clearer. One place to start might be with the sixteenth-century Flemish painting, entitled *De Bakker van Eeklo*. This vibrant canvas tells of how troubled people could access the user-friendly, community-based mental health service of their day, in the bakehouse of the village of Eeklo. In this unlikely setting, diagnosis by a good doctor led the client straight into an early version of 'high-intensity treatment' – the first stage of which entailed the removal of their head with an axe and its replacement with a fresh cabbage, intended to staunch the flow of blood. Thus pacified, the client sat patiently, while their severed cranium was 'kneaded, sprinkled with flour, and rubbed with "wondercream", before being purified by the heat of the oven', and then returned, freshly rebaked, to its rightful place upon the shoulders of its owner.[65] A crude method of mental cleansing, but so much more direct and honest, when compared with what passes for healing of the soul, in the age of psychological science.

8
The Therapy Market – From the Third Wave to 'Happiness'

I wonder now whether inner coldness and desolation may not be the precondition for making the world believe, by a kind of fraudulent showmanship, that one's own wretched heart is still aglow.

W.G. Sebald[1]

INSTITUTIONAL AND COMMERCIAL PRESSURES ON THE TALKING TREATMENTS

Therapists like to emphasise the humanitarian nature of their mission. But, as in any other industry, they also experience pressures and incentives to continually develop the services that they provide and to distinguish them from the others that jostle in the marketplace. If the talking therapists have always had an uneasy relationship with psychiatry, then this has been almost equally so for their relations with each other. In the US health care system, for instance, it is common wisdom that 'a buyer's market exists for psychotherapy'[2] and that all practitioners need to know that they are 'going into a profession with fierce competition',[3] which is subject to an unspoken hierarchy. Psychotherapists are deemed superior to counsellors, with psychoanalysts at the apex (for those who believe, and are willing to pay for their services), even though there has never been a shred of evidence for any differences between them in effectiveness. In an act of candour unusual for the field, this situation led John McLeod, professor of counselling at the University of Dundee, to quip in 1999 that the only difference between a counsellor and a psychotherapist was about £8,000 in fees.[4]

Just like the meaningless psychiatric diagnoses that have proliferated in recent years, new talking therapies continue to multiply. 'Dialectical behaviour therapy' (DBT), 'eye movement desensitisation and reprocessing' (EMDR), 'acceptance and commitment therapy' (ACT), 'cognitive analytic therapy' (CAT), 'cognitive mindfulness therapy' (CMT) and 'Sorenson's treatment for instability of mood',[5] are just a few of the more recent entrants, most of them rendered into technical sounding acronyms and in search of as many mental disorders as possible. Thus, DBT might be prescribed for BPD or NPD,[6] and EMDR, for PTSD, GAD, or SAD, for instance. Like so many other trends, this one can be traced to Freud, when the first British edition of his work turned him 'into an English gentleman and a confident doctor', by translating his vernacular German into a latinised, medical vocabulary – whence the plain *das Ich* ('the I') and *das Es* ('the it'), became the much more intriguing 'ego' and 'id', respectively.[7]

Modern-day psychological treatments likewise sound arcane and mysterious, but the notions and activities behind them belie this impression, to say the least. EMDR is described by enthusiasts as 'the silicon chip of psychotherapy',[8] and is used to treat people who are suffering from a mental trauma, or, increasingly, from anxiety, depression and a host of other problems. As we saw in Chapter 4, the treatment technique is straightforward; the EMDR practitioner waves his or her finger back and forth in front of the seated or recumbent client, while they track it with their eyes, thus 'reprocessing' the offending memories into the 'correct' bits of the client's brain.[9]

The suspicion grows that many practitioners have coined pseudo-scientific names for their treatments for the same reasons that pharmaceutical companies choose portentous titles for their psychoactive drugs: to secure an exclusive brand-name identity for their product, and because marginal and placebo treatments give best results, when stamped with an impressive, technical label.[10]

In contrast to pharmaceutical remedies, few of the talking ones are owned, or patented, by multimillion-dollar companies, but exceptions do exist and they are instructive. Neuro-linguistic programming (NLP), for instance, is a slickly packaged, commercialised version of CBT, which teaches people to manage their misery and boost their enthusiasm by, allegedly, tinkering with the neural circuits that underlie positive and negative thoughts and the moods that they produce. Like EMDR, it relies in part upon the monitoring and deliberate use of eye movements (looking to the right or the left, for example) to ensure that the client is 'engaging' the 'correct' side of their brain, as they upgrade their mental software, by generating new, life-changing affirmations.[11] Qualified psychologists are prone to sneer at NLP for its lack of empirical grounding. Seen with a clearer eye, its abiding tenet, that we can reprogramme ourselves to be more dynamic and creative, perhaps to become paragons of boldness and resolve – is a less bashful version of the theories and practices espoused by the advocates of NLP's more respectable siblings.

In the world of scientifically based psychotherapy, the official manuals (and other training materials) are usually in copyright. The publication of books and journals, the delivery of training packages by renowned therapists and academic institutes and their graduates can be a rewarding business. You cannot become qualified in some of the more fashionable therapies, like DBT, for instance, unless you have undertaken an approved training, for a high fee.[12]

In Britain, since the 1980s, the NHS has been gradually (and often stealthily) shifted by successive governments in the direction of a business culture, ruled by competition for an internal market of health care.[13] Psychologists and other health professionals have learned to talk of performance indicators and targets, audit and quality control, as if they had never bothered before to consider (or to try to measure) how their patients felt about their treatment. In the new NHS Foundation Trusts, there is an emphasis upon the marketing of psychology and psychological skills to other 'stakeholders', including the voluntary and private sector, the universities and, of course, other Foundation Trusts.[14]

Authoritarian forms of management have replaced more democratic lines of accountability. Clinical knowledge is regarded as an off-the-shelf product, to be shaped and directed by managers, in harness with organisational goals and with the requirements of enormously expensive (and often dysfunctional) computer systems.[15] If you talk to psychologists up and down the country, it is clear that in many institutions they are preoccupied with the 'business plans' that increasingly shape or dictate their activities, and they are encouraged to vie for performance and innovation awards, analogous to the prizes used by commercial companies to motivate employees who build cars within lean production schedules.[16] Never mind that the disturbed human beings that they try to help are not machines, or customers, or that thousands of vehicles made by one such company had to be recalled because of safety concerns about their braking systems.[17]

At the time of writing, the UK government has been proposing to open up psychological services for adults in primary care to private or other non-NHS providers. Such a move will be smoothed along by policies for rationalising treatment; first, via the introduction of 'payment by results' for clinicians, and secondly, by the allocation of patients with more serious psychological problems to separate 'clusters', in which they will be grouped according to their troubles, and then channelled into the care and treatment 'pathways' and 'packages' deemed suitable.[18]

However, this notion of payment by results ignores the strong evidence, collected by academic psychologists, that if you begin to reward people for those aspects of their work that they find *intrinsically worthwhile*, then their creativity and performance can drop, sometimes drastically.[19] Similarly, the grouping of patients and their problems and treatments into 'clusters' cannot be the advance in treatment and care proclaimed by its advocates in the Department of Health. Since each 'cluster' is defined by its own set of diagnoses and associated NICE guidelines for therapy – and eventually for social care, as well – then the machinery will continue to be driven by dubious psychiatric thinking.

Some clinicians, dubbed 'psychopreneurs' by their more sceptical colleagues,[20] have welcomed these changes and the idea of private-sector 'involvement' as an opportunity to sell psychological services and to expand their pay cheques. On the other hand, many of their colleagues object to what they see as the break-up of the NHS system of universal, equitable, free, state-provided health care into a more disjointed and competitive one, likely to increase health inequalities.[21] The reluctance of the British Psychological Society (BPS) to take a stand on this issue,[22] and its failure to contribute to a key House of Commons Health Committee inquiry into the workings of NICE,[23] are yet further signs that psychologists are no more free of business imperatives than people in other industries. In the sharp-elbowed world of marketised care, it becomes difficult to speak a more measured and modest language about what can be achieved, and still more difficult to ask searching questions about the shaky scientific, clinical and ethical basis of the whole.

MINDFULNESS, OR MINDLESSNESS? THIRD-WAVE CBT

Over the last 30 years, CBT has found its way into every nook and cranny of the modern mental health industry, pushing out most of its competitors. Despite its success, however, enthusiasts have come to acknowledge that CBT is not always so effective in treating people whose problems are deeply rooted or who live in harsh circumstances.[24] In part, 'Third-wave CBT' is a response to these challenges. Therapists still claim to modify the client's thinking, feelings and behaviour, but the new element concerns how this is done. It is no longer necessary to avoid or counter unwanted or disturbing thoughts. Instead, the client should learn to coolly observe them. The resulting powerful beam of attention will dispel these troubled clouds and open up a clearer space in the client's mind, from which new and more sensible or productive courses of action can be seen and chosen, or may even emerge spontaneously, given enough time.[25] Most of these third-wave approaches explicitly embrace mindfulness practices and visualisation exercises of Buddhist or Hindu origin, designed to cultivate more awareness of the somatic manifestation of emotions and moods, together with greater calmness, stoicism and compassion toward self and others. Buddhism as a philosophy is concerned with purging the mind and body of desire, aversion and delusion,[26] and it is easy to see how western therapists (always looking for new ideas) were able to map these concerns on to the declared domains of psychoanalysis, behaviourism and cognitive therapy, respectively, and then onto the general template of an integrative approach like CBT. This third wave is therefore quite the magpie, having also borrowed psychodynamic ideas on the importance of the mutual transference of feelings between client and therapist as a key to better insight, ideas from family therapy about how clients can get trapped in mutually destructive patterns of communication with their nearest but not so dearest, and, now, meditative mindfulness.[27] Promoted as having a role in the prevention as well as cure of mental illness, the mindfulness-based therapies affirm any (and sometimes all) of several different conceptions of mental health – ranging from the more humble aim of freedom from distress, to adaptation to the world as it is and then upward, into individual fulfilment and even mystical transcendence.[28] Besides clinical treatment, these techniques are used by individual therapists in their quest to better their own emotional resilience and wisdom, and they are deployed by public-sector and commercial organisations, intent upon improving the morale and stress-fitness of their employees, especially those who work in health, education and social care.[29]

Third-wave treatments owe at least part of their popularity to the fact that most of them are fully manualised, making them fairly easy to deliver and teach, and ensuring that purchasers know exactly what they are buying. They come in many varieties and they have spawned a correspondingly large number of acronyms. For the sake of brevity, I will concentrate on four of what are perhaps among the best known, which include acceptance and commitment therapy (ACT), mindfulness-based cognitive therapy (MBCT), dialectical behaviour therapy (DBT) and integrative couples behaviour therapy (ICBT).

In their methods and philosophy, both ACT and MBCT remain closest to the outlook of traditional Mahayana Buddhism. Acceptance and commitment therapy,[30] sometimes known simply as 'ACT', has been widely applied to the treatment of depression, anxiety and of obsessive (or ruminative) worries and compulsions. Reasonably enough, ACT therapists try to help the client develop an improved awareness of their body as the gateway to learning to relax and let go of unwanted feelings and thoughts. ACT embraces an extended definition of self, encompassing the people and places that help to shape the client's conduct and to define who they are. MBCT emphasises the neutralisation of so-called 'secondary emotions', our 'worries about our worries', through meditation – for example, the anxiety that arises from the knowledge that we are hosting depressive thoughts.[31] Both of these approaches can make use of Hindu compassion meditations, designed to increase interpersonal warmth and acceptance, and to neutralise feelings of anger, resentment, or jealousy, for instance. These two styles are perhaps closest to traditional Buddhism, both in their emphasis on the central importance of meditation, and because the therapist is also a teacher, who deliberately models the calm and mentally focused attitudes that the client seeks to emulate.

By contrast, DBT[32] is used mainly to treat people with so-called personality disorders; that is, individuals who experience intense and unpredictable shame, rage, guilt, or fear, often rooted in a history of abuse and rejection stretching back to early childhood. Clients with these problems may regularly hurt themselves in non-fatal ways; for example, by scraping the skin on their forearms, or by taking overdoses of non-prescription painkillers. DBT therapists offer a treatment package intended to help the distressed individual control and tolerate these uncomfortable emotions, communicate their feelings more effectively, and build mindfulness methods both into their daily routines and into the management of personal crises. The necessary skills are usually taught in a once-weekly group or classroom format, matched with private individual CBT sessions designed to offer alternative, less destructive ways of responding to emotional pain. When struggling with the urge to hurt themselves, clients also have the option of phoning their practitioner (or therapy team) for advice and comfort, should they feel the need.[33] Because of the strong and cyclical nature of their destructive urges, DBT recipients also enter into contracts in which they promise not to harm themselves; any breach of the bond eventuates in reduced contact with the psychological healer. Intended to prevent the client from extracting additional emotional gain from their self-injury in the form of heightened therapist attention and concern, this rule is not designed as a form of punishment, although some clients seem to experience it as such. The 'dialectical' aspect of DBT refers to the dynamic tension between, on the one hand, the mindfulness strategies designed to improve self-acceptance, and, on the other, the active, behavioural and cognitive strategies intended to bring about personal change.

Integrative couples behaviour therapy (ICBT) aims to help partners to acknowledge the normality of love and hate within any deep human bond.[34] The therapist will teach skills in conflict resolution and negotiation, intended to help the couple to upgrade their relationship into a mutually accepting and benevolent one. Mindfulness exercises are unleashed to increase mutual emotional sensitivity, and visual meditations are put to use in heightening feelings of acceptance, warmth and kindness.[35]

To many, these new variants of CBT seem to offer a significant advance upon their predecessors. They place more emphasis upon embodiment, upon how things feel to us, and upon how these feelings might influence our thoughts and reactions. Some of them also give more weight to procedural or tacit knowledge – to knowing what to do in a situation, as opposed to analysing or talking about it endlessly, in therapy. Sometimes they also focus upon the emotionally tangled circumstances in which some people are stuck.

Clients report many benefits from these practices, couched, unsurprisingly perhaps, in the language and declared goals of each variety of therapy. In the case of the mindfulness approach, they say that they are more open to the world around them, appreciative of its beauty, and at peace with themselves and others: towards whom they are also more sensitive, patient and kind. They talk about the value of realising that their thoughts are just thoughts – no longer part of who they are and thus to be ignored or even let go of, when most troubling. In some studies, a small number of people who practice mindfulness report a complete realignment of their priorities, a determination to value each moment, to be less acquisitive, competitive and materialistic.[36] Health care workers who undergo mindfulness training have also reported reduced anxiety, and an improved ability to make decisions, to prioritise and concentrate upon their work.[37] Daily mindfulness practice is claimed to yield improvements in mental health as assessed by conventional outcome scales, such as the PHQ,[38] and the Beck depression inventory, for example.[39]

How revolutionary are these therapies in reality? Upon close inspection, some of the ideas behind the third-wave therapies are not quite as new as they seem. For instance, the concept of heightened attention (albeit on the part of the therapist rather than the client) was central to the work of the early analysts, and featured significantly in their writings. Freud and later Karen Horney and Wilfred Bion had noted the importance of maintaining an evenly spread awareness toward the client, all the better to capture whatever might arise in the act of freely associating their thoughts.[40] For Freud, this was a device for collecting as much information about the analysand as possible. For Horney, Bion and other practitioners in the late twentieth century, such as Peter Lomas,[41] it could also help the therapist to be more intuitive and hence more acute in their interpretations and advice. This focus on the power of unmediated insight has some resonance with Zen Buddhist teachings, and indeed, Karen Horney had an enduring interest in this school. She came to believe that the therapist's ardent, whole-hearted absorption in the client's story could be healing in itself, a warm laser of compassion. Humanist therapists share this assumption, some of them also having written on the importance of attending closely to their own somatic sensations as they arise during therapy, as clues to what the client might be feeling.[42] With more openly hieratic intent, R.D. Laing had advocated the power of meditation to free people of the dead weight of their past and of the petty restrictions of the present.[43]

For all of their apparent novelty, third-wave CBT approaches share the same magical belief that we can overcome the weight of deep-seated personal problems and of a troublesome world through insight. The outcome research in this field replicates every fault that we find in the wider field of psychotherapy research, discussed in Chapter 3. Investigators have not felt the need to bother with rigorous experimental methods, because they have assumed from the outset that the cognitive techniques that they deploy are effective. There is the same absence of proper control groups, the same reliance upon limited and unreliable checklist measures of outcome, and inadequate independent assessment and long-term follow up.[44]

Take, for instance, a study that examined the imparting of acceptance and commitment therapy (ACT) techniques to 72 nurses and allied staff – many of then senior practitioners and managers

– in a British NHS service for people with learning disabilities who display disturbing, aggressive, or self-injurious behaviour.[45] Such environments can sometimes be tense and unsettling, and never more so than during periods of institutional upheaval, such as the NHS was experiencing at the time.[46] This particular study was an example of what is known as a 'train the trainers' approach, in which the latest ideas and techniques are enthusiastically 'cascaded' from psychologists to their health service colleagues, who then pass the new practices on to others, in turn. To begin with, a group of volunteers from the service were taught the basics of ACT, and then given the change to rehearse their newfound skills each day, *in situ*. Having grasped the mindfulness methods, six individuals were then chosen to transmit them to their colleagues and subordinates, via a series of workshops. To assess the helpfulness of this coaching, each workshop attendee was asked to anonymously complete a pack of questionnaires before and then directly after the instruction period, and then once again, six months later. Amongst other things, these feedback sheets probed each participant's levels of anxiety and emotional exhaustion, their sense of personal accomplishment and of the adequacy of workplace resources and of collegial support. The results were good. Those who returned their forms were generally satisfied with their ACT tuition, and said that it had helped them to feel more content in their work, healthier overall and less worried, depressed and pressured. These outcomes, presented at a regional seminar in the UK, were enthusiastically received, as yet one more demonstration of the power of mindfulness to help employees cope with difficult jobs, made more difficult by mounting workplace demands. They had learned to cultivate *'increased awareness and acceptance of stressors'*.[47] It only needs a moment's reflection to see that none of these claims are justified.

The people who teach techniques like these are often enthusiastic, even idealistic. They sing a popular song about the power of the mental over the physical, and for many, they are persuasive thereby. From a research point of view, this is not fatal. It becomes deadly, however, when investigators fail to any set of people receiving mindfulness instruction with a comparable one receiving a dummy treatment, delivered with at least token eagerness and conviction. In this one grave omission, this study is far from unusual. An even more serious fault lies in the researchers' failure to see another, rather obvious, point: that in a tough climate of organisational downsizing and job insecurity, few employees are likely to say things that might be construed as critical of superiors who are either endorsing this kind of training as fellow workshop attendees, or perhaps delivering it.[48] This is true even when such comments are collected via a seemingly anonymous survey sheet. There is every reason to believe that people gave the answers that were expected of them, at least for those who bothered to return their questionnaires – after the passage of six months, less than a fifth of the participants were doing so. In its poor research methods and blindness to the realities of power relationships, this study is typical of the whole field.

In addition to the traditional illusions that go with standard CBT, the third-wave approaches have added their own confusion in the form of hype about the power of mindfulness, presented as an altered form of consciousness, in which new and more insightful ways of thinking will dramatically crystallise. These claims disregard the critical evidence that meditation is a form of rest that, by itself, leads to no special changes in the working of the brain or the mind. It is usual for a state of relaxation to manifest in hormonal and neurological adjustments, feelings of pleasure, resistance to discomfort and pain, and sharpened self-awareness that all correspond closely with the results of formal meditation.

In the 1980s, the American researcher David Holmes carried out two large meta-analyses of studies that had examined relaxation and meditation procedures of various kinds.[49] Holmes looked at the effects of these two practices upon biochemical, neurological and other measures of organic activity, looking for evidence that meditation might be a unique method, distinct from ordinary repose. Holmes found no basis for this claim, although, clearly, we should be wary of any approach that tries to strip away the context in which people act. Doubtless, the brains and bodies of people in these two groups would have been subtly different: because of their differing situations, expectations, received instructions and therefore ... experiences. Contemporary brain imaging methods – more sensitive than the electrical brain recordings (made from the scalp) that were typical of Holmes' time – sometimes show differences between mediators and relaxers, which may reflect the practices in which they are engaged.[50] Nevertheless, we also need to treat the results of brain-scanning research in this area – as in so many others – with prudence. Participants are studied in what is a very unusual, not to say bizarre, situation, with their head placed inside a large, noisy, ring-shaped magnet, while the investigators rely upon computer software that is prone to discover exactly what they are looking for:[51] as in a recent experiment that claimed to find 'emotional excitation' in the brain of a salmon, as it was shown pictures of people arguing. Even worse, the fish was dead.[52]

In our present state of knowledge, then, it is fair to say that meditation guarantees nothing more than a temporary and refreshing break from our cares, along with insight into the transience and contingency of self, should we wish to contemplate the idea.[53] However, many traditional Buddhist practitioners do not regard this insight by itself as having any fundamental significance, unless regularly attained (which is difficult) *and* backed up by institutions, traditions, rituals, and the ethics that they embody – that is, by social and cultural settings that nurture and sustain the enlightened person. Traditional practitioners of these arts strove to become mindful for spiritual purposes, as part of an integrated network of beliefs and ethical teachings, allied to a wider community. Equanimity and well-being were not the main goals, and it was not possible to attribute these subjective effects to any one part of the system alone.[54]

If we consider how the development of psychotherapies has reflected not the advance of science but the efforts of practitioners to market their skills, then we can see that the third-wave treatments are a logical continuation. First, the psychologists tried behaviourism, and when that didn't work as well as they had hoped, they borrowed ideas about unconscious bias and cognitive distortions from Freud to create CBT; when it became painfully obvious that that didn't work very well either, for quite a few people, then the psychologists took from Buddhist and Hindu teachings. Borrowing is fine if it leads to progress, which in this case is questionable. The mindfulness therapies fit well with the main currents in western culture in the early twenty-first century. Third-wave CBT approaches derive some of their kudos from the claim that they represent an effort to integrate western science with the wisdom of more traditional societies in general, and with the authority of the mysterious East in particular. If anyone should doubt the appeal of these ideas for the public and for practicing therapists alike, then they would be well advised to visit any conference or professional gathering that features a fair selection of leading therapies, including third-wave CBT. New Age notions about 'holism', 'spirituality' and mysticism jostle merrily with the wilder fringes of speculations about quantum mechanics and 'the new physics' as applied to 'healing'.[55] Of course, in their public pronouncements about their work, cognitive practitioners allude – stridently at times – to the literature of cognitive science and 'evidence-based medicine', but there is little doubt that the appeal of third-wave approaches owes something to the exotic and the arcane.

WHAT IS POSITIVE PSYCHOLOGY?

The last decade has seen an explosion of popular and academic publications on the theme of emotional well-being – or, more colloquially (and no less vaguely) 'happiness'.[56] Self-help books and DVDs on this theme take up many feet of shelving space in bookstores and libraries. There is even an academic journal devoted to the study of this subject.[57] Hundreds of positive psychology courses are available in US colleges, and in two major universities in London. In 2007, all state schools in England were directed to begin teaching 'social and emotional intelligence' or 'happiness lessons', according to the media.[58] In combination with its close cousins, 'emotional intelligence' and 'multiple intelligences', positive psychology seemed to promise empowerment and achievement for all. The British Prime Minister and others have decided that political and economic policies should be measured, not just by conventional economic costs and benefits, but also by their effects upon a national happiness index.[59] This surge of interest in well-being seems to reflect several trends that have come to fruition in recent years. These trends include an accumulating body of research in economics and psychology suggesting that affluent people are not much happier than the poor, the ensuing debates that this has generated among philosophers, academics and policy 'think tanks', and perhaps most of all, a growing disquiet about the values and directions that early twenty-first-century western society is taking.[60]

In the US, the positive psychology movement is most strongly linked with Martin Seligman, the former chair of the American Psychological Association (the professional organisation of psychologists in that country). In 2000, Seligman and his colleague Mihályi Czíkszentmihályi issued a manifesto for the new century, in a leading article of a special issue of *American Psychologist*, the premier publication for US psychology.[61] They urged that the whole field should abandon its traditional focus upon personal pathology and failure, and embrace individual flourishing as the new basis for study, and for intervention. In Britain, this positive or happiness psychology movement is associated with Richard Layard,[62] an academic economist and policy advisor to the last New Labour government, and to a lesser extent with psychotherapists and social commentators such as Oliver James.[63] Layard is unique in having been able to turn many of his ideas into national policy, but all of these individuals have written well-known books on the psychology and science of happiness.

If we are to believe the promoters of positive psychology, we are at a unique point in history. During the last few millennia of recorded history, writers, thinkers and ordinary individuals might have had some useful ideas on the subject of contentment and how to attain it, but it is only in the last decade or so, with the benefit of psychological science, that we have really come to know about it. Positive psychology is an attempt to improve well-being through psychological techniques. Positive psychologists understand well-being as feelings of joy and gratitude for the good things that have happened in our lives, together with greater acceptance of our selves and of others. Writing letters of thanks, making positive affirmations every day, pursuing activities that require intense concentration and that therefore help us to forget ourselves and to 'flow in the moment' are all actions associated with positive psychology. Sketching, disco dancing, mountain climbing, juggling, meditation, coarse fishing, creative writing; ice skating, jogging, painting in pastels, karate, cooking, tai chi, playing a guitar, talking with a friend, star gazing, acrobatic exercise, playing tiddlywinks, writing a computer programme, making love, scoring with a basketball, singing in a choir, paragliding, closing a business deal, performing open heart surgery, or weaving a rug: all of these activities and more can hike our happiness quotient. The intense concentration that they demand leads to a total immersion in the task, or what leading well-being theorist Czíkszentmihályi calls 'flow', a state of being joyfully present in the moment, allowing us to temporarily ignore our own concerns.[64] Positive psychologists also endorse the familiar methods of CBT as a way of brushing aside the cobwebs of negativity that get in the way of achieving these goals, and they claim to have experimental evidence showing that these simple techniques are effective and have lasting effects.

Although there are differences of emphasis amongst the theorists of happiness, the main tenets of the movement are remarkably consistent. These elements are as follows: we can all agree on what 'happiness' is, it can be accurately measured, and it is not just the absence of worry or distress – but a state of heightened mood and optimism that we can deliberately cultivate, so as to get more out of our lives. The happy individual is at ease both with themselves and with others, energetic and focused when required, warm and caring, creative, humorous, open-minded and committed to the present, while sanguine about the future. In principle, this condition of grace is attainable by all. Some psychologists, particularly the European writers, believe that it can be more easily achieved if we find or cultivate friendships and join in cohesive communities, as these defend against loneliness and despondency.[65]

How then is happiness attained? For the positive psychologists, it is all a matter of learning the right skills for rational thinking, and with a hint of mysticism – not unlike that espoused in a famous space opera film – thrown in for good measure:

> The fact is that we can train our feelings. We are not simply victims of our situation, or indeed of our past – exaggerated ideas associated with Karl Marx and Sigmund Freud, respectively. Instead, we can directly address our bad feelings and replace them by positive feelings, building on the positive force that is in each of us, our better self.[66]

> Through systematic experimentation [modern cognitive therapy] has found ways to promote positive thinking and to systematically dispel the negative thoughts that affect us all. In recent years these insights have been generalized to 'positive psychology', to offer a means by which all of us, depressed or otherwise, can find meaning and increase our enjoyment of life.[67]

It is also about doing the right things. Martin Seligman recommends that we discover and exploit our unique combination of what he calls our 'signature strengths', which include, humanity, temperance and persistence.[68] This vision of cheerfulness combines the virtue ethics of Confucius, Mencius and Aristotle with modern psychological theories of motivation. Seligman's conclusion is that happiness has three dimensions that can be cultivated: the 'Pleasant Life', the 'Good Life' and the 'Meaningful Life'. The first of these is realised if we learn to savour and appreciate such basic pleasures as companionship, the natural environment and our bodily needs. We can remain enjoyably stuck at this stage or we can go on to experience the 'Good Life', which is achieved through discovering our unique virtues and strengths, and employing them creatively to enhance our lives.

According to Seligman:

> 'The very good news is there is quite a number of internal circumstances ... under your voluntary control. If you decide

to change them (and be warned that none of these changes come without real effort), your level of happiness is likely to increase lastingly.'[69]

The positive psychologists root these claims in the results of international surveys, designed to probe the relationship between happiness and wealth. For people living in western countries, these investigations seem to show that contentment rises in line with earnings only for people at the bottom end of the income scale, and that once a certain threshold has been crossed, further jumps in wealth do not add much to reported well-being. This threshold is surprisingly modest, at around the average income of a typical middle-class family. Moreover, people living in much poorer Third World societies seem to report levels of happiness that compare well with their western counterparts, and according to some surveys are more buoyant in outlook.[70] This observation has an ambiguous relationship with the income inequalities hypothesis of health and illness discussed in Chapter 5. In addition, if we track the reported happiness of individual people over months and years, then we find that the levels do not vary much in the long run, despite ups and downs in finance, work, habitation, family arrangements, and health and vigour. For the positive psychologists, these findings suggest two things. First, good cheer is an internal psychological state that has only limited reference to external circumstances; and secondly, it is a condition that the individual can cultivate, given enough determination and expert advice. Few of these psychologists go so far as to baldly say that their methods will directly increase one's stock of personal contentment, but this is obviously the implicit claim.

There are some important differences between the professors of contentment, however, and these divisions speak to their professional allegiances and quite possibly to their varying cultural outlooks. Layard, for example, has advocated a two-pronged approach involving social and economic policies designed to reduce inequalities in income as well as to provide more cognitive therapy.[71] Seligman, from a characteristically American standpoint, has leant more toward the psychological devices that individuals can supposedly deploy if they are to improve their lot. Foremost amongst these are the familiar methods of cognitive therapy, designed to dispel negative thoughts, methods that Seligman regards as scientifically vindicated. Oliver James is doubtful about the efficacy of short-term CBT treatments, and instead looks toward long-term psychodynamic therapy as a partial answer to widespread misery, while admonishing each of us to become less competitive and acquisitive.[72]

For the professionals, this kind of happiness psychology is the great success story of the last decade. On both sides of the Atlantic, it has been widely taken up in business, and in the fields of education and health promotion, as a revolutionary approach. Yet we have been here before. Many of the basic ideas of the movement echo the nineteenth-century creed of romantic individualism, as propounded by writers like Emerson and Thoreau, who believed that all individuals must nurture their exclusive qualities apart from the surrounding society. Through this expression of a unique, authentic self, each would achieve personal gratification and satisfaction – an idea that finds its expression in the prized self-actualisation of the therapy industry and in the promises of the positive psychologists. Indeed there were other twentieth- and nineteenth-century movements that mooted the power of the individual to overcome their ills through belief, diligence and better adaptation to the world as it is. This was a time of quack entrepreneurial and spiritual movements promising good health, happiness and material success. Prominent among them was the cult of 'New Thought', which, according to Elizabeth Towne, one of its main proponents, entailed a 'cheerful right-thinking attitude of mind [that] will cure any kind of disease, except broken bones'.[73] Townes's claim is not far distant from any recent article by one of the many twenty-first-century positive psychologists, who extol the curative power of positive emotions, credited with boosting overall happiness, lowering levels of blood cortisol and the risk of heart attack and stroke, and with raising bodily resistance to the rhinoviruses that cause colds and influenza. Like its nineteenth-century counterparts, positive psychology has faith in the power of mind to control and even heal the body, a faith that reflects the split between soul and matter that is emblematic of Christianity and of western civilisation.

But there are many difficulties with the positive psychology outlook. There is the basic question of whether a subjective thing like happiness can be measured at all, closely followed by the issue of whether we really can choose to modify our well-being to order, especially over the longer term. Then there are the effects of positive psychology upon the individuals who use it and upon the wider society. The more closely we scrutinise each of these topics, the less the field looks like science and the more it comes to resemble make-believe, and this in turn raises further questions about why this enterprise has flourished in recent years. In the following sections, we will look at each of these issues.

CAN HAPPINESS BE MEASURED?

As we have seen, Richard Layard and other academics think so. They base this claim upon self-report data from surveys that pose questions such as the following: 'Taken altogether, how would you say things are these days – would you say you are very happy, pretty happy or not too happy?'[74] This questionnaire data cited by Layard is incapable of addressing the particulars of human life, because it tries to fit the subtle nuances of lived experience into the square holes of a handful of insipid questions about one's 'happiness'. A serial killer and a vicar might declare themselves equally pleased with their situation in life, with the degree to which they have been able to meet their personal goals, but if you bothered to ask them, then their visions of the good life would be rather different.

Furthermore, is it sensible to believe that the high levels of happiness reported by some of the poorest of people in the world are a sure sign that well-being has little to do with wealth, or material conditions? Since there are grounds for thinking that people in western countries, when asked, will evaluate their well-being by reference to what they know of the conditions of life in the rest of the world (including the very worst places), then it is unlikely that the people in the rich countries are using the same standards as those in poor countries to judge their happiness. When queried about how they feel about their lives, it may be that the poorest give answers that suggest that things are not too bad, but their words scarcely seem to match their objective situation, unless they (or we) are blind, or deluded. To live in a shantytown in which the streets are open sewers, to be worn down by back-breaking labour, the omnipresence of violent crime, disease and the prospect of premature death – both for one's loved ones and for oneself – these are only the beginnings of the travails faced by the destitute in most parts of the planet. Could it be that in these circumstances, when they are asked about their contentment, the impoverished are cutting the cloth of their answers to fit the status of the person asking the questions on the one hand, and the constraints of their own lives on the other?[75]

Throughout history, colonised people, subjugated women and slaves have all learned to assure the master of their contentment with their lot, and have sometimes even come to believe in it themselves, especially with the help of organised religion.[76] And we don't have to travel all that far to find this kind of thing, as shown by the researcher Simon Charlesworth, in his study of the lives of impoverished working-class people in South Yorkshire.[77] Most of his interviewees seemed to be acutely aware of the fallacy of believing that there must be a higher aspect of human life, rising above the gritty level of the capital that one embodies or has. Charlesworth notes that when it is openly expressed, this outlook renders working-class people crude and offensive in the eyes of middle-class interlocutors, ignorant of how much of their own 'dignity, respect and sophistication and faith in other human beings have been purchased by their relative wealth and good fortune'.[78] By contrast, the poor and the marginalised eke out a living upon this cold basement level of British life. The most 'contented': the ones who have fully given up the ghost, and who are 'happy to live within the range of possibilities that are available'.[79]

We can see a similar pattern in the lives of people from other downtrodden groups, such as those who are designated as learning disabled. When asked, they will often describe themselves to researchers or to government assessors as contented and 'happy' – not because things are necessarily going well for them, but because, having been forced to lead narrow lives, they lack an idea of how things could be better. A woman who has for many years gone no further than the end of her street might say that she is content, and in a sense, she is, because she does not know what she is missing. This kind of distortion will be all the more likely if the questions are asked in the perfunctory tick-box manner, that is typical of surveys conducted by social scientists.[80]

Such problems become more severe in light of the possibility that what we tell ourselves about our own motivations and feelings is not always reliable. The social scientist Daniel Haybron has argued that people can become detached from their true feelings about situations where there is little incentive for this kind of reflection, or where it is discouraged. Even when self-scrutiny is allowed, we can get so used to our circumstances that we cease to register our own feelings about them. Haybron makes this argument with reference to the scientific claim that most of us have a fairly stable level of reported happiness that varies only modestly with changes in circumstance, and instead reflects an individual and genetically wired 'set point' in our happiness level. Haybron suggests that this apparently constant plane of contentment might just as easily speak of our tendency to *consistently report* a given amount of well-being, perhaps irrespective of what we might actually be feeling. Simple tick-box checklists elicit the equivalent of the emptily polite greetings that people give each other every day as they pass in the street, or in the Monty Python film as the trout swim past each other in their endless circuit around their familiar gourmet restaurant tank, cheerfully bidding each other 'good morning'.

A further problem with these surveys is that it is very difficult and perhaps impossible to reach the more disturbed, discontented and chaotic people in the population who are least likely to participate, but who might also be supposed to be the least happy. Their relative absence from this research may skew the findings in significant and unpredictable ways.

IS IT ALWAYS GOOD TO SMILE?

There are good grounds for thinking that positive psychology is actually harmful, as the American journalist and critic Barbara Ehrenreich shows in her vivid account of the rise of happiness psychology in the US and beyond. Ehrenreich reveals the inanities of a motivational training industry that offers expensive but well-attended seminars designed to teach you that you can get a job just by visualising the kind of person that you want to be, or by making earnest imprecations to a 'higher power'. This is a multimillion-dollar industry aimed at white-collar unemployed jobseekers; it thrives upon hoodwinking the jobless into believing that their situation is their own fault, and nothing to do with the condition of the US economy, or the new corporate regime that has made everyone expendable who is below upper management.[81]

When Ehrenreich was diagnosed with breast cancer and encouraged to join a therapeutic support group of fellow patients, it became apparent just how far this kind of outlook had crept into other facets of modern life. She was encouraged to believe that talking about her cancer with other sufferers would help to cure it – especially if she could view her life-threatening illness as an opportunity for spiritual renewal. The peculiar nature of this way of thinking – a creepy mixture of Walt Disney sentimentality and God-fearing determination to succeed – was summed up in the pink teddy bears given out by the clinicians at the cancer clinic to all newly stricken women, some of whom went to their death burdened with guilt for their failure to fight the disease with 'positive energy'. The dark side of being relentlessly upbeat is that you grow to be preoccupied with monitoring the extent of your happiness and your ability to sustain it, so that well-being becomes a source of anxiety in its own right. In this way, positive psychology leads people to be obsessed with policing themselves and less inclined to ask disruptive questions about the kinds of treatments that they receive and how they are administered, or even about why they have fallen ill to begin with.[82]

There is no good evidence for any of these claims, which are based largely upon correlational studies that do not tell us anything about what the underlying causes of the observed relationships might be. Like all other areas of applied psychology, the studies that have been conducted yield a familiar tale: the more carefully controlled the investigation of happiness boosting techniques, the more carefully that possible health effects are measured, then the closer the effect upon serious illness approaches zero.[83] It is true that many studies have found that those who report themselves to be happy and in control of their lives seem to enjoy better general health. Psychologists habitually assume that this is a demonstration that positive beliefs lead to healthy outcomes.

However, it is just as likely that the arrows of influence point not from sound mind to sound constitution, but the other way around. People with the most health and well-being are more inclined to say that they are happy. But their vigour is likely to reflect not so much their inner mental strength, as the good fortune of having lived the more comfortable, stable and well-resourced kind of life that helps create both a good physical constitution and a more sanguine outlook.[84]

Indeed, Ehrenreich makes a good case that the popularity of happiness psychology has led to a harmfully over-optimistic view of the world. Besides helping to blind people to the widespread misery caused by redundancy and job instability, this mandatory joyfulness may have helped to fuel the unrestrained speculation that brought about the collapse of the financial markets in 2008. In the twenty-first century, a sinister version of Mr Micawber is alive and well, and he may hold a psychology degree.

Positive psychology also has effects upon conceptions of right and wrong. It promotes the Pollyanna-ish belief that virtue, contentment and a life of security and ease all dine together at the same table. This is a distorted and unrealistic view of ethics, not to mention history. The philosopher Susan Neiman observes that because of his realism on these matters, Kant is usually portrayed as a dour and puritanical defender of virtue, when in fact he wanted goodness to yield joy, just as much as the rest of us, but unfortunately, 'He simply tells us the truth: that it often does not.'[85] Humanist philosophers in the eighteenth and nineteenth centuries viewed happiness not as a pleasant psychological state but as a political condition that meant democratic choice, freedom from arbitrary persecution and the liberty to live the life that one chose, within the limits of respecting the rights of others.

For many writers and thinkers down the ages, 'happiness' – to the extent that the word signified anything at all – meant living to some purpose, which can be a difficult job. Even if their lives were a struggle and often 'miserable' in terms of Seligman's emotional calculus, what they were doing seemed to be worthwhile, because it pointed to a future: to the creation of new ideas, doctrines, scientific discoveries, or practical inventions that might benefit many other people, besides themselves. In other words, their lives had a wider purpose beyond narrow personal satisfaction. To live with one eye on the future in this way is to court anxiety and doubt instead of bliss, because none of us can know what the years ahead will hold, beyond our own certain death. Thinkers as varied as Nietzsche, Camus and Voltaire have rejected a self-congratulatory feeling of happiness as a pallid substitute for what they saw as the only valid way to live – that is, to face up to the harsh facts of mortality, of the enigma and likely indifference of the universe, and to strive, as best we can, for a meaningful existence within these terms.[86] To avoid this task is to build despair into the heart of our existence, even though we might be outwardly upbeat – marking off the answers in the psychologist's question sheet that confirm optimism and good cheer.[87]

WHY THE POSITIVE PSYCHOLOGISTS ARE STILL SMILING

The field of positive psychology has flourished during the last ten years or so. The standard explanation for this development is that we are witnessing the advance of science, but this will not do, if only because, as we have seen, the foundations of this whole field are so nebulous, not to say vacuous. The ideas behind happiness psychology have a long history as philosophy and in popular culture. There are other reasons behind this expansion.

One of them must surely be to do with the slow loss of faith in the chemical cure. Less than 20 years ago, in books, newspaper articles and television interviews, both psychiatrists and psychologists were extolling the benefits of a new generation of psychiatric drugs as the cure for depression and as the high road to happiness for those of us who had lost our self-confidence or become jaded with our lives. Reputable clinicians talked seriously about 'better living through Prozac'. The latest class of antidepressants are now viewed by the public and by growing numbers of professionals with wariness if not suspicion, in light of the mounting evidence for their harmful side effects and limited efficacy. Similar doubts, though more muted, have been gathering in relation to the so-called anti-psychotics that psychiatrists widely prescribe for 'schizophrenia' and other serious diagnoses. For some time, there has been need of a replacement for chemically induced good spirits, in order to help keep the mental health industry afloat, and doubtless to meet the need of the public, schooled to expect professional solutions to their problems.

These cracks in the bulwark of biomedicine and Big Pharma have not been quite the boon to the talking therapy professions that some might have hoped. In the US, managed care, and in Europe, the advent of manualised therapy, clinical audit and payment by results have all helped to reduce the income, freedom and status of this group. In large measure, the positive psychology movement reflects the anxieties and the marketing ambitions of the psychology industry. The parallel with psychiatric drugs is a close one, because the pharmaceutical industry has a long history of developing new substances and then working hand-in-hand with the medical profession to create new disorders to match them.[88] As so often, and contrary to shallow economic theories that pretend that everything happens in a free market, it is supply that leads people to create demand, and the positive psychologists have taken their lessons from the drug industry. They have developed brand new markets for their premier product – that is, CBT. In the tradition of commercial advertising, the placement of the word 'positive' with 'psychology' creates a strong association between the two, and helps to insulate the new discipline from critical thinkers from both within and outside the parent tradition, so that mind cures are foregrounded, while questions of social justice and well-being recede into the distance.

One reason that positive psychology has been championed, then, is because it offers a way of restoring diminished credibility, but there is more to the story than this. In the West, religious authority has declined without anything to replace it. People are less certain about what is wrong or right or what the purpose of life should be, beyond a commitment to self-fulfilment and personal honesty. These are the humanist values of therapy culture, incarnate in the many politicians who extol sincerity as the touchstone of moral worth and the yardstick by which actions should be judged.[89]

Positive psychology offers to fill the moral vacuum in our lives by purporting to tell us what our aims should be and how to reach them. It also has a talent for being all things to all men. It wraps together many of the traditional teachings of the theistic religions, of eastern belief systems and some of the key tenets of New Age philosophy within a single, seemingly respectable scientific package, large and flexible enough to appeal to any sector of the health promotion industry, and to consumers and health service planners of almost any political persuasion.

The attractions of happiness psychology for many politicians are obvious. It appeals to leaders who wish to appear wise, caring and at the leading edge of social and scientific policy, and who welcome cheap and fast solutions to complex and deep-rooted social problems.

The irony is that, in their focus on the importance of social life, the positive psychologists celebrate the individual actor as supreme. They enjoin us to change our ways by finding our own solutions. Nowhere is there much hint of what people should do if they are not part of a welcoming community, if they do not have a job, or a family that brings them into meaningful contact with others, if their neighbours are not saviours, but distrustful, obstructive, or even predatory. These kinds of problems are more likely to arise for the large minority of citizens who live in a zone of poverty, poor health and insecure or casual labour. But middle-class people are also feeling the chill. To read the positive psychologists is to think that the workplace is ultimately humane and benign, and that earnest efforts to reason with intransigent bosses and defensive or competitive colleagues will result in positive change. In reality, employees are being squeezed to achieve maximal productivity as the economy flounders, and this kind of pressure does not always bring out the best in people.[90]

Were happiness largely a matter of insight then most of us would have already chanced upon these ingredients of a better life by now. After all, people have been thinking and writing about the power of mind over matter for the last 2,000 years and more. Back in the 1930s, the philosopher Bertrand Russell came up with a set of prescriptions for well-being that strongly resembled Layard's and Seligman's. The main difference was that Russell saw stoicism and rational thought as only one side of the coin. They were qualities that emerged from good character, which in turn could grow only from humane social institutions rather than from a world like our own, in which constant busyness and the getting of wealth are the main – often the only – official goals.[91]

The ideas of the positive psychologists are so commonplace that we could have culled their words straight from almost any of the more sentimental pop songs, films, novels, or poems of the last hundred years (the trite homilies of the British author 'Patience Strong' come to mind).[92] If love, hope and perseverance are always enough, then the reality that most of us have not been able to match our lives to these exhortations must be saying something about the true connection between right thinking, wealth and 'happiness', if only we are willing to listen:

> Marxism may possibly be a mistaken theory, but it is a useful instrument for testing other systems of thought, rather like one of those long-handled hammers with which they tap the wheels of locomotives. Tap! Is this wheel cracked? Tap! Is this writer a bourgeoise? A crude question ... and yet it is surprising how often a pretentious book will seem suddenly hollow if you apply to it the simple question: Does this writer or does he not, take account of the economic basis of society?'[93]

'Ask yourself if you are happy', averred John Stuart Mill, 'and you cease to be so.' Anyone who has to grapple too long with the hoary platitudes of positive psychology is likely to agree. The vision of happiness that we are invited to entertain resembles the commercials for Redi-Brek porridge, as seen on British television: an enveloping aura of warmth that turns the possessor into something like a large, glowing jelly baby. Yet the idea that good cheer is not much more than sensations of bliss and good will towards everyone is simplistic at best and dangerous at worst. Whatever else happiness may be, it is a subjective state that cannot be detached from ethics and values and still less from the cultural and social world that gives rise to them, such that one person's positivity really can be the wretchedness of another, and misery is a lot easier to measure. We can say with some confidence that the larger and more visible the gaps in wealth and status within any industrialised society – and the more exploitative those relationships – then the greater the likelihood of widespread strife, distress and mutual suspicion, not to mention poorer physical health. To the degree that these things can be alleviated then we can be made happier. But as for an objective science of well-being, this is a misguided attempt to put the cart before the horse. Even when we allow that beyond dull repose or bovine contentment, a positive mental state means different things to different people, it cannot be manufactured at will. Instead, if we are lucky, if we have the choices, then an unself-conscious satisfaction can arise as a byproduct of our actions, from our engagement with the world. It is the work of clinicians and researchers who have tried to grasp the fundamental importance of this engagement – but in the context of distress, rather than of joy – that we will consider next.

9

Towards a Psychology that Reflects what the Therapy Industry Will Not Tell Us

Today, we need social theory as never before, but we need it to reunite us with our estranged bodies, and to rediscover the sense of a humility which a view of the world at this scale entails.

A.F. Robertson[1]

Some clinicians have recognised the limitations of their trade, and have questioned received ideas about why people are unhappy and what they can do about it. A few of these writers are well known, some of them have been unjustly forgotten, or dismissed as relics of a bygone time. Their work, however, remains important because it speaks strongly of the terrain that has been mapped out in previous chapters. It shows that people do not always choose to be whom or how they are, and that the individualistic approach of psychiatry and psychotherapy is necessarily limited as an endeavour. In this chapter, a selection of this work is critically reviewed and then intertwined with a discussion of recent philosophical and scientific developments. The aim being to suggest a theoretical structure upon which to build a sounder understanding of the nature of personal suffering; beyond the pseudo-science of psychiatry and the rhetoric of talking therapy.

It is often forgotten that Freud had the good sense to admit that personal troubles had something to do with personal circumstances. His story of the unconscious, of how it was moulded by family experience and then became an instrument of conflict as it ran up against the grain of civilised life – was an improvement upon the misplaced ideas of the biological psychiatry of his day. When it counted most, however, he turned away from realist interpretations of the causes of misery, notably in his claim that the childhood sexual abuse reported by some of his female analysands was pure fantasy.[2] The external world became little more than a set of props, enabling or hindering the unconscious mind, the main actor, as it performed its tragicomic roles.[3] As the twentieth century ground onwards, with its catastrophic wars and huge social upheavals, not all psychoanalysts could accept this view. Some of them came to see that misery might owe much more to what was happening outside of the person's head, and not only during their childhood. The idea that personal disturbance might be a form of 'social neurosis', brought about by the constant need to compete with others in an unstable capitalist economy was fruitfully developed by the analysts Alfred Adler,[4] Karen Horney[5] and Harry Stack Sullivan,[6] during the interwar years of the twentieth century. All of them found their success as émigrés to the United States and many of them had had first-hand experience of political despotism.[7] In the post-Second World War years, this group were followed by the 'Frankfurt School' of Marxist-inspired critics such as Erich Fromm,[8] who found it increasingly difficult to separate the distress of the individual from the nature of the world around them. Despite their trenchant criticisms of what the relentless pursuit of money did to people, however, none of these thinkers could bring themselves to abandon their faith in the value of individual treatment. The pre-war psychoanalytic writers fell out of fashion, particularly in the US. A revival of their general outlook had to wait for the work of the British psychiatrist R.D. Laing and his colleagues in the (misnamed) anti-psychiatry movement of the 1960s.[9]

R.D. LAING AND 'ANTI-PSYCHIATRY'

Laing was one of Britain's most revolutionary and creative psychiatrists. To some extent, this could be attributed perhaps to his lifelong (and anguished) agnosticism, and his non-conformist Scottish educational background – at odds with the dry empiricism favoured by the English universities, and by the psychiatric establishment that he would later challenge.[10] A public intellectual and perhaps the only British psychiatrist to count as a philosopher, Laing applied the insights of the European existentialist and phenomenological writers and later on, theories of communication to his work with people labelled 'schizophrenic'.[11]

Although not a systematic thinker – there is no Laingian school of therapy – his work traces a continuous thread in its concern for the diminished life, lived without meaning or feeling.[12] From his early days as a National Service army psychiatrist, at Glasgow's Gartnavel Royal Hospital, Laing sought to dissolve the barrier between the mad and the sane by entering into the experience of those written off by his colleagues as irreparable 'cases'. For Laing, their sorry condition was in part a response to the dull barbarisms of institutional psychiatry, which had made them resemble Homer's ghosts, dwelling in Hades, 'across Rivers of Fear'.[13] He rejected the psychoanalytical method – the probing of deviant conduct for signs of concealed emotional struggle – as just one more device for ignoring what the patient was experiencing in the here-and-now. The therapist was no longer a fully detached observer but more like the reader of a difficult but rewarding novel; willing to engage with the narrative on its own terms, through an act of sympathetic imagination. But this was no excursion into the wilder fringes of speculative thought. He always kept close to the patient's experience.[14]

In his first book, *The Divided Self*,[15] published in 1960, Laing argued that psychotic experience was not the random fizz of faulty neurons, but an enduring state of being, which he termed 'ontological insecurity'. An intrusive, and often loveless, upbringing had compelled the sufferer to create a divided or schizoid self comprised of a false, outer persona, shielding their vulnerable inner core from the unwelcome scrutiny of others. From the sufferer's point of view, there was an empty, almost two-dimensional quality to life, imperilling their existence as an embodied, separate and stable being, teetering on the edge of painful engulfment by the rest of the world. Guarded, inflexible and cold, the main stance of the insecure person was one of alienation and passivity. They might get by, but they were never far from psychosis, and because they could not understand themselves, they often seemed opaque or simply crazy to others. When engulfment happened, it could lead to a loss of self and to the diagnosis of 'schizophrenia'. It was the psychiatrist's job to aid the sufferer in regaining their trust in the solidity of the world and of themselves, that is, their knowledge of who and what they were.

In *Sanity, Madness and the Family*,[16] published three years later, Laing and his colleague Aaron Esterson wrote of their study of eleven families of people who bore the diagnosis of schizophrenia. They argued that, within these families, it was paradoxical and chronically frustrating communications that had played the key role in the growth of psychosis. Rather than being ill, the designated psychiatric patient was all too often the unhappy repository for the unexpressed miseries, conflicts and fears of the rest of the family. The assignment of the diagnostic label was a convenient means of stopping these shared fears and guilty secrets from seeing the light of day, and was an act of conspiracy against the patient.

For all of the groundbreaking qualities of their work, Laing and Esterson's environmentalist account of the genesis of madness has never been followed up with further research in the half-century since its publication, an undeserved fate, given its importance on the one hand, and its scientific short-comings as a small-scale uncontrolled study, on the other. If nothing else, this omission surely speaks to the conservative nature of the mental health field in the early twenty-first century.[17]

Laing was not the only person in the field to see things this way. In the mid-1960s, the British psychiatrist R.D. Scott wrote a series of articles about this process of diagnostic closure, which he called 'the betrayal funnel'. He set up what we might now call a 'family therapy service', unique at the time, in which a team of nurses and doctors trained by Scott worked with both family and patient to prevent hospital admission. They did this, via an effort to negotiate between the different views of the family members and to use the results to encourage change in entrenched patterns of behaviour toward the patient – and sometimes by simply encouraging them to exit the toxic familial home.[18]

Scott did not publish widely, but Laing and like-minded colleagues such as David Cooper continued to write about their ideas and practice, and were wrongly dubbed as 'anti-psychiatrists' by the British media. Laing, at least, never rejected the idea of psychiatry itself, only its biological foundations.[19] Indeed, he helped to establish the Philadelphia Association. A voluntary British organisation, it offered asylum (in the true sense of the word) and talking treatment for people with psychiatric problems, initially at Kingsley Hall, a community settlement building, in a grim district of East London. In a series of publications, he offered a compelling account of psychotic experience as a rational response to a mad world, and then moved on to trace the contradictions and insanities of this world, gripped in an interminable Cold War and seemingly poised to destroy itself with nuclear weapons.[20] By the early 1970s, Laing was a celebrity. Perhaps in part because of this, he seemed to lose interest in his own critique of psychiatry. His attraction to mysticism became all consuming and, together with his inclination to romanticise mental breakdown as a journey of discovery, began to lose him support.[21] In the end, it was probably not so much Laing's retreat from western science, his growing alcoholism and chaotic personal and professional life – nor, even, his increasingly bitter confrontations with his critics – but the wider political and cultural changes of the 1980s that did most harm to his radical thesis.

THE DEMISE OF ANTI-PSYCHIATRY

It is no accident that the 'anti-psychiatry' movement took off during the 1960s; a time when western institutions and their alliance with capitalism and colonialism came in for a good deal of questioning, especially by the rising generation. The 1960s was also a period of unparalleled prosperity. Middle-class young people in particular were enjoying a surplus of money and time that could be turned to social criticism, and protest.[22] But the economic climate grew colder: 'The tightening of the fiscal screws that began with the 1973 oil crisis may not have been a conspiracy ... but it has certainly worked out to the advantage of the powerful.'[23] By the 1980s, graduates found themselves in a shrinking job market and facing the first waves in the long retrenchment of the welfare state. The taste for social protest and experiment was on the wane.

A further significant change that came with this decade was the sudden and unexpected rebirth of biomedicine. With fresh confidence, psychiatrists and researchers could be heard declaiming that mental illness was akin to physical illness and more importantly, that it was all about all about bad genes, bad brains and the drugs to repair them.[24] There was a ready audience for these ideas, helped along if not created by the promotions of the pharmaceutical industry, and by the rising fashion both in academia and in popular culture for individualised explanations for everything.[25] Rational choice theory in economics created the notion (or perhaps the spectre) of the human being as a canny trader, making every important decision according to the same calculus of personal profit and loss.[26] Throughout the social sciences, postmodern theories waxed boldly, many of them declaring the death – or at least the dissolution – of the subject into a haze of discourse, and the importance of an ever-expanding range of personal identities, beginning with the ethnic, the gendered and the sexual.[27]

THE GHOSTS OF RADICAL PSYCHIATRY

Good ideas never die completely, however. The work of Laing's Philadelphia Association continues. Funded on a shoestring, it offers a haven where seriously distressed men and women are allowed to go through what they have to go through, in the company of others, at their own pace and without the well-intentioned intrusions of psychiatry or family.[28] Many of Laing's insights have survived within current mental health care practices, though seldom attributed to him. For instance, the work that psychologists have carried out with the families of the sufferers of 'schizophrenia', within a 'CBT' framework and aimed at reducing the expression of hostility and criticism toward the sufferer clearly owe much to Laing's ideas.[29] However, as the clinical psychologist Lucy Johnstone points out, in her seminal book, *Users and Abusers of Psychiatry*, these modern doctors of 'high expressed emotion' studiously avoid any implication that the family might have helped to cause the client's problems in the first place, despite this being an obvious implication of their work.[30] Over the last 30 years, there has been the rise of the service user movement and the drive toward de-institutionalisation, which has been matched by a growing emphasis upon 'customer satisfaction' within the British National Health Service.[31] While Laing would not have allied himself with the political paymasters for these changes or with how they have worked in practice, he contributed more than most to the climate of opinion – both popular and academic – that helped sustain them.[32]

The spirit of Laing's ideas persisted in the writings of a handful of other thinkers, such as the academic psychologist, David Ingleby, who in the early 1980s edited a volume of politically, sociologically and psychoanalytically influenced analyses of the mental health system, entitled *Critical Psychiatry*.[33] Its release delayed by an ambivalent publisher and largely ignored in most professional mental health journals, this book has gained in reputation over the years. Ingleby, the author of a weighty backlist of articles and papers, was unable to secure tenure at Cambridge, a circumstance that owed much to the intercession of a hostile establishment psychiatrist at the time, which was vocally protested by many of his colleagues and students.[34] Ingleby decided to migrate to The Netherlands, where he found a more open-minded reception, taking a chair in developmental psychology at the University of Utrecht.[35] It is easy to see why Ingleby garnered so much support. His book presented a broad spectrum of views on the contours and roots of psychological suffering, and a sceptical stance toward the health professionals.

Ingleby and his co-authors shared Laing's general outlook, but their arguments had more nuance. Possible genetic or temperamental influences upon mental health and disturbance were not dismissed altogether, but were understood, not as destiny, but as context dependent. What mattered was not the person's physical condition,

but how they were able to live it out. There was a
against the one-sided positivist approach of conventio'
which sought to treat human beings as if they were like el.
particles, disturbed mechanically by their illnesses or by u.
environments in the same way that an electron might be deflected
by a magnetic field.[36]

The psychoanalyst Joel Kovel showed that psychotherapy and
counselling had become essential components of the capitalist
economy, especially in the United States, turning socially induced
misery into false questions of self-management or improvement.[37]
The sociologist Peter Conrad wrote about the first tide in the
'diseasing' of restless American schoolchildren as 'hyperkinetic'
– the precursor of the diagnosis of ADHD.[38] In contrast, Ingleby
and his colleagues argued that humans should only be understood
as subjects who actively interpret their world (and their own
unhappiness) in meaningful ways, something that psychiatry had
to take seriously if it was to call itself a science, let alone aspire to be
helpful. Ingleby himself drew upon psychoanalytic ideas, to reveal
the limitations of a diagnostic checklist approach to understanding
personal troubles, and to show how emotional suffering caused
by one's situation could run very deep, forming a hidden reservoir
of emotional pain that eluded all attempts at superficial mapping,
still less a 'quick cure'.[39] He recognised that patients did not always
see how their troubles might reflect the wider political world, as
opposed to their immediate personal struggles, and he argued that
therapists should strive to offer interpretations that transcended
the sufferer's own view of themselves. These tricky questions of
construal and understanding, of whose account should have the
most authority, remain unresolved, and have been largely avoided
by subsequent therapists of a critical ilk.[40]

CRITICAL PSYCHIATRY IN THE TWENTY-FIRST CENTURY

Indeed, the title of Ingelby's book has been taken up as a banner
for the currently active field of 'critical psychiatry', formed from
an alliance between disaffected psychiatrists, mental health
practitioners and 'users' of the mental health system. In its numerous
publications and conferences, the UK Critical Psychiatry Network
challenges the authority of clinical neuroscience in psychiatry, seeks
to introduce a strong ethical and cross-cultural perspective into
psychiatric knowledge and practice, and to politicise mental health
issues.[41] Critical psychiatrists such as Pat Bracken, Duncan Double,

Joanna Moncrief and Sammi Timimi are sceptical of assertions that psychosis and other forms of emotional distress can be best explained as products of aberrant brain function alone, and they question the claims made by the pharmaceutical industry for the role of psychotropic drugs in the 'treatment' of this distress. They look to social causes of emotional disturbance, including poverty, bad housing, loneliness, stigma, discrimination and racism. They ask whether behaviour judged odd or deviant by white middle-class doctors is inevitably a form of madness, as opposed to spiritual ecstasy, crisis, or healing ritual. Their position reflects scientific evidence on the roots of distress (see Chapter 5), as well as the tendency for most people who use psychiatric services to view these environmental influences as more important for their recovery than the drugs that their doctors prescribe.[42]

The existence and outlook of critical psychiatry is also a response to the complex and sometimes contradictory politics of mental health care in the twenty-first century. For example, it is in part a reaction to the authoritarianism of recent governments, intent upon enforcing psychiatric drug treatment and other coercive measures upon patients living 'in the community', and that targets young black men in particular for these measures, in what is widely seen as a form of institutional racism. The growth of critical psychiatry also reflects the influence of the mental health service user's movement in the design and evaluation of British treatment and care services, where policies require that mental health workers at least give lip service to sharing power and working 'in partnership' with their 'users'.[43] A further influence is the globalisation of the world economy, most apparent in the multicultural nature of early twenty-first-century Britain. Minority ethnic academics and user groups justifiably question western notions of self, sanity and madness, and seek recognition for the detrimental effects of the hostility that many of them have endured (and continue to endure) from their 'host' communities.[44]

The critical or post-psychiatry movement is 'a loose coalition of thinkers and actors whose ideas display certain family resemblances', in the words of David Ingleby.[45] One of those familial trends is a widespread acceptance of postmodernist ideas of mental illness and of its treatment, which suggest that any form of severe distress is just another form of discourse, as valid in its own way as any other. This idea owes most to the writings of the French philosopher Michel Foucault, who argued that insanity had been created by the language and practices of psychiatry – 'a monologue by reason about madness'.[46] Thus, many people in the post-psychiatry movement practice some version of narrative therapy, as one element in their clinical toolkit, which can also include psychotropic drugs (used sparingly) and asylum (in the true sense of the word). From the narrative standpoint, if we listen respectfully to someone who describes their auditory hallucinations or voices as a religious or mystical experience, then we are helping them toward self-accept-ance and perhaps toward a calmer and happier state of being. This way has much to recommend it on humanistic grounds, but taken to an extreme, it can also be an invitation to paradox and perhaps confusion. If the creation of a congenial story by therapist and client becomes the sure path to mental health (a realist claim), but that tale does not have to be 'accurate' in any absolute sense (an anti-realist claim), then which is most important, truth or pretence? Most recipients of talking therapy find the new account of their problems that emerges to be helpful because they believe that it captures something real about their lives, not because it is 'just another story'.[47] One of the few things that talking treatment might reliably do is to help people to see through their own self-deception. If it is hard to build a good life upon falsehood, then it is unclear how a narrative method can help people to cleave to the truth (however defined), when more pleasing, self-serving stories await invention. Experimental evidence suggests that the more we re-tell any tale about ourselves, the more partial our account (and our memories) become.[48] For most of us, the distinction between fact and fiction remains an important one.

The narrative outlook has become a staple of the humanities and social sciences, as the supposedly fundamental account of human nature, and a moral blueprint for how we should live and make sense of our lives. The philosopher Galen Strawson suggests that this narrativist orthodoxy has triumphed because it reflects the circumstances of those who write about it, and who enjoy top positions within academia, and the rest of society.[49] Critical psychiatrists appear to embrace other varieties of psychological therapy, but in their understandable rush to disown most of biomedicine, they do not seem to acknowledge the likely impotency of the talking cure, as discussed in Chapter 4.

Still, experience can sometimes be a great teacher. In some circumstances, it is impossible, despite one's professional allegiances, to avoid the conclusion that unhappiness depends upon the weight of biography and of the world that surrounds each one of us. In her account of how psychiatry works to conceal the social origins of distress and to pass off normative and moral judgements as neutral medical ones, the clinical psychologist Lucy Johnstone shows how troubled and abusive family life, chronic poverty, the constraints of gender roles, and the drudgery of meaningless or repetitive work can all engender forms of desperation that appear bizarre and 'mad' to an unsympathetic onlooker, particularly to someone trained to describe behaviour in the flat medical language of mental and behavioural 'symptoms'. Instead, Johnstone looks back to the work of Laing, Scott and other pioneering psychiatrists of the 1960s, together with feminist authors who saw madness as the result of having to live in a mad world, while lacking the ability to change it. Johnstone is surely correct to argue that, in contrast to psychiatry, the psychologist's willingness to talk with patients about their disturbing experiences as an expression of their biography (rather than of a mysterious 'chemical imbalance') is a more legitimate undertaking – on both scientific and ethical grounds.

There are many other therapists who share Johnstone's views. Drawing upon their own clinical work and upon the research literature, including the publications of people who regularly cut or burn themselves, the clinical psychologists Babiker and Arnold take a similar path.[50] They show that what is anaemically described by health professionals (and often the sufferers) as 'self-harm', is in fact a way of soothing otherwise unbearable emotional pain, by exchanging with its more manageable physical counterpart and, above all, of evading the censorship of family and community to express what cannot be uttered: it is, in their words, 'a language of injury'. In western culture, the majority of people who hurt themselves in this way and, as we have noted, who experience depression and other maladies, are women. The last 30 years have witnessed the flourishing of feminist therapies, which have sought to acknowledge this reality and to mould their assumptions and methods to the experience of women, as a subjugated and often exploited group.[51] Feminist critics from Elaine Showalter[52] to Geoffrey Masson[53] and Jane Ussher[54] have revealed the patriarchal nature of the main schools of psychotherapy, for example, in their fondness for interpreting the silent protest of the housewife or child-bearer as clinical anxiety or depression. Some of these authors have revealed the astonishing levels of abuse perpetrated by some leading male therapists against their female clients. In contrast to the broader feminist movement however, women-centred therapies have not been as potent a force for social change as some had hoped. This is perhaps because some practitioners have leant heavily upon complex psychoanalytic theory that is inscrutable to the uninitiated, and because it is hard in practice to deliver on promises of empowerment made via any kind of therapeutic programme, be it for an individual, or for a group.[55]

There are many other ways in which the language of mental health practitioners can fail to match up to the subjective turmoil that it is supposed to describe and illuminate. It is surprising that few people have asked whether psychotherapy provides an accurate map of the nature and roots of personal problems from the sufferer's point of view, or whether it helps them to be understood or helped by others. In pursuit of an answer to these questions, the psychologist Dawn Leeming,[56] as part of a larger study of the experience of the emotion of shame, interviewed 22 adults who suffered from serious psychological problems, and had had extensive experience of psychiatric and psychological treatments. Most of them mentioned environmental causes of their ills, including early physical and sexual abuse, domestic violence, emotional loss and adult bullying.

These narratives are valuable for their exploration of how psychological states manifest themselves. Not just as images and words, but as physical sensations. Think, for example, of how it feels, in the pit of your stomach, to sit through a gruelling job interview, to be deeply humiliated or embarrassed, or to be let down by a loved one. Leeming tried to get at these issues by asking her participants what they thought about how well their psychiatric and psychological treatments helped them and their associates to understand their problems. Most of their interviewees were highly ambivalent about psychiatric 'explanations' that inflated flawed biochemistry over the unhappy circumstances and cruel histories that most of them viewed as fundamental to their anguish.

In her joint discussion of this work with her colleagues, Mary Boyle and James McDonald, Leeming argues that psychological explanations of distress offer the most faithful picture of how suffering clings to the contours of personal history and circumstance. However, talking therapists should find better ways of helping people to understand how their troubles relate to their environment and that 'failure to cope' need not equate with personal slippage, or blame. Leeming and colleagues suggest that therapists need to embrace the stubbornly physical dimension of anguish, but without falling into the pseudo-medical language of psychiatry. This study also shows how hard it is for some people to accept that 'the mind' is not like reprogrammable computer software. Simplistic notions of self and personal change seem to enjoy wide currency.

INSIGHTS FROM PEOPLE WITH LEARNING DISABILITIES AND ORGANIC IMPAIRMENTS

For therapists, this rule seems to weaken for some client groups, whose misery all too obviously bears the stamp of their circumstances – as acknowledged, by a group of writers on CBT who, in a widely cited volume, explore the value of cognitive therapy for adults with learning disabilities.[57] What is of most interest is the primacy, reluctantly accepted, of the client's social and material environment for clinical progress. These therapists are unanimous in warning that therapeutic gains cannot be sustained in the absence of genuine choice for the client and of continuing efforts from carers to help them consolidate what they have learned. As one of the editors of this book later observed

> … without a reasonable world to enter outside of the consulting room, the benefits of such therapy will at best be limited. Clients may end up in confusing situations where, for example, they may be encouraged to be assertive and independent by therapists, only for this to bring them into conflict with carers or relatives who do not value these traits. Worse than this, many people with Learning Disabilities continue to suffer emotional, physical and sexual abuse in childhood and adulthood – something which services have been unable to prevent.[58]

This is as close to an admission of the inadequacy of individual psychological treatment as any mainstream psychological therapy practitioner is likely to come. Frankness comes more easily when writing about health services directed at people with undeniable organic impairments which limit their scope for learning and action, and who have a long history of being fourth-class citizens, their survival and well-being dependent upon the dispensations of others. But Stenfert Kroese and colleagues should not have been shocked. In the 1930s, British psychologists had been calling for change in how children with learning disabilities and their families were handled by public institutions and communities, as *the key* to their better health and happiness.[59] In the early twenty-first century, some clinical psychologists believe that their profession has lost sight of its former focus upon the environments that cause distress and 'challenging behaviour' in children and adults in this group. They call for a renewed focus upon prevention, support, respite and advice, as opposed to individual therapy.[60]

Adult learning disability services share these features with elder and child psychology provision in the UK. Rather than directly spotlighting that distressed individual, psychologists who work in these settings have sometimes focused upon the network of relatives, carers, institutions and amenities around the designated patient, as more suitable targets for change. These so-called 'systemic' or 'family' therapies are widely practiced in public health agencies in the UK and the United States, and particularly in child and adolescent therapy services – perhaps because the approach lends itself to multi-agency working.[61] In its willingness to look beyond the individual as the locus and cure for distress, family therapy is several steps ahead of traditional psychological treatment. However, it is questionable that the apparent changes can be sustained beyond the boundaries of the consulting room, given the many external pressures that such families face on the one hand, and the heavy weight of personal disposition and acquired habits, on the other. When carefully scrutinised, the evidence for the effectiveness of these methods looks no better than that for any other psychological therapy.[62]

COMMUNITY PSYCHOLOGY

Another group of psychologists who look to the sufferer's world as the source of their problems (indeed, whose outlook is defined by this view) are the community psychologists. Their approach is an ecological one. Rather than seeking to treat individual patients, they try first to help ordinary people to diagnose the mentally toxic aspects of their world and then work alongside them, to reduce these harms. Community psychology is multidisciplinary in nature, drawing upon the kind of epidemiological literature discussed in Chapter 5. Social power is a central concept. Practitioners share a commitment to social justice, to working in partnership with the laity and to the strengthening of communal connections and of economic and material resources. Community practitioners often use an action research framework, with a view to identifying communal strengths and weaknesses, and useful themes and ideas for achieving shared goals, which are put into practice and then tested and modified in the field. In seeking these aims, they have borrowed concepts such as 'empowerment' and 'social capital' from the disciplines of community work and political science, respectively.[63]

In principle, community psychology interventions can run from neighbourhoods to nations – in the case of advice on health and social policy, for example. In practice, most such projects remain quite small, little more than extensions of therapeutic group work. A good example would be the handful of British NHS-based schemes, described in an undergraduate textbook intended to showcase a representative sample of UK community psychology practice.[64] These are discussion and education groups, designed, respectively, to give ordinary members of the public, long-term mental health service users, and women and men with learning disabilities an opportunity to critique key aspects of their world and to achieve a measure of solidarity otherwise lacking. Founded with one eye on their potential for changing the health and social care services that support them, these groups run the gamut from creative writing, news gathering (in regard to the failings of the mental health care system) to the elucidation of noxious mental environments.

Projects like these can sometimes demonstrate lively invention. For instance, the British clinical psychologist Guy Holmes has made use of the beauty of his native Shropshire landscape as a setting for what he calls 'Walk and Talk'. Organised and run in collaboration with mental health service users and with members of the general public, advertised locally and open to all, this is an annual summertime endeavour – intended to bring people together around a shared interest rather than a shared diagnosis. In a once-weekly countryside stroll along the banks of the River Severn, participants discuss personal concerns and wider questions about the causes and prevention of distress, and some of them make new friends along the way. Holmes and his colleagues have also created a series of 'Psychology in the Real World' courses, that attract a similarly broad array of people, but within a more conventional seminar format, designed to explore some of the bread-and-butter topics of community psychology and their implications for civic life and well-being.[65]

Despite the enthusiasm of their members, however, most of the psychology groups discussed here have remained focused chiefly upon mutual support – their creators fittingly modest in their claims for what has (and might be) achieved.[66]

One of the best-celebrated community psychology schemes, initiated by clinical psychologist Sue Holland in the 1980s and known eventually as WAMH – Women's Action for Mental Health – was wider in scope, and has proved to have unusual staying power. This project was notable for the remarkable level of commitment shown by Holland. She lived and worked for over ten years in the deprived White City public housing estate in West London, and allied herself with local mental health service users and other residents in order to tackle street-lighting and crime, and to establish a crèche and a refuge house for psychiatric emergencies. As well as providing individual therapy, she also set up a mutual self-help network of ex-clients, trained them in therapeutic techniques, and attended community development meetings. This work was 'disrespectful of existing professional boundaries' and challenged the vested interests of many expert groups.[67] Holland does not talk about her own feelings or her general health, but her many roles and responsibilities must have been demanding ones – both personally and professionally. It is unlikely that anyone could sustain this level of commitment without some loss of health and vitality, not to mention their private family life. The writings of other community psychologists hint strongly at such conflicts and costs.[68]

In order to be successful, community projects often depend upon unusually committed and perhaps charismatic individuals, with a stomach for political confrontation when required. But how easy can it ever be to argue with the king who pays the shilling?[69]

These are not the only problems facing the community practitioner. If we adopt a reasonable standard of evidence – of the kind that would be required in the field of epidemiology, for instance – then the vast majority of studies in support of community psychology appear far less conclusive than we might hope. As William Epstein has observed in a series of wide-ranging surveys of the US community-work literature – any thorough assessment of community projects seldom shows them to be effective in reducing the rate or severity of psychological distress, or of any other personal or social problem – even, for example, where tangible (and easy-to-measure) outcomes are concerned, such as increased employment or reduced poverty. This is because of credulous and poorly planned research that depressingly echoes the outcome literature for talking therapy. Few of these community projects have been rated for helpfulness by people who are independent and without a personal, political, financial, or professional stake in the outcome. Furthermore, the assessments have tended to focus upon what people say about changes in their community, instead of focusing upon possible changes in what they actually *do*. There is for instance, a very big difference between someone saying that they feel safer and being able to show that there has been a genuine drop in the rate of violent crime, consequent upon a particular neighbourhood initiative. Most of these investigations are conducted in the absence of control assessments, of any attempt to look at how similar communities elsewhere might have fared in the absence of the given community intervention. To add to these difficulties of interpretation, there have been few efforts to follow up on what the longer-term effects of any given project might be – beyond the typical one- or two-year period of the programme itself.[70]

In the US throughout the post-war period, charitable and voluntary community action programmes have made little impact upon the ills that they were explicitly designed to attack, such as community decay, crime and drug addiction. What, indisputably *has* made a difference is national government action, in the form of more generous and humane social policies in health, social care, education and housing; but these periods of generosity are rare, prompted by economic and social catastrophe. Even a cursory glance at the UK community psychology literature, such as the dozens of studies discussed in Jim Orford's compendious and scholarly review,[71] shows that these scientific shortcomings are not unique to the American literature.

We have seen that some therapists and virtually all community practitioners have acknowledged the difficulty of attaining individual cure through psychological techniques. We have also seen that even radical and environmental alternatives to traditional talking therapy may have severe limitations of their own. Is there a coherent body of knowledge that might help us to make sense of what has confronted us, so far? One step in this direction might be into the territory of the behavioural psychology that we touched upon in Chapter 1. At first glance, this might look like a backward step, given that this brand of psychology is now out of fashion. However, not all of the reasons for its recent decline are good ones. It is worth considering behaviourism because it is one of the few approaches that try to view the individual (and the sufferer) as an *expression* of the landscape in which they are embedded.

BEHAVIOURISM – EMBARRASSING UNCLE, OR HONOURABLE ANCESTOR?

From its inception in the late nineteenth century, psychology as a science has aspired to the goals of understanding, prediction and control. Human beings have always been difficult to read and their actions still harder to foresee, at least as far as individuals are concerned.

Over the years, psychologists have tried to deal with these problems. Psychodynamic and humanist writers described a rich inner world of thought and feeling. By contrast, the behaviourists focused upon what people do and say, in response to the contingencies of reward and punishment in the world around them. Their core contention: that mind was a by-product of action, of interest only to the extent that it could be understood as observable activity, such as speech, gesture or writing, as, for instance, the American academic psychologist Burroughs F. Skinner felt that he was able to demonstrate, when he showed that pigeons could be trained to play table tennis, by shaping their behaviour through successive rewards.[72]

While the behaviourist project wore the costume of science, it failed because it was unable to meet its goals of rigorously controlling and predicting what people did outside of the aseptic laboratory walls, and because, for many, there was something lacking in a science of human life that treated people as crude automatons. Attempts to incorporate the inventiveness of language as an internal or 'secondary signalling system' became complex and unwieldy, and still further removed from the goal of prediction.[73] It might be possible to increase the amount that someone talked by nodding and smiling (rewarding them) every time that they said something, but who could tell how a specific individual would respond to the next question in a banal conversation, still less to an enquiry about their philosophy of life? Human beings were just too intricate and subtle, their actions prompted by too many influences – internal and external, symbolic and tangible – to bear comparison with pigeons, rewarded with food pellets.

The behavioural approach convinces only where the researcher has almost full control over the situation and is dealing with an organism less complex than themselves. Nevertheless, the behaviourists had the virtue of realism, when they gave the environment its due. What psychologists need is some way of combining this clear focus upon the world with a recognition that private thoughts and feelings, if not fully autonomous, are indispensible for understanding how it is that this world can work its evils upon so many of us.

Skinner was derided by most of his colleagues for ignoring subjective experience. But they were wrong, because radical behaviourism was in fact defined, not by its denial of private events, but by its unique take upon them:

A science of behaviour must consider the place of private stimuli as physical things, and in doing so, it provides an alternative account of mental life. The question then, is this: What is inside the skin, and how do we know about it? The answer is, I believe, the heart of radical behaviourism.[74]

In this regard, the European psychologists Alvarez and Sass offer a thoughtful overview of the similarities between Skinnerian behaviourism and phenomenological psychology. This is a tradition that takes subjective experience as the starting-point for any attempt to understand another human being, while situating that experience in the particularities of time, place, relationships, and the body of the subject – as young or old, male or female, and so on. On the one hand, Alvarez and Sass acknowledge the importance of this inner experience in any account of what it means to be human and to struggle with difficult circumstances, and on the other, they recognise that these supposed inner and outer worlds are not separate, but mutually reinforcing.[75] In their efforts to understand and help people who suffer madness, these writers suggest that the behaviourist notion can be illuminating, if it is recast, in terms of the phenomenological notion of the 'lived world'. On the other hand, behaviourism needs to recognize the importance of symbolic culture – the role of meaning as the ground of all that we do, say and feel. In behavioural terms, the main idea is that what we might call 'stimulus' and 'response' are not separate things – that is, the external trigger and the action that it brings forth – but are complementary to one another and part of a continuous loop. In common with simpler animals, we are constantly seeking knowledge about our world and in doing so, by where and how we look, for example, we change the way in which that world impinges upon us, even if only in subtle ways, but enough to show that the supposed separation between us and our surrounds is a false duality – a point that was made in the nineteenth century by the American philosopher and educationalist John Dewey.[76]

That 'inner' and 'outer' might be two sides of the same coin was also a key concern for Ludwig Wittgenstein, who noted that we perceive affective states in ourselves, and others, by observing conduct in characteristic contexts that can be publicly identified. The very nature of a given emotion, its status as anger or shame, for instance, is inseparable from physiological states, ways of behaving and certain attitudes toward the world. The emotions are also shaped by cultural expectations and by what people are allowed to say, in virtue of their social status. Historical and sociological studies, for example, suggest that the passions of anger and pride have always been distributed according to social and political power, and far less available to people in denigrated categories, including women and slaves.[77] The philosopher Maurice Merleau-Ponty – famous for challenging the traditional dualisms of mind and body, and of self and others – captured something of this complex picture. He did not reject the reality of subjective life, but doubted that our thoughts form an entirely private and autonomous universe:

> We must reject the prejudice that makes 'inner realities' out of love, hate, or anger, leaving them accessible to one single witness: the person who feels them. Anger, shame, hate and love are not psychic facts hidden at the bottom of another's consciousness. They are types of behaviour or styles of conduct that are visible from the outside. They exist on this face or in these gestures, not hidden behind them.[78]

That all feeling, ideation and expression might be rooted in the material and social world brings us to recent enactive theories of consciousness and perception, which claim that such faculties cannot be reduced to information processing inside the brain, but arise instead from transactions between body, central nervous system and setting.[79] The boundary between self and context is far more permeable than conventional cognitive psychology supposes. For instance, the implements and devices that we use can come to feel that they are part of who we are: extensions of our bodies. Mind tools, such as writing, mathematical notation and diagrams not only increase our scope for action, they are the skeletons upon which our thoughts can grow, assisting us to unravel problems and invent new ones. Language is not just a set of rules but a social practice, part of our lives, as we can see in the comparison of non-English speaking-immigrants and their children. The latter acquire the new tongue so much more easily than their parents, in part because their brains are more flexible, but also because their whole being is thoroughly immersed in the new culture. It is from such experiences that we become creatures of habit and skill, with little need to interpret a world given to us already, through our implicit learning: 'At a very basic level, we are involved, that is to say, tangled up – with the places we find ourselves. We are of them.'[80]

The enactive approach offers yet another bridge between the seemingly irreconcilable subjective and behaviourist viewpoints, explaining inner states by appeal to external and observable actions, by the skills and habits that the person uses to respond to their environment. On the other hand, this framework retains the traditional notion that internal mental events – ideas, memories and attention, for instance – can influence behaviour, even while these hidden processes are downgraded in potency, as just another set of threads, in an endless web of mutual influence.[81]

Bringing Up the Bodies – How the World Gets Under the Skin

Are we now any closer to understanding the realities of psychological distress and the limitations of conventional talking treatments? This section will contrast the work of the American researcher, Martin Seligman, with that of two British psychologists, John Cromby and Dave Harper, to show how near but also far away psychologists can get in trying to understand the external roots of distress, and how deeply these roots can reach into us.

Martin Seligman's popular theory of 'learned helplessness' has sought to account for the genesis of depression from a lack of perceived influence over oneself and one's circumstances. In the late 1960s, Seligman, a young academic researcher, had started with a largely behaviourist conception of how enduring sadness and apathy might come about, via experiments with dogs, held in a special harness and trained to press a pedal to avoid painful electric shock. Seligman then wired a second group of dogs in series with the first, but without the benefit of a similar pedal, so that each animal in this group received the same punishment schedule but without any way of being able to influence it. Subsequently, Seligman and his collaborator, Steven Maier, tested all of the animals in a shuttle box – now free to learn to escape the electric shocks, by leaping over a low barrier. At this new task, however, most of the canines in the second group did very poorly. They quickly gave up the ghost, and ended up in a huddle on the floor of the box, allowing themselves to be continually shocked. These unfortunate dogs had learned two inescapable lessons: that they could no longer control the worst things that were happening to them, and that there was no point in taking evasive action. They looked, for want of a better word, 'depressed'.[82]

Rather than taking these observations as the starting-point for a sober analysis of what causes profound unhappiness and of what can and cannot be done about it, Seligman and his colleagues have since proceeded to turn the concept of learned helplessness outside-in, so that it is no longer a matter of the tight interweaving between an individual and their tough circumstances, but a largely mental entity. That is, a set of negative expectancies sit inside each depressed or pessimistic person's head,[83] awaiting correction by means of psychological techniques, as expressed in Seligman's more recent notion of 'learned optimism', whereby any of us can incrementally talk and work ourselves into a rosier outlook and a better life.[84]

Not all theorists and clinicians share Seligman's views. John Cromby and Dave Harper take the subjective experience of paranoia, not as the starting-poisnt for a self-transformation cookbook, but for placing this kind of unhappiness squarely inside the body that hosts it *and* in the world that produces it.[85] They acknowledge that paranoia is a feature of psychiatric 'illnesses' such as 'paranoid schizophrenia' and 'delusional personality disorder'. However, they argue that psychiatric thinking turns what is in reality a complex phenomenon into a simple medical label, concealing the skeins of malign social and family conditions that give rise to it. Paranoia is often a feature of many people's day-to-day lives. Irrational beliefs such as faith in the supernatural and everyday suspicion and mistrust are highly prevalent. Witness for instance, the CCTV cameras that adorn almost every high street in the UK, the country with the most watched citizenship in the world.[86] What distinguishes those who come into contact with mental health services because of 'paranoia' and those who do not are the levels of misery, conviction and preoccupation associated with their beliefs, and how much they are seen as a nuisance or a threat.

The authors take their cue from the work of the neuroscientist Antonio Damasio, who has shown in studies of brain-damaged and normal people that in real life, the best decisions are never made in harness to the cold rationality of *Star Trek*'s Mr Spock. Instead, they are informed by a mixture of calculation and of feelings – states of arousal that flow from low-level brain structures to muscles and glands and back again – in the form of visceral feeling tones that tinge our outlook, and help create the hunches that inflect preference and choice. These subtle feelings faithfully bear the imprint of our personal history and are the primary ground from which we engage with everything and everyone.[87] Damasio says little about how intuitions like these might speak of our place in the world, but if we are concerned with the genesis of mental suffering, this becomes an all-important question.

Where safety, self-worth, or competency have been undermined over many years, and where the individual has met with little in the way of countervailing friendship or affection from others, then it is scarcely surprising that they might acquire a profound distrust, in the manner that a crustacean gradually builds up its protective shell. The frequent rejection and disdain of others solidifies, gradually, into defensive unease, and then into a hostile vigilance that becomes a self-fulfilling prophecy, underwritten by the mental health system: 'Once you are diagnosed you have to live knowing that you have less rights than a criminal, knowing that you can be forcibly drugged and that 46% of consultant psychiatrists want to erode your rights further by introducing compulsory treatment orders.'[88]

The first of these authors has written a similar account of how the profound and enduring sadness commonly known as 'depression' can arise from a punishing existence, over which the individual has little leverage, try though they might to exert it. Besides the neuropsychological framework described above, Cromby draws upon the German Critical Psychology of Klaus Holzkamp, Frigga Haug and others.[89] These scholars related the extent of subjective freedom and choice – what they called the 'subjective possibility space' – to external (objective) material and economic conditions: 'The poor tend to live in a long unchanging present while the rich have a future to look forward to.'[90] Cromby also draws upon the work of anthropologists who suggest that certain patterns of conversation can sometimes channel people into a depressive identity. He argues that individuals diagnosed as depressed have learned to embrace one of three main scripts about themselves – as hopeless, powerless, or worthless. Just as the lines in a play need a flesh-and-blood actor to breathe life into them, so these scripts go far beyond mere words, and represent a wide constellation of feelings and actions that reflect a plot and scenery that is only partially of each actor's making. Helplessness, for instance, burdens people with a general sense of inability and so drags them downwards into apathetic withdrawal, whereas powerlessness, in which self-worth is usually at stake, might lead to agitation and defensiveness, insomnia and weight loss. On the other hand, the worthlessness script can foster self-deprecation, crippling guilt and anxiety, and gloom about the future. Because every option literally *feels* as threatening as each of the others, then the sufferer is effectively denied the usual guidance of bodily sensation in their decision making, which becomes agonised and clumsy.

If all of these scripts entail the compaction of 'subjective possibilities', then they can also be modified by conscious action. But the difficulty of doing so should not be underestimated. Apart from the weight of habit, divisions of class, gender and ethnicity, for example, constrain the ideas to which people are exposed, and what they can say and do in their ordinary lives. For poor people living in western consumer societies, for instance, the daily grind of earning and getting by, the patronising arrogance and pettiness of the welfare officials upon whom many of them depend, the contrast between public opulence on the one hand, and bare survival and private squalor on the other – all reinforce the message of low self-worth.[91] Over time, such feelings become ingrained, densely connected to memories and experiences through multiple neural networks, and in consequence, always primed to surge forth and overwhelm, making future attempts at escape more unlikely, even if circumstances should change for the better.

These observations go some way in accounting for the intransigence of this mental and bodily state and for its great variability between individuals – something that psychiatric diagnostic systems have largely ignored.[92] An important implication is that psychological therapy aimed at shifting stubborn patterns of 'negative thought' is unlikely by itself to do much good. What most individuals need instead is a reliably safe haven, a place that offers belonging, validation and direction. It is their situation rather than their mind that needs to change for the better.[93]

In this emphasis upon the material body and world, the insights offered by Cromby are almost the inverse of those presented by Seligman, and are far less likely to lead to the belief that wearing rose-coloured spectacles is the same as strewing the streets with petals. Although we humans have the capacity to tell ourselves that things are not so bad after all, on the level of feelings and – to a large degree – of our actions, we are more like Seligman's dogs than we might prefer to believe. We are made miserable, in the end, not just by the strength of our beliefs, but by the weight of hard and all-too-real situations, as they bear downward, robbing us of control.

DAVID SMAIL – FROM ILLUSION TO REALITY?

If all of this seems rather obvious, then few clinicians have been able to even glimpse it, let alone abandon their faith in the potency of the talking cure. But apostates do exist. Perhaps one of the best known is the British clinical psychologist, David Smail, who began his career in the early 1960s, at a therapeutic community in the Claybury Psychiatric Hospital, in Essex. This experience sensitised him to the influence of situations upon human mentality, an outlook that Smail carried into his subsequent career as head of the community-based clinical psychology service in Nottingham, for almost 30 years from 1968. From the outset, he had puzzled over what the research literature and his own clinical experience might teach him about the practice of therapy, which, in common with many others at the time,[94] he came to see, not as a technical procedure, but as a personal encounter, for which there could be no predictable or standardised outcome.[95] But his doubts did not end there. From the late 1970s to the early twenty-first century, Smail's writings reveal a gradual shift of viewpoint. At the start, here is someone who believes (guardedly) that treatment can offer improved self-awareness and perhaps ameliorative action, if not cure.[96] At the end, there is the realisation that unhappiness treated by clinicians has much more to do with the sufferer's situation than with anything about themselves, and for those with few privileges, this unhappiness is pretty well beyond the reach of therapeutic or any other conversation. It was the experience of trying to help some of the casualties of Thatcherism and of the 1980s 'business revolution' that finally convinced Smail of the near-irrelevance of his trade.[97]

By the mid-1980s, he found himself starting to treat more and more middle-class professionals suffering from emotional troubles as sudden as they were puzzling. Almost every one of these individuals saw their unhappiness as a mark of their own failure in this era, in which 'shock capitalism' was introduced into Britain. Public services and nationalised industries were forced to embrace free market ways and deregulation, backed up by a widespread official commitment to 'business values'. Many of these professionals found themselves struggling with workplaces where long-accepted practices, values and ethics had been shoved aside in favour of 'no-nonsense' profit making, 'efficiency' and 'competition'. Sartorial changes marked this transformation of political and social outlook. Heads of university, hospital, or accountancy departments suddenly appeared at their offices in shoulder- padded 'power suits', as if the characters from American soap operas that extolled money making as the apex of existence had strode from their film sets, straight into the humdrum scenery of British working life. Even social workers swapped their corduroy jackets and dungarees for sensible suits and smart ties, especially if they aspired to be managers. The psychotherapy and counselling professions underwent a big expansion, not because of any new scientific advances, but because of the assiduous self-promotion of their practitioners and their openness to the doctrines of business.

Almost every one of Smail's patients attributed their 'anxiety' or 'depression' to their own weakness, when in truth, their sorrows pointed to the arrival of an altogether chillier and unnerving era. Unless we live in unusual circumstances, the script for what it means to be a good employee, woman, man, or even a person, is not just our own invention. It is largely gifted by the society in which we live. When these directions become ambiguous or contradictory, and when there are penalties for our 'mistakes' in our public and personal lives, then we are likely to experience the resulting confusion as emotional turmoil and a sign of our own personal or moral failings. For most victims, this 'inability to cope' was the only verdict offered by the psychotherapy and counselling industries, and by the transnational and corporate interests that profited from these unsettling circumstances.

The remarkable thing about Smail's work was not so much these observations in themselves – supported by psychiatric survey data and other health indices such as rising suicide rates for young men, all of which revealed the shadow side of 1980s Britain – but that so few of his colleagues seemed to have noticed what was happening. His writings are widely cited in academic and popular texts that question foundations of talking therapy, and are often mandatory reading on mental health training courses, especially the parts dealing with ethics. In common with many other critics, however, his ideas have yet to reach very far into the world of clinical theory and practice, even as they continue to develop in to what Smail in his most recent work has called a 'social-materialist psychology'.[98] This is so named, because it does not treat encounters between people as fluid games open to manipulation at the whim of the players (as assumed in so much academic and therapeutic psychology), but as situations that are soaked through and through with power. Where some actors will be afforded plenty of room to choose their course, others, in the worst cases, will be constrained to servitude. Indeed, power rules the social world into which we are born and comes in a variety of forms – economic, coercive and ideological, and works through appeals to our perceived self-interest, even though there is enormous social pressure to deny this. Our concern with money, for instance, falls outside of the bounds of polite conversation, although our economic status remains central to our well-being and features in the daydreams and nightmares of a good many of us. Power is also embodied, as noted by the late French theorist Pierre Bourdieu,[99] acquired through formal and informal learning, and gradually accumulated into our physical appearance, our styles of expression and movement, and in our suite of talents and dispositions, which can themselves be traded for other forms of influence. In essence, our 'supposed "inner strengths" are really no more than the reflection of outer advantages'.[100]

Embodied power is never absolute. Even quasi-biological endowments, such as 'good looks' or 'high intelligence' can shift in value, according to social and political currents. Intellectuals, for instance, can suffer drastically when political regimes turn dictatorial. A world geared to endless profit making ensures that some of us will always have a lot more control than others, and that those with the least will have more precarious and miserable lives. They will also be the ones most vulnerable to shifts in the more distant forms of influence that move almost everyone. This is evident, for example, when stock markets falter and in response, politicians set about dismantling the public services upon which those of low and middling income depend for employment and protection. The irony of this situation is that these most distal powers, the ones with the most potency to shape where and how we live, work and play (and in the end, who and what we *become*) are also the ones of which we are least aware. Above all, when it comes to accounting for the distress to which they give rise and which we feel only in the most proximal way: inside of our bodies.

In Smail's work, the image of the unconscious as a set of dynamic forces has been rehabilitated, but its operations moved, with more scientific credibility, *beyond* the skin of the individual. If we want to understand why people are unhappy, then, rather than the traditional idea of insight into a mythical interior psychological space, we need to cultivate *outsight* into the external world.[101]

CONCLUSION: 'IT'S REALITY – BUT NOT AS WE (ALWAYS) KNOW IT ... '

This chapter has looked at the work of some psychologists and theorists who have been prepared to acknowledge that people can be paranoid because they have been persecuted, or depressed because their world is depressing. The suggestion is that the social-materialist outlook might offer an account that makes the best match with the territory explored in this chapter and in the rest of this book.[102]

However, this standpoint does not and cannot claim to be the final word in the effort to understand how people become distressed and what, if anything, can be done about it. To say the least, there are many details to be filled in and ideas to be elaborated. We have scarcely begun to study the myriad ways in which circumstances can work their way into the feelings and thoughts of the person, into their hopes and fears, not to mention their biology. Moreover, distress is not a fixed thing. The hysteria that afflicted women and, it is increasingly recognized – men – in the nineteenth century, is a rare phenomenon today. Instead, many of us suffer from 'depression' or from the 'flashbacks' of PTSD. Who is to say of what psychological ills our grandchildren will complain?

From a realist or scientific perspective, the social-materialist viewpoint seems to offer a number of advantages in comparison to the offerings of the therapy industry on the one hand, and of biomedical psychiatry on the other. It can do justice to the epidemiological literature on psychological disturbance that we discussed in Chapter 5. Unlike positivist psychiatry, it acknowledges that the vicissitudes of life do not have a fixed effect, like exposure to a bacillus, but depend upon how they are construed and negotiated by each person, at both a conscious but more often unconscious level. It can also accept that biological or temperamental differences might make some people more prone to demoralisation in the face of adversity, but without descending into the worst kinds of biological reductionism. Uniquely, it acknowledges the poor evidence for the effectiveness of psychological treatments that we have reviewed earlier in this book, and indeed *requires* that talk alone cannot be a potent lever of personal change. What counts are world, body, power interactions. The social-materialist view shares with psychoanalysis the tendency to depose conscious deliberation from its throne. However, it avoids the subtle blame of Freud's approach, in which the individual is responsible both for their own lack of insight and their failure to act upon it. It answers the still-pertinent arguments of an earlier generation of critics such as Peter Sedgwick, who took Laing and Foucault to task for fear that their rejection of the concept of mental illness denied the human suffering involved, and would prove rather convenient for governments and some of their voters, eager to wash their hands of social responsibility.[103] No such possibility is entailed here. The perspectives that we have examined confront this suffering not as an illness, but as an anguish that is all too tangible and that cannot be argued away, or ignored.

In their overview of the scientific literature on the prevention of mental suffering written nearly 40 years ago, the American psychologists Marc Kessler and the late George Albee observed that no disease has ever been eliminated or even brought under control by a cure alone. In every case, from the Broad Street pump onwards, prevention led the way: 'Everywhere we looked, every social research study we examined, suggested that major sources of human stress and distress generally involve some form of excessive power.'[104] These conclusions remain valid today. Before the discovery of the malarial parasite and the route of its transmission via the mosquito, people used to drain malarial swamps because of what they took to be their 'bad airs', long thought to be the cause of the sickness. This theory was of course wrong in almost every detail, but close enough to the wider truth to work. The same lesson applies to the genesis and reduction of personal distress. We don't necessarily need to know every pathway that leads to misery in every individual. If anguish and madness are caused by material things happening to material bodies: on one side, traumatic abuse and persecution; and on the other, soul-deadening labour, squalid impoverishment, the boredom of joblessness, the moralising sermons of the privileged – to name but a handful of the officially approved torments – then it seems sensible not to try to talk people out of their unhappiness, but to change the world from which it springs. A concerted effort to take the plight of the poor and the marginalised seriously, to redistribute wealth, and to give them more say over their own future might not solve every one of these ills, but it would be a good place to start.

Notes

INTRODUCTION

1. DeRubeis, R.J., Webb, C.A., Tang, T.Z. and Beck, A. (2010) 'Cognitive Therapy', in Dobson, K. (ed.), *Handbook of Cognitive Behavioural Therapies* (3rd edn). New York: The Guilford Press, p. 292.
2. Mills, C.W. (1959, 2000) *The Sociological Imagination. Fortieth Anniversary Edition.* Oxford: Oxford University Press.
3. See Porter, R. (2002) *Blood and Guts: A Short History of Medicine.* Harmondsworth: Penguin; Wootton, D. (2007) *Bad Medicine: Doctors Doing Harm Since Hippocrates.* Oxford: Oxford University Press.
4. Rose, N. (1999) *Governing the Soul: The Shaping of the Private Self.* London: Free Association Press (originally published 1989).
5. *Hunger in America: 2012 United States Hunger and Poverty Facts* <http://www.worldhunger.org/articles/Learn/us_hunger_facts.htm> retrieved 19 November 2012.
6. NAHO (2009) *Roadmap to End Childhood Hunger in America by 2015.* National Anti-Hunger Organizations <http://www.hungercenter.org/publications/naho-roadmap-to-end-childhood-hunger-in-america-by-2015/> retrieved 28 December 2012.
7. Elliot, L. and Atkinson, D. (2007) *Fantasy Island.* London: Constable Robinson.
8. With apologies to the British urban folk group, Half Man Half Biscuit. The line is taken from the title of one of their songs, 'The Light at the End of the Tunnel (is the Light of an Oncoming Train)', from the album, *Camell Laird Social Club.*

CHAPTER 1 MISERY, MIND CURES AND FASHION

1. Illich, Ivan (1972) *Deschooling Society.* Harmondsworth: Penguin, p. 132.
2. Porter, R. (1987) *A Social History of Madness: Stories of the Insane.* London, Routledge; see Boyle, M. (2002) *Schizophrenia: A Scientific Delusion?* London: Routledge.
3. Gross, D.M. (2008) *The Secret History of Emotion: from Aristotle's Rhetoric to Modern Brain Science.* Chicago, IL: University of Chicago Press.
4. See the discussion of this fascinating takeover in Boyle, *Schizophrenia: A Scientific Delusion?*
5. Seabrook, J. (2007) 'Cities of Fear', in Seabrook, *Cities (Small Guides to Big Issues).* London: Fennwood Publishing, Pluto, Palgrave Macmillan and Oxfam.
6. Scull, A. (2009) *Hysteria: The Biography.* Oxford University Press.
7. Micale, M. (2008) *Hysterical Men: The Hidden History of Male Nervous Illness.* Cambridge, MA: Harvard University Press, p. 280.

8. Beard, M. (1881) *American Nervousness: Its Causes and Consequences, a Supplement to Nervous Exhaustion (Neurasthenia)*. New York: Putnam; see Pietikainen, P. (2007) *Alchemists of Human Nature*. London: Pickering and Chatto.

9. Pietikainen, P. (2005) 'Neurosis and the Theory of Infectious Diagnoses', in Pietikainen, P. (2005) (ed.) *Modernity and its Discontents: Sceptical Essays on the Psychomedical Management of Malaise*. Stockholm: Ax:son Johnson Foundation.

10. Pietikainen, *Alchemists of Human Nature*.

11. Scull, *Hysteria: The Biography*, pp. 136–8.

12. See Webster, R. (1995) *Why Freud Was Wrong: Sin, Science and Psychoanalysis*. London: HarperCollins.

13. Attributed to the clinical psychologist Don Banister: personal communication, from Dr John Cromby.

14. Gutheil, T. and Gabbard, G.O. (1993) 'The Concept of Boundaries in Clinical Practice: Theoretical and Risk-Management Dimensions', *American Journal of Psychiatry* 150: 188–96.

15. Brown, J.A.C. (1964) *Freud and the Post-Freudians*. Harmondsworth: Penguin.

16. Pilgrim, D. and Treacher, A. (1992) *Clinical Psychology Observed*. London: Tavistock and Routledge.

17. Webb, T.F. (2006) '"Dottyville" – Craiglockhart War Hospital and Shell-shock Treatment in the First World War', *Journal of the Royal Society of Medicine* 99(7) (July): 342–6.

18. Goggin, J.E. and Goggin, E.B. (2001) *Death of a 'Jewish Science': Psychoanalysis in the Third Reich*. Ashland, OH: Purdue University Press.

19. Pilgrim and Treacher, *Clinical Psychology Observed*.

20. Rose, N. (1989) *Governing the Soul: The Shaping of the Private Self*. London: Routledge.

21. Jacobs, M. (2006) *The Presenting Past. The Core of Psychodynamic Counselling and Therapy*. Open University and McGraw Hill.

22. Scull, *Hysteria*; Fancher, R. (1995) *Cultures of Healing: Correcting the Image of the American Mental Health Professions*. San Francisco, CA:. W.H. Freeman.

23. The diagnosis of 'neurasthenia' never died out in China, where it remains a highly prevalent diagnosis. See, for example, Kleinman, A. (1986) *Social Origins of Distress and Disease: Depression, Neurasthenia and Pain in Modern China*. New Haven, CT: Yale University Press and Watters, E. (2010) *Crazy Like Us: The Globalization of the American Psyche*. New York: Free Press.

24. Burnham, J.C. (2005) *What is Medical History?* London: Polity.

25. Freeman, W. (1968) *The Psychiatrists: Personalities and Patterns*. New York and London: Grune and Stratton.

26. Hunt, A.W. (1964) 'Enforcement in Probation Casework', *British Journal of Criminology* 4: 239–52; Friedlander, K. (1947) *The Psychoanalytical Approach to Juvenile Delinquency*. London: Kegan Paul, Trench, Tubner.

27. See Pilgrim, D. (2008) 'CBT and the Layard Thesis', in House, R. and Lowenthal, R., *Against and For CBT: Towards a Constructive Dialogue?* Ross-On-Wye: PCCS Books Ltd, p. 260.

28. See Skinner, B.F. (1953) *Science and Human Behavior*. New York: Macmillan.

29. Pilgrim and Treacher, *Clinical Psychology Observed.*

30. Martin, D.V. (1962) *Adventure in Psychiatry.* Oxford: Bruno Cassirer.

31. See, for example, Proctor, G. (2002) *The Dynamics of Power in Counselling and Psychotherapy: Ethics, Politics and Practice.* Ross-On-Wye: PCCS Books Ltd.

32. Doward, J. (2010) 'One in Five Britons has Consulted a Counsellor or a Psychotherapist', *Observer:* 1 August <http://www.guardian.co.uk/society/2010/aug/01/counselling-psychotherapy-survey> retrieved 28 January 2011.

33. NHS Choices (n.d.) *Can I Get Free Therapy or Counselling?* <http://www.nhs.uk/Conditions/stress-anxiety-depression/Pages/free-therapy-or-counselling.aspx> retrieved 30 November 2012.

34. Stivers, R. (2004) *Shades of Loneliness: Pathologies of a Technological Society.* Oxford: Rowman and Littlefield.

35. Iliffe, S. (2008) *From General Practice to Primary Care: The Industrialisation of Family Medicine.* Oxford: Oxford University Press.

36. See Pollock, A. (2004) *NHS Plc: The Privatization of Our Health Care* (2nd edn). London: Verso.

37. As persuasively argued by David Ingleby. See, for example, his chapter 'Transcultural Psychiatry', in Double, D.B. (ed.) (2008) *Critical Psychiatry: The Limits of Madness.* London: Palgrave Macmillan.

38. Moncrieff, J. (2008) *The Myth of the Chemical Cure: A Critique of Psychiatric Drug Treatment.* London: Palgrave Macmillan.

39. Schofield, W. (1964) *Psychotherapy: The Purchase of Friendship.* Hemel-Hempstead: Prentice Hall.

40. Pilgrim and Treacher, *Clinical Psychology Observed*; Smail, D. (1978) *Psychotherapy: A Personal Approach.* London: Dent.

41. Fancher, R. (1996) *Cultures of Healing: Correcting the Image of American Mental Health Care.* San Francisco, CA: W.H. Freeman and Company; see also Pilgrim and Treacher, *Clinical Psychology Observed.*

42. For an American perspective, see Cushman, P. (1995) *Constructing the Self, Constructing America.* Cambridge, MA: Perseus Publishing. For a British viewpoint, see McLeod, J. (2012) *An Introduction to Counselling.* Milton Keynes: McGraw Hill Higher Education, Open University Press.

43. Parker, I. (2007) *Revolution in Psychology.* London: Pluto.

44. Bowers, J. (1990) 'All Hail the Great Abstraction: Star Wars and the Politics of Cognitive Psychology', in Parker, I. and Shotter, J. (eds), *Deconstructing Social Psychology.* London: Sage Publications, pp. 127–40. See also Latour, B. (1987) *Science in Action.* Milton Keynes: Open University Press.

45. Kline, P. (1987) *Psychology Exposed: or The Emperor's New Clothes.* London: Routledge.

46. Beck, A.T., Rush, A.J., Shaw, B.F. and Emery, G. (1979) *Cognitive Therapy of Depression.* New York: The Guilford Press; Hofmann, S.G. (2011) *An Introduction to Modern CBT: Psychological Solutions to Mental Health Problems.* New York: Wiley-Blackwell.

47. The quotation is from William Shakespeare's *Hamlet.* Act 2. Scene 2, line 240, in Harris, B. (ed.) (2009) *Oxford Dictionary of Quotations.* Oxford: Oxford University Press, p. 701. A similar statement to this effect, deriving this time from the classical Stoic philosopher, Epictetus, can be found in Ellis, A. (1962) *Reason and Emotion in Psychotherapy.* Oxford: Lyle Stuart, p. 54. CBT enthusiasts less often observe that Epictetus was a former slave.

48. Bolsover, N. (2004) 'Psychotherapy and Evidence', *Journal of Critical Psychology Counselling and Psychotherapy* 4(2): 68–77.

49. Pilgrim and Treacher, *Clinical Psychology Observed*.

50. See, for example, Tarrier, N., Haddock, G., Barrowclough, C. and Wykes, T. (2002) 'Are All Psychological Treatments for Psychosis Equal? The Need for CBT in the Treatment of Psychosis and not for Psychodynamic Psychotherapy', *Psychology and Psychotherapy: Theory, Research and Practice* 75: 365–74.

51. Pilgrim, D. (2011) 'The Hegemony of Cognitive Behaviour Therapy in Modern Mental Health Care', *Health Sociology Review* 20(2) (June): 120–32.

52. Cayoun, B. (2011) *Mindfulness Integrated CBT: Principles and Practice*. Chichester: John Wiley and Sons.

53. See Loewenthal, D. and House, R. (2010) *Critically Engaging CBT*. Maidenhead: McGraw Hill Higher Education, Open University Press; Spinelli, E. (2000) *The Mirror and the Hammer*. London: Sage.

54. Hallam, R.S. and O'Connor, K.P. (2002) 'A Dialogical Approach to Obsessions', *Psychology and Psychotherapy* 75 (Pt 3) (September): 333–48.

55. Cameron, D. (2000) *Good to Talk?: Living and Working in a Communication Culture*. London: Sage.

56. Pilgrim, D. and Rogers, A. (2010) *A Sociology of Mental Health and Illness* (4th edn). London: Open University Press and McGraw Hill.

57. For a discussion of this concept as a social, moral and political aspiration, see Elliott, C. (2003) *Better Than Well: American Medicine Meets the American Dream*. London and New York: W.W. Norton and Company.

58. Many confident claims are made about the power of CBT in Padesky, C. and Greenberger, D. (1995) *Mind Over Mood. Clinician's Guide to Mind Over Mood*. New York: Guildford Press.

59. See, for example, Feltham, C. (ed.) (1999) *Controversies in Psychotherapy and Counseling*. London: Sage.

60. Johnstone, L. and Dallos, R. (eds) (2006) *Formulation in Psychology and Psychotherapy: Making Sense of People's Problems*. London: Routledge.

61. See, for example, Loewenthal, D. (2011) *Post-existentialism and the Psychological Therapies: Towards a Therapy without Foundations*. London: Karnac Books; Postle, D. (2007) *Regulating the Psychological Therapies: From Taxonomy to Taxidermy*. Ross-On-Wye: PCCS Books Ltd.

62. A good example of a sceptical position in regard to the extent to which psychotherapy can be theorised, researched, taught, dispensed and evaluated as a kind of medical treatment, see House, R. and Totton, N. (1998) *Implausible Professions: Arguments for Pluralism and Autonomy in Psychotherapy and Counselling*. Ross-On-Wye: PCCS Books Ltd.

63. Gordon, P. (2009) *The Hope of Therapy*. Ross-On-Wye: PCCS Books, Ltd; King, L. (2003) 'Telling Like It Is', in King, L. and R. Randall (eds), *The Future of Psychoanalytic Psychotherapy*. London: Wurr.

64. See, for example, Postle, D. (2007) *Regulating the Psychological Therapies: From Taxonomy to Taxidermy*. Ross-On-Wye: PCCS Books Ltd.

CHAPTER 2   THE PSYCHOPATHOLOGY OF EVERYDAY LIFE

1. Illich, I. (1975) 'Medical Nemesis', Chapter 2 in his *The Medicalization of Life* <http://www.soilandhealth.org/03sov/0303critic/030313illich/Frame.Illich.Ch2.html> retrieved 8 August 2012.

2. Fitzpatrick, M. (2001) *The Tyranny of Health: Doctors, and the Regulation of Lifestyle*. London: Routledge.

3. Kessler, R.C. et al. (1994) 'Lifetime and 12-month Prevalence of DSM-111-R Psychiatric Disorders in the United States', *Archives of General Psychiatry* 51: 8–19.

4. McManus, S., Meltzer, H., Brugha, T. and Bebbington, P. (eds) (2007) *Adult Psychiatric Morbidity in England, 2007: Results of a Household Survey*. Leeds: The NHS Information Centre for Health and Social Care; Horwitz, A.V. and J.C. Wakefield (2008) *The Loss of Sadness: How Psychiatry Transformed Normal Sorrow into Depressive Disorder*. Oxford: Oxford University Press.

5. Marcia, A. (2011) 'The Epidemic of Mental Illness: Why?', *New York Review of Books* LVIII(11) (23 June–13 July): 20–22.

6. Murray C.J.L. and Lopez, A.D. (eds) (1996) *The Global Burden of Disease: A Comprehensive Assessment of Mortality and Disability from Diseases, Injuries and Risk Factors in 1990 Projected to 2020*. Cambridge, MA: Harvard School of Public Health on behalf of the World Health Organization and the World Bank (Global Burden of Disease and Injury Series, Volume 1).

7. Gergen, K.J. (1990) 'Therapeutic Professions and the Diffusion of Deficit', *Journal of Mind and Behavior* 11(3–4) (1990): 353–67.

8. Showalter, E. (1985) *The Female Malady: Women, Madness, and English Culture, 1830-1980*. New York: Pantheon Books.

9. Wolfensberger, W. (1994) 'The Growing Threat to the Lives of Handicapped People in the Context of Modernistic Values', *Disability & Society* 9(3): 395–413; Thomson, M. (1998) *The Problem of Mental Deficiency: Eugenics, Democracy and Social Policy in Britain, c. 187 –1959*. Oxford: Clarendon.

10. World Health Organization (2011) *International Statistical Classification of Disease and Related Health Problems*, 10th revision. Geneva: World Health Organization.

11. American Psychiatric Association (1994) *DSM IV TR (Diagnostic and Statistical Manual of Mental Disorders)* (4th edn). Washington, DC: American Psychiatric Association.

12. Chen Y.F. (2002) 'Chinese Classification of Mental Disorders (CCMD-3): Towards Integration in International Classification', *Psychopathology* 35(2–3): 171–5.

13. White, K. (2006) *The Sage Dictionary of Health and Society*. London: Sage.

14. Kutchins, H. and Kirk, S. (1997) *Making Us Crazy: DSM – the Psychiatric Bible and the Creation of Mental Disorders*. New York: The Free Press.

15. Read, J. and Sanders, P. (2010) *The Causes of Mental Health Problems (Straight Talking Introductions)*. Ross-On-Wye: PCCS Books Ltd.

16. Slater, L. *Opening Skinner's Box. Great Psychological Experiments of the 20th Century*. London: Bloomsbury.

17. Rosenhan, D.L. (1973) 'On Being Sane in Insane Places', *Science* 179(4070) (January): 250–58.

18. Horwitz, A.V. and Wakefield, J.C. (2008) *The Loss of Sadness: How Psychiatry Transformed Normal Sorrow into Depressive Disorder*. Oxford: Oxford University Press; see also Kirk, S.J. (2005) *Mental Disorders in the Social Environment: Critical Perspectives*. New York: Columbia University Press.

19. Kutchins and Kirk, *Making us Crazy*.

20. See American Psychiatric Association (2012) *DSM-V Facts* <http://dsmfacts. org> retrieved 28 December 2012/>.

21. Kutchins and Kirk, *Making us Crazy*.

22. Angell, M. (2011) 'The Illusions of Psychiatry', *New York Review of Books* 14 July 2011 <http://www.nybooks.com/articles/archives/2011/ jul/14/illusions-of-psychiatry/?pagination=false&printpage=true> retrieved 10 October 2012.

23. Spitzer, R.L., Sheehy, M. and Endicott, J. (1977) 'DSM III: Guiding Principles', in Rakuff, V.M., Stancer, H.C. and Kedward, H.B. (eds), *Psychiatric Diagnosis*. New York: Brunner/Marzel, p. 3.

24. Holmes, G. (2012) Personal communication: words attributed to Peter Breggin, speaking at a critical mental health conference held in Shropshire, UK, in 2000.

25. Bentall, R. (2010) *Doctoring the Mind: Why Psychiatric Treatments Fail*. London: Penguin Books.

26. Whitaker, R. (2010) *Anatomy of an Epidemic*. New York: Crown.

27. Healy, D. (2012) *Pharmageddon*. Berkeley: University of California Press.

28. Breggin, P. (1991) *Toxic Psychiatry*. London: Fontana.

29. Warner, R. (2004) *Recovery From Schizophrenia: Psychiatry and Political Economy* (3rd edn). London: Routledge.

30. Healy, D. (1997) *The Anti-Depressant Era*. Cambridge, MA: Harvard University Press; Johnstone, L. (2010) 'The Anti-depressants: A Historical Analysis', in Rapley, M., Moncrieff, J. and Dillon, J. (eds), *De-Medicalising Misery: Psychiatry, Psychology and the Human Condition*. London: Palgrave Macmillan, and Kirsch, I. (2010) 'Anti-depressants and the Placebo Response', in ibid.

31. Johnstone, L. (2006) 'The Limits of Biomedical Models of Distress', in Double, D. (ed.), *Critical Psychiatry: The Limits of Madness*. Basingstoke: Palgrave Macmillan.

32. Moncrieff, J. (2010) 'Psychiatric Diagnosis as a political device', *Social Theory and Health* 8(4): 370–82, at 373.

33. Healy, *Pharmageddon*.

34. Carlton, T., Ferriter, N., Hubbard, N. and Spandler, H. (2008) 'A Systematic Review of the Soteria Paradigm for the Treatment of People Diagnosed With Schizophrenia', *Schizophrenia Bulletin* 34(1): 181–92.

35. Whitaker, R. (2002) *Mad in America: Bad Science, Bad Medicine, and the Enduring Mistreatment of the Mentally Ill*. New York: Basic Books.

36. Jablensky, A. (1992) 'Schizophrenia: Manifestations, Incidence and Course in Different Cultures', *Psychological Medicine*, 20 (monograph): 1–95, and Hopper, K. (2000) 'Revisiting the Developed Versus Developing Country Distinction in Course and Outcome in Schizophrenia', *Schizophrenia Bulletin* 26 (2000): 835–46.

37. Whitaker, R. (2010) *Anatomy of an Epidemic: Magic Bullets, Psychiatric Drugs, and the Astonishing Rise of Mental Illness in America*. New York: Crown.

38. Whitaker, *Mad in America*.

39. Breggin, P. (1991) *Toxic Psychiatry*. London: HarperCollins; Healy, *Pharmageddon*, and Warner, *Recovery From Schizophrenia*.

40. Bentall, R. (2009) *Doctoring the Mind*. London: Allen Lane, Penguin; Boyle, M. (2002) *Schizophrenia: A Scientific Delusion*. London: Routledge.

41. Wakefield, J.C. and Horwitz, A.V. (2012) *All We Have to Fear: Psychiatry's Transformation of Natural Anxieties into Mental Disorders*. Oxford: Oxford University Press.

42. Healy, *Pharmageddon*.

43. Healy, D. (2004) 'Shaping Discontent: The Roles of Science and Marketing', in Pietikainen, P. (ed.), *Modernity and Its Discontents: Sceptical Essays on the Psychomedical Management of Malaise*. Stockholm: Axel and Margaret Ax:son Johnson Foundation.

44. Healy, *Pharmageddon*.

45. Angell, 'The Illusions of Psychiatry'.

46. Davies, H. (2001) 'The role of the private sector in protecting the human subject', *Institute of Medicine* <http://www.acrohealth.org/testimony. php?yr=2001> retrieved 6 August 2012.

47. Healy, *Pharmageddon*.

48. At least half of all papers dealing with clinical drug trials, by the estimate of David Healy: ibid.

49. Angell, 'The Illusions of Psychiatry', p. 22.

50. Healy, D. (2007) 'The Engineers of Human Souls and Academia', *Epidemiologica e Psichiatria* 16(3): 205–11.

51. Conrad, P. (2007) *The Medicalization of Society: On the Transformation of the Human Conditions into Treatable Disorders*. Baltimore, MD: Johns Hopkins University Press.

52. Woloshin, S. and Schwartz, L. (2006) 'Giving Legs to Restless Legs: A Case Study of How the Media Makes People Sick', *PLoS Med* 3(4) <http://www.plosmedicine.org/article/info%3Adoi%2F10.1371%2Fjournal.pmed.0030170> retrieved 11 February 2013.

53. Moncrieff, J. (2003) *Is Psychiatry for Sale?* London: Institute of Psychiatry.

54. American Psychiatric Association (1994) *DSM IV TR*. Washington, DC: American Psychiatric Association.

55. American Psychiatric Association (1980) *Diagnostic and Statistical Manual of Mental Disorders III (DSM III TR)*. Washington, DC: American Psychiatric Association.

56. Young, Allen (1995) *The Harmony of Illusions*. Princeton, NJ: Princeton University Press.

57. Linder, M. (2004) 'Creating PTSD', in Caplan, P. and Cosgrove, L. (eds), *Bias in Psychiatric Diagnosis*. Lanham, MD: Aronson; Summerfield, D. (2001) 'The Invention of Post-Traumatic Stress Disorder and the Social Usefulness of a Psychiatric Category', *BMJ* 322: 95.

58. Kutchins and Kirk, *Making Us Crazy*.

59. See, for example Furedi, F. (2008) *Paranoid Parenting*. London and New York: Continuum.

60. APA, *DSM IV TR*.

61. Scott, S. (2006) 'The Medicalisation of Shyness: From Social Misfits to Social Fitness', *Sociology of Health & Illness* 28(2): 133–53, at 19.

62. Grandin, M. and Scariano, M.M. (2005) *Emergence: Labeled Autistic*. New York: Warner Books.

63. Baron-Cohen, S. (1998) *Asperger Syndrome: The Facts*. Oxford. Oxford University Press.

64. Billington, T. (2000) *Separating, Losing and Excluding Children: Narratives of Difference*. London: Routledge, Falmer.

65. Billington, T. (2006) 'Working with Autistic Children and Young People: Sense, Experience and the Challenges for Services, Policies and Practices', *Disability and Society* 21(1): 1–13, at 4. See also Buller, D.J. (2005) *Adapting Minds: Evolutionary Psychology and the Persistent Quest for Human Nature*. Cambridge, MA: MIT Press.

66. Tamimi, S., Gardner, N. and McCabe, B. (2010) *The Myth of Autism: Medicalising Men's and Boys' Social and Emotional Competence*. London: Palgrave Macmillan.

67. Holmer-Nadesen, M. (2005) *Constructing Autism: Unravelling the Truth and Understanding the Social*. London: Routledge; Moloney, P. (2010) '"How can a chord be weird if it expresses my soul?" Some Critical Reflections on the Diagnosis of Aspergers Syndrome', *Disability and Society* 25(2): 135–48.

68. Illousz, E. (2008) *Saving the Modern Soul*. London: Routledge.

69. Fitzpatrick, M. (2009) *Defeating Autism: A Damaging Delusion*. London: Routledge.

70. See the website for the Institute for the Study of the Neurotypical <http://isnt.autistics.org> retrieved 20 November 2012.

71. Angell, 'The Illusions of Psychiatry'.

72. Tamimi, S. (2009) *A Straight-talking Introduction to Children's Mental Health Problems* (Straight Talking Introductions series, Bentall, R. and Tudor, P., series eds). Ross-On-Wye: PCCS Books Ltd.

73. Reay, D. (2006) 'The Zombie Stalking English Schools: Social Class and Educational Inequality', *British Journal of Educational Studies* 54(3) (September): 288–307.

74. These effects range from growth inhibition and stroke in the case of stimulants, to suicidal thinking and violence in the case of the SSRIs, and dyskenesia plus obesity and diabetes, for the anti-psychotics: Breggin, P., *Toxic Psychiatry*; Healy, *Pharmageddon*.

75. Boyle, D. (2003) 'The Syndrome that Became an Epidemic', *New Statesman*, 6 October: 27–8.

76. According to the *New York Times*, a Rutgers University study found that children from low-income families were four times more likely to receive anti-psychotic medication when compared with children from families that had private healthcare insurance (see Angell, 'The Illusions of Psychiatry', p. 22).

77. Healy, D., Harris, M., Cattell, D., Michael, P., Chalassani, P. and Hirst, D. (2005) 'Service Utilisation in 1896 and 1996: Morbidity and Mortality Data from North Wales' *History of Psychiatry* 16: 27–41.

78. Healy, 'The Engineers of Human Souls and Academia'.

79. Pilgrim, D. and Rogers, A. (2010) *A Sociology of Mental Health and Illness* (4th edn). Basingstoke: Open University Press and McGraw Hill Educational.

80. Rose, D. and Thornicroft, G. (2010) 'Service User Perspectives on the Impact of a Mental Illness Diagnosis', *Epidemiol Psychiatr Soc.* 19(2) (April–June): 140–47.

81. Barham, P. and Hayward, R. (1991) *From Mental Patient to Person*. London: Routledge.

82. See Whitaker, *Anatomy of an Epidemic*; Pilgrim, D. and R. Bentall (1999) 'The Medicalisation of Misery: A Critical Realist Analysis of the Concept Depression', *Journal of Mental Health* 8(3): 261–74.

83. Johnstone, L. (2006) *The Limits of Biomedical Models of Distress*, in Double, *Critical Psychiatry*.

84. These responses can also be highly individual and unpredictable. See, for example, Barrett, M. (2007) *Casualty Figures: How Five Men Survived the First World War*. London: Verso.

85. See Bambury, B. (2012) 'Are We Over-diagnosing Autism? The Psychiatric Debate', CBC News. 27 January <http://www.cbc.ca/news/health/story/2012/01/27/f-vp-bambury-autism.html>. These were Spitzer's words to British film-maker, Adam Curtis.

CHAPTER 3   THE 'CEO OF SELF' ... ?

1. Fodor, J. (2000) *The Mind Doesn't Work That Way: The Scope and Limits of Computational Psychology*. Cambridge, MA: MIT Press, p. 100.

2. Draisma, D. (2009) *Disturbances of the Mind*. Cambridge: Cambridge University Press.

3. See Kozuch, B. and Nichols, S. (2011) 'Awareness of Unawareness: Folk Psychology and Introspective Transparency', *Journal of Consciousness Studies* 18 (11–12): 135–60.

4. Tomasky, M. (2011) 'The "CEO of Self"', review of *This is Herman Cain!: My Journey to the White House* by Herman Cain, *New York Review of Books*: 22 December <http://www.nybooks.com/articles/archives/2011/dec/22/herman-cain-ceo-self/?pagination=false&printpage=true> retrieved 4 October 2012.

5. Lutz, C. (1985) 'Depression and the Translation of Emotional Worlds', in Kleinman, A. and Good, B. (eds), *Culture and Depression: Studies in the Anthropology and Cross-Cultural Psychiatry of Affect Disorder*. Berkeley: University of California Press, p. 65.

6. Hoffman, S. and Asmundson, J.G. (2008) 'Acceptance and Mindfulness-based Therapy: New Wave or Old Hat?', *Clinical Psychology Review* 28(1): 1–16.

7. Baars, B. (1997) *In the Theatre of Consciousness: The Workspace of the Mind*. New York: Oxford University Press; Beck, A. (1995) *Cognitive Therapy: Basics and Beyond*. New York: Guilford Press.

8. Bruner, J. (2004) *Making Stories: Law, Literature, Life*. Cambridge, MA: Harvard University Press.

9. Kelly, A.E. (2000) 'A Self-Presentational View of Psychotherapy: Reply to Hill, Gelso, and Mohr (2000) and to Arkin and Hermann (2000)', *Psychological Bulletin* 126(4): 505–11, at 507; emphasis added.

10. Danziger, K. (1994) *Constructing the Subject*. Cambridge: Cambridge University Press; Lyons, W. (1986) *The Disappearance of Introspection*. Cambridge, MA: MIT Press.

11. Schwitzgebel, E. (2011) *Perplexities of Consciousness*. Cambridge, MA: MIT Press.

12. Hulbert, R.T. and Schwitzgebel, E. (2008) *Describing Inner Experience? Proponent Meets Skeptic*. Cambridge, MA: MIT Press.

13. Grimes, J. (1996), 'On the Failure to Detect Changes in Scenes Across Saccades', in Akins, K. (ed.), *Perception* (Vancouver Studies in Cognitive Science, 2), New York: Oxford University Press, pp. 89–110.

14. Blackmoore, S. (2005) *Consciousness: A Very Short Introduction*. Oxford: Oxford University Press.

15. Simons, D.J. and Levin, D.T. (1998) 'Failure to Detect Changes to People During a Real-world Interaction', *Psychonomic Bulletin and Review* 5(4): 644–9.

16. Mack, A. and Rock, I. (1998) *Inattentional Blindness*. Cambridge, MA: MIT Press.

17. Simons, D.J. and Chabris, C.F. (1999) 'Gorillas in our Midst: Sustained Inattentional Blindness for Dynamic Events', *Perception* 28: 1059–74.

18. Schiffman, N. (2005) *Abracadabra! Secret Methods Magicians and Others Use to Deceive their Audience*. New York: Prometheus Books.

19. Noe, A. (2002) 'Is the Visual World a Grand Illusion?', *Journal of Consciousness Studies* 9(5–6): 1–12.

20. Haybron, D.M. (2008) *The Pursuit of Unhappiness: The Elusive Psychology of Well-Being*. Oxford: Oxford University Press.

21. Bhuyar, P., Banarjee, A., Pandve, H., Padmnabhan, P., Patil, A., Duggirala, S., Rajan, S and Chaudhury, S. (2008) 'Mental, Physical and Social Health Problems of Call Centre Workers', *Industrial Psychiatry Journal* 17(1): 21–25.

22. Bargh, J. (2008) 'Free Will is Unnatural', in Baer, J., Kaufman, J.C. and Baumeister, R.F. (eds), *Are We Free? Psychology and Free Will*. Oxford: Oxford University Press.

23. Doris, J. (2002) *Lack of Character: Personality and Moral Behaviour*. Cambridge: Cambridge University Press.

24. See, for example, Hirstein, W. (ed.) (2010) *Confabulation: Views From Neuroscience, Psychiatry, Psychology and Philosophy*. Oxford: Oxford University Press.

25. Nisbett, R. and Wilson, T. (1977) 'Telling More Than We Can Know: Verbal Reports on Mental Processes', *Psychological Review* 84(3): 231–59.

26. Caldini, R. (1994) *Influence: The Psychology of Persuasion*. New York: Morrow.

27. Latane, B. and Darley, J.M. (1970) *The Unresponsive Bystander: Why Doesn't He Help?* New York: Appleton Century Crofts, p. 124.

28. Marsh, J. (2011) *Class Dismissed: Why We Cannot Teach or Learn Our Way Out of Inequality*. New York: Monthly Review Press.

29. Blaxter, M. (1997) 'Whose Fault is it? People's Own Conceptions of the Reasons for Health Inequalities', *Social Science and Medicine* 44(6): 747–56, at 754.

30. Marmot, M. et al. (2010) *Fair Society Healthy Lives: Strategic Review of Health Inequalities in England post-2010*. London: The Marmot Review.

31. Rollnick, S., Miller, W. and Butler, C. (2007) *Motivational Interviewing in Health Care: Helping Patients Change Behavior*. New York: Guilford Publications.

32. Baumeister, R.F. and Tierney, J. (2011) *Will Power: Rediscovering the Greatest Human Strength*. New York: Penguin Press.

33. Throop, E.A. (2009) *Psychotherapy, American Culture, and Social Policy: Immoral Individualism*. Basingstoke: Palgrave Macmillan, p. 21.

34. Clark, D.A. (1995) 'Perceived Limitations of Standard Cognitive Therapy: A Reconsideration of Efforts to Revise Beck's Theory and Therapy', *Journal of Cognitive Psychotherapy* 9(3): 153–72.

35. Coyne, J. (1989) 'Thinking Postcognitively about Depression', in Freeman, A., Simon, K.M., Beutler, L.E. and Arkowitz, H. (eds), *Comprehensive Handbook*

of *Cognitive Therapy*. New York: Plenum Press; Hall, K. and Iqbal, F. (2010) *The Problem with Cognitive Behavioural Therapy*. London: Karnac.

36. Moore, M.T. and Fresco, D.M. (2007) 'Depressive Realism and Attributional Style: Implications for Individuals at Risk for Depression', *Behavior Therapy* 38: 144–54.

37. Beck, A.T. (1976) *Cognitive Therapy and the Emotional Disorders*. New York: International Universities Press.

38. Fancher, R. (1996) *Cultures of Healing: Correcting the Image of American Mental Health Care*. San Francisco, CA: W.H. Freeman and Company.

39. Ilardi, S. and Craighead, W.E. (1994) 'The Role of Non-specific Factors in Cognitive Behavioural Therapy for Depression', *Clinical Psychology Science Practice* 1: 138–56.

40. Sotsky, S.M., Glass, D.R., Shea, M.T., et al. (1991) 'Patient Predictors of Response to Psychotherapy and Pharmcotherapy: Findings of the NIMH Treatment of Depression Collaborative Research Program', *American Journal of Psychiatry* 148: 997–1008.

41. Imber, S.D., Pilkonis, P.A., Sotsky, S.M., et al. (1990) 'Mode-specific Effects Among Three Treatments for Depression', *Journal of Consulting and Clinical Psychology* 58: 352–9.

42. Longmore, R. and Worrell, M. (2006) 'Do We Need to Challenge Thoughts in Cognitive Behavior Therapy?', *Clinical Psychology Review* 27: 173–87, at 185.

43. Duncan, B.L., Miller, S.D., Wampold, B.E. and Hubble, M.A. (eds) (2010) *The Heart and Soul of Change. Delivering What Works in Therapy* (2nd edn). Washington, DC: American Psychological Association.

44. Beck, A.T. and Alford, B.A. (2009) *Depression: Causes and Treatments* (2nd edn). Philadelphia: University of Pennsylvania Press.

45. Teasdale, J.D. (1997) 'The Relationship Between Cognition and Emotion: The Mind-in-place in Mood Disorders', in Clark, D.M. and Fairburn, C.G. (eds), *The Science and Practice of Cognitive Behaviour Therapy*. Oxford: Oxford University Press.

46. See, for example, the discussion of this issue in Epstein, W.M. (2002) 'The Willow World of Virtue', in *American Policy Making: Welfare as Ritual*. Lanham, MD: Rowman and Littlefield; Epstein, W.M. (2006) 'Cognitive Behavioral Therapy as Christian Science' in *Psychotherapy as Religion*. Reno: University of Nevada Press. Where researchers have bothered to look for relationships between negative thoughts and prevailing (sometimes subtly prevailing) circumstances, then they have often found them. See, for instance, Stoppard, J.M. (1998) *Understanding Depression: Feminist Social Constructionist Approaches*. London: Routledge.

47. *The Beezer*. London: D.C. Thomson.

48. Wegner, D.M. (2002) *The Illusion of Conscious Will*. Cambridge, MA: MIT Press.

49. Pronin, E., Wegner, D.M., McCarthy, K. and Rodriguez, S. (2006) 'Everyday Magical Powers: The Role of Apparent Mental Causation in the Overestimation of Personal Influence', *Journal of Personality and Social Psychology* 91: 218–31.

50. Wegner, D.M. (2008) 'Self is Magic', in Baer, Kaufman, and Baumeister (eds), *Are We Free?*, pp. 227–8.

51. Dennet, M. (2008) 'Some Observations on the Psychology of Thinking About Free Will', in Baer, Kaufman and Baumeister (eds), *Are We Free?*
52. Dennett, D. (1992) *Consciousness Explained*. London: Allen Lane, Penguin.
53. Blackmore, S. (2001) 'Consciousness', *The Psychologist* 14: 522–5.
54. Claxton, G. (1999) 'Whodunnit? Unpicking the "Seems" of Free Will', *Journal of Consciousness Studies* 6(8–9): 99–113.
55. Donald, M. (2001) *A Mind So Rare: The Evolution of Human Consciousness*. New York: Norton.
56. Wegner, *The Illusion of Conscious Will*.
57. Ibid.

CHAPTER 4   DOES THERAPY WORK?

1. Hubble, M.A., Duncan, B.L, Miller, S.D. and Wampold, B.E. (2010) 'Introduction', in Duncan, B.L., Miller, S.D., Wampold, B.E. and Hubble, M.A. (eds), *The Heart and Soul of Change: Delivering What Works in Therapy*. Washington, DC: American Psychological Association, p. 42.
2. Fancher, R.A. (1996) *Cultures of Healing: Correcting the Image of American Mental Health Care*. San Francisco, CA: W.H. Freeman and Company, p. 12.
3. Heine, R.W. (1953) 'A Comparison of Patients' Reports on Psychotherapeutic Experience with Psychoanalytic, Nondirective and Adlerian Therapists', *American Journal of Psychiatry* 112: 321–7; 'Some Implicit Common Factors in Diverse Methods of Psychotherapy', *American Journal of Orthopsychiatry* 6: 412–15; Rogers, C. (1942) *Counseling and Psychotherapy*. Boston, MA: Houghton Mifflin.
4. Eysenck, H.J. (1952) 'The Effects of Psychotherapy: An Evaluation', *Journal of Consulting Psychology* 16: 319–24.
5. Epstein, W. (1993) *The Illusion of Psychotherapy*. New Brunswick, CT: Transaction; Eysenck, H.J. (1963) 'Behaviour Therapy, Spontaneous Remission and Transference in Neurotics', *American Journal of Psychiatry* 11: 867–71.
6. Bergin (1971) reanalysed Eysenck's data and found evidence, using less stringent criteria (which counted the people who dropped out of the studies as having 'recovered'), that individuals in the treated groups showed substantial improvement: Bergin, A.E. (1971) 'The Evaluation of Therapeutic Outcomes', in Bergin, A.E. and Garfield, S.L. (eds), *Handbook of Psychotherapy and Behavior Change: An Empirical Analysis*. New York: John Wiley & Sons, pp. 217–70.
7. Little, J.H. (2010) 'Evidence Based Practice: Evidence or Orthodoxy?', in Duncan et al. (eds), *The Heart and Soul of Change*.
8. Lambert, M.J. and Ogles, B.J. (2004) 'The Efficacy and Effectiveness of Psychotherapy', in Lambert, M.J. (ed.) (2004) *Bergin and Garfield's Handbook of Psychotherapy and Behavior Change* (5th edn). New York: John Wiley & Sons, p. 140.
9. Smith, M.L., Glass, G.V. and Miller, T.I. (1980) *The Benefits of Psychotherapy*. Baltimore, MD: Johns Hopkins University Press.
10. Lambert, M.J., Shapiro, D.A. and Bergin, A.E. (1986) 'The Effectiveness of Psychotherapy', in Garfield and Bergin (eds), *Handbook of Psychotherapy and Behavioral Change*.

11. For instance, Roth, A. and Fonagy, P. (2006) *What Works for Whom: A Critical Review of Psychotherapy Research* (2nd edn). New York: The Guildford Press.

12. For example, Barak, A., Hen, L., Boniel-Nissim, M. and Shapira, M. (2008) 'A Comprehensive Review and a Meta-Analysis of the Effectiveness of Internet-Based Psychotherapeutic Interventions', *Journal of Technology in Human Services* 26 (2/4): 109–60. See also, Duncan et al. (eds), *The Heart and Soul of Change*, and Roth and Fonagy, *What Works for Whom*.

13. See Loewenthal, D. and House, R. (eds) (2010) *Critically Engaging CBT*. Maidenhead: McGraw-Hill, Open University Press.

14. Breggin, P.R. and Cohen, D. (1999) *Your Drug May Be Your Problem: How and Why To Stop Taking Psychiatric Medications*. Cambridge, MA: Perseus Books.

15. Hubble et al., 'Introduction', in Duncan et al. (eds), *The Heart and Soul of Change*.

16. Montaigne, M. de (1572) *Essays*. Trans. J.M. Cohen, 1958. Harmondsworth: Penguin Classics.

17. Moerman, D. (2002) *Meaning, Medicine, and the 'Placebo Effect'*. Cambridge: Cambridge University Press.

18. Jopling, D. (2008) *Talking Cures and Placebo Effects*. Oxford: Oxford University Press.

19. Fisher, S. and Greenberg, R. (1998) From Placebo to Panacea: Putting Psychiatric Drugs to the Test. New York: John Wiley & Sons.

20. Ibid.

21. Moerman, *Meaning, Medicine, and the 'Placebo Effect'*.

22. Fisher and Greenberg, *From Placebo to Panacea*, p. 31.

23. Sutherland, I. (1992) *Irrationality: The Enemy Within*. London: Constable.

24. Shapiro, F. and Silk-Forrest, M. (1997) EMDR: The Breakthrough 'Eye Movement' Therapy for Overcoming Anxiety, Stress, and Trauma. New York: Basic Books.

25. Casement, P. (1985) *On Learning from the Patient*. London: Routledge.

26. Gendlin, E. (1981) *Focusing*. New York: Bantam.

27. Ilffe, S. (2008) *From General Practice to Primary Care: The Industrialization of Family Medicine*. Oxford: Oxford University Press.

28. Davies, D. (1997) *Counselling in Psychological Services*. Milton Keynes: Open University.

29. Kearny, J. (1996) *Culture, Class and Politics: Undisclosed Influences in Therapy and Counselling*. Ross-on-Wye: PCCS Books Ltd.

30. Sands, A. (2000) *Falling for Therapy*. London, Macmillan.

31. See Bohart, A.C. and Talman, K. (2010) 'Clients: the Neglected Common Factor in Psychotherapy', in Duncan et al. (eds), *The Heart and Soul of Change*.

32. Stivers, R. (1999) *Technology as Magic: The Triumph of the Irrational*. New York: Continuum.

33. Hansen, S. et al. (2003) *Beyond Help: A Consumer's Guide to Psychology*. Ross-on-Wye: PCCS Books Ltd.

34. Geertz, C. (1975) 'On the Nature of Anthropological Understanding', *American Scientist* (63): 47–53, at 48.

35. Throop, E.A. (2009) *Psychotherapy, American Culture, and Social Policy: Immoral Individualism*. Basingstoke: Palgrave Macmillan.

36. Thomas, K. (2008) *The Ends of Life: Roads to Fulfillment in Early Modern England*. Oxford: Oxford University Press.

37. Ibid.

38. Cushman, P (1995) *Constructing the Self, Constructing America*. Cambridge, MA: Perseus Publishing.

39. Bohart and Tallman, 'Clients: the Neglected Common Factor in Psychotherapy'.

40. France, A. (1989) *Consuming Therapy*. New York, Free Association Books.

41. See Halmos, P. (1965) The Faith of the Counsellors: A Study in the Theory and Practice of Social Case Work and Psychotherapy. New York: Schocken Books.

42. Feltham, C. (2010) 'Whatever Happened to Free Will and Willpower?', in *idem, Critical Thinking in Counselling and Psychotherapy*. London: Sage.

43. Ellis, A. (1998) The Practice of Rational Emotive Behaviour Therapy. New York: Free Association.

44. Rogers, C. (2003) Client Centred Therapy: Its Current Practice, Implications and Theory. London: Constable.

45. Baumeister, R.F. and Tierney, J. (2010) *Willpower: Why Self-Control is the Secret of Success*. London: Penguin.

46. Rose, N. (1989) *Governing the Soul: The Shaping of the Private Self*. London: Routledge.

47. Hill, C.E., Gelso, C.J. and Mohr, J.J. (2000) 'Client Concealment and Self-presentation in Therapy: Comment on Kelly', *Psychological Bulletin* 126(4) (July): 495–500; discussion 505–11.

48. Kelly, A.E. (2000) 'A Self-Presentational View of Psychotherapy: Reply to Hill, Gelso, and Mohr (2000) and to Arkin and Hermann (2000)', *Psychological Bulletin* 126(4) (July): 505–11.

49. Rosenthal, R. (1976) *Experimenter Effects in Behavioral Research* (enlarged edn). New York: Irvington. These effects have been known about from the 1930s (Rosenzweig wrote one of the very first papers on this topic) and have been researched extensively since the 1960s. See Duncan, B.L. (2010) 'Prologue: Saul Rosenzweig: The Founder of the Common Factors', in Duncan et al. (eds), *The Heart and Soul of Change*, p. 19.

50. Rosenthal, L.R. and Jacobson, L. (1992) *Pygmalion in the Classroom: Teacher Expectation and Pupils' Intellectual Development* (expanded edn). New York: Irvington.

51. Blanck, P.D., Rosenthal, R. and Hazzard Cordell, L.D. (1985) 'The Appearance of Justice: Judges' Verbal And Nonverbal Behaviour In Criminal Jury Trials. The Board of Trustees of the Leland Stanford Junior', *Stanford Law Review* November <bbi.syr.edu/publications/blanck_docs/1985.../38StanLRev89.pdf> retrieved 11 February 2013.

52. Ambady, N., LaPlante, D., Nguyen, T., Rosenthal, R., Chaumeton, N. and Levinson, W. (2002) 'Surgeons' Tone of Voice: A Clue to Malpractice History', *Surgery* 132: 5–9.

53. Epstein, W. (2006) *Psychotherapy as Religion: The Civil Divine in America*. Reno: University of Nevada Press.

54. Mair, K. (1992) 'The Myth of Therapist Expertise', in Dryden, W. and Feltham, C. (eds), *Psychotherapy and its Discontents*. Buckinghamshire: Open University.

55. Schinka, J.A. and Velicer, W.F. (2003) *Handbook of Psychology, Research Methods in Psychology*. New York: John Wiley & Sons.

56. Longmore, R. and Worrell, M. (2006) 'Do We Need to Challenge Thoughts in Cognitive Behavior Therapy?', *Clinical Psychology Review* 27 (2007): 173–87, at 185. See also the discussion in Wampold, B.R., Minami, T., Tierney, S.C., Baskin, T.W. and Bhati, K.S. (2005) 'The Placebo Is Powerful: Estimating Placebo Effects in Medicine and Psychotherapy From Randomized Clinical Trials', *Journal of Clinical Psychology* 61(7): 835–54.

57. Howard, A. (2005) *Identity and Counselling*. London: Palgrave; Kline, P. (1992) 'Problems of Methodology in Studies of Psychotherapy', in Dryden and Pilgrim (eds), *Psychotherapy and its Discontents*.

58. Boyle, M. (2002) *Schizophrenia: A Scientific Delusion?* (2nd edn). London: Routledge; Littell, 'Evidence Based Practice: Evidence or Orthodoxy?'.

59. Holmes, J. (2002) 'All You Need Is Cognitive Behavior Therapy?', *British Medical Journal* 324: 288–91; Mair, K. (1992) 'The Myth of Therapist Expertise', in Dryden and Pilgrim (eds), *Psychotherapy and its Discontents*.

60. Epstein, *Psychotherapy as Religion: The Civil Divine in America*.

61. Davies, *Counselling in Psychological Services*.

62. Erwin, E. (1997) *Psychotherapy and Philosophy*. London and New York: Sage.

63. Epstein, W. (1996) *The Illusion of Psychotherapy*. New York: Transaction.

64. Epstein, *Psychotherapy as Religion: The Civil Divine in America*.

65. Epstein, W. (2013) *Empowerment as Ceremony*. Piscataway, NJ: Transaction Publishers.

66. See Schwartz, N (1999) 'Self-Reports: How the Questions Shape the Answers', *American Psychologist* 54(2): 93–105. Schwartz observes that reports of general experiences (such as the experience of psychotherapy) capture people's 'beliefs about their experience rather than the experience itself' (p. 14).

67. Epstein, *Psychotherapy as Religion: The Civil Divine in America*, p. 220.

68. Bohart, A.C. (2000) 'The Client is the Most Important Common Factor: Client's Self Healing Capacities and Psychotherapy', Journal of Psychotherapy Integration 10: 127–50. See also Cooper, M. (2008) *Essential Research Findings in Counselling and Psychotherapy: The Facts are Friendly*. London: Sage.

69. Bohart and Tallman (2010) 'Clients: The Neglected Common Factor in Psychotherapy'.

70. Pilgrim, D. (1997) *Psychotherapy and Society*. Sage: London.

71. Richards, B. (1995) 'Psychotherapy and the Hidden Injuries of Class', *BPS Psychotherapy Section Newsletter* 17: 21–35.

72. Kearny, A. (1996) *Culture, Class and Politics: Undisclosed Influences in Therapy and Counselling*. Ross-on-Wye: PCCS Books Ltd.

73. Schofield, W. (1964) Psychotherapy: The Purchase of Friendship. New York: Transaction.

74. See Illouz, E. (2008) *Saving the Modern Soul: Therapy, Emotions, and the Culture of Self-Help*. Berkeley: University of California Press.

75. Falconnier, L. (2010) 'Social Class and Work Functioning in Treatment for Depression', *Psychiatric Services* 61(7): 718–21.

76. Mahrer, A. (1998) 'Embarrassing Problems for the Field of Psychotherapy', *BPS Psychotherapy Section Newsletter* 23(3): 3–25; Smail, D.J. (1978) *Psychotherapy, a Personal Approach*. London: Dent.

77. Sparks, J.A. and Duncan, B.L. (2010) 'Common Factors in Couple and Family Therapy: Must All Have Prizes?', in Duncan et al. (eds), *The Heart and Soul of Change*; see Mair, 'The Myth of Therapist Expertise'.

78. Masson, G. (1989) *Against Therapy*. London: Fontana.

79. Weldon, F. (1999) 'Mind at the End of its Tether', in Feltham, C. (ed.), *Controversies in Psychotherapy and Counseling*. London: Sage.

80. See, for example, Duggan, C., Huband, N., Smailagic, N., et al. (2007) 'The Use of Psychological Treatments for People with Personality Disorder: A Systematic Review of Randomized Controlled Trials', *Personality and Mental Health* 1: 95–125. They sound an unusual note of caution: 'these results frequently come from a few centres with charismatic leaders', p. 122.

81. Baldwin, S.A., Wampold, B.E. and Imel, Z.E. (2007) 'Untangling the Alliance Outcome Correlation: Exploring the Relative Importance of Therapist and Patient Variability in the Alliance', *Journal of Clinical and Consulting Psychology* 75: 842–52.

82. Feltham, C. (1999) 'Against and Beyond Core Theoretical Models', in Feltham (ed.), *Controversies in Psychotherapy and Counseling*.

83. Johnstone, L. (2006) 'Controversies and Debates about Formulation Psychology and Psychotherapy', in Johnstone, L. and Dallos, R. (eds), *Formulation in Psychology and Psychotherapy*. Hove, Sussex: Routledge.

84. Chadwick, P. et al. (2003) 'Impact of Case Formulation in Cognitive Behaviour Therapy for Psychosis', Behaviour Research and Therapy 41: 671–80, at 675.

85. Johnstone, 'Controversies and Debates about Formulation Psychology and Psychotherapy', p. 218.

86. Hubble et al., 'Introduction', in Duncan et al. (eds) *The Heart and Soul of Change*.

87. Feltham, C. (1998) 'Against and beyond core theoretical models', in Feltham (ed.) *Controversies in Psychotherapy and Counselling*, p. 187.

88. Durlak, J. (1979) 'Comparative Effectiveness of Paraprofessional and Professional Helpers', *Psychological Bulletin* 86: 80–92.

89. Shapiro, D.A. and Shapiro, D. (1982) 'Meta-analysis of comparative Therapy outcome Studies. A Replication and Refinement', *Psychological Bulletin* 92: 581–604; Weisz, J.R., Weiss, B., Alicke, M.D. and Klotz, M.L. (1987) 'Effectiveness of Psychotherapy with Children and Adolescents. A Meta-analysis for Clinicians', *Journal of Consulting and Clinical Psychology* 55: 542–9.

90. Nietzel, M.T. and Fisher, S.G. (1981) 'Effectiveness of Paraprofessional and Professional Helpers. A Comment on Durlak', *Psychological Bulletin* 89: 555–65.

91. Hattie, J.A., Sharpley, C.F. and Rogers, J.H. (1984) 'Comparative Effectiveness of Professional and Paraprofessional Helpers', *Psychological Bulletin* 95(3) (May): 534–41, at 534.

92. Berman, J.S. and Norton, N.C. (1985) 'Does Professional Training Make a Therapist More Effective?', *Psychological Bulletin* 98: 401–6, at 405.

93. Dawes, R.M. (1994) *House of Cards: Psychology and Psychotherapy Built on Myth*. New York: The Free Press, p. 5.

94. Stein, D.M. and Lambert, M.J. (1995) 'Graduate Training in Psychotherapy: Are Therapy Outcomes Enhanced?', *Journal of Consulting and Clinical Psychology* 63: 182–96.

95. Cooper, M. (2008) *Essential Research Findings in Counselling and Psychotherapy: The Facts are Friendly*. London: Sage; Duncan et al., *The Heart and Soul of Change*; Mcleod, J. (2009) *An Introduction to Counselling* (4th edn). Basingstoke: Open University Press.

96. Also, see the discussion in McLenan, J. (1998) 'Becoming An Effective Counsellor: Are Training And Supervision Necessary?', in Feltham (ed.), *Controversies in Psychotherapy and Counselling*.

97. Stolk, Y. and Perlesz, A.J. (1990) 'Do Better Trainees Make Worse Family Therapists? A Follow-Up Study of Client Families', *Family Process*, 29: 45–8; Strupp, H.H. and Hadley, S.W. (1979) 'Specific Versus Nonspecific Factors in Psychotherapy: A Controlled Study of Outcome', *Archives of General Psychiatry* 36: 1125–36.

98. Stolk and Perlesz, 'Do Better Trainees Make Worse Family Therapists?'.

99. Davies, D. (1997) *Counselling in Psychological Services*. Buckinghamshire: Open University Press; Bostock, J. (1990) 'Clinical Training and Clinical Reality', *British Psychological Society Psychotherapy Section Newsletter* 8: 2–7.

100. Dryden, W. (1995) The Stresses of Counselling in Action. London: Sage; Holmes, G. (2001) 'So Farewell Then, CMHTs', Clinical Psychology 6: 7–10.

101. Deutsch, C.J. (1984) 'Self-reported Sources of Stress Among Psychotherapists', *Professional Psychology* 15: 833–45; Epstein, *The Illusion of Psychotherapy*.

102. Dineen, T. (1998) *Manufacturing Victims: What the Psychology Industry is Doing to People*. London: Constable; Epstein, *The Illusion of Psychotherapy*.

103. Bickman, L., Guthrie, E.R., Foster, E.M., Lambert, E.W., Summerfelt, W.T., Breda, C.S. and Heflinger, C.A. (1995) *Evaluating Managed Mental Health Services: The Fort Bragg Experiment*. New York: Plenum Press; Bickman, L. (1996) 'A Continuum of Care: More is Not Always Better', *American Psychologist* 51: 689–701.

104. Bickman, L., Summerfelt, W.T., Firth, J. and Douglas, S. (1997) 'The Stark County Evaluation Project: Baseline Results of a Randomized Experiment', in Northrup, D. and Nixon, C. (eds), *Evaluating Mental Health Serivces: How Do Programs for Children 'Work' in the Real World?* Newbury Park, CA: Sage Publications – quoted in Dineen, *Manufacturing Victims*, p. 198.

105. London School of Economics (2006) *The Depression Report: A New Deal for Depression and Anxiety Disorders*. London: Centre for Economic Performance's Mental Health Policy Group, LSE.

106. Shapiro, F. (2012) *Getting Past Your Past: Take Control of Your Life with Self-Help Techniques from EMDR Therapy*. New York: Rodale.

107. See, for instance, Lilienfeld, S.O. (1996) 'EMDR Treatment: Less than Meets the Eye', *Skeptical Inquirer* 20(1): 25–31. For an update, see Lilienfeld, S.O. (2011) *EMDR Treatment: Still Less than Meets the Eye* <http://www.quackwatch.com/01QuackeryRelatedTopics/emdr.html> retrieved 22 February 2012.

108. Seligman, E.P. (1995) 'The Effectiveness of Psychotherapy: The Consumer Reports Study', *American Psychologist* 50(12): 965–74.

109. See the discussion in Howard, *Identity and Counselling*.

110. Dawes, *House of Cards*, p. 59.

111. See Duncan et al. (eds), *The Heart and Soul of Change*.

112. Epstein, W. (1998) 'The Ineffectiveness of Psychotherapy', in Feltham (ed.), *Controversies in Psychotherapy and Counselling*.

113. For example, Cooper, *Essential Research Findings in Counselling and Psychotherapy*; and Duncan et al. (eds), *The Heart and Soul of Change*.

114. Arnold, E.L. (2007) 'Political Zeal as Theological Science', *Journal of the American Academy of Child and Adolescent Psychiatry* 46(8) (August): 1088–191, at 1090.

115. Ibid., p. 1091.

116. See Miller, S.D., Hubble, M.A., Duncan, B.L. and Wampold, B.E. (2010) 'Delivering What Works', in Duncan et al. (eds), *The Heart and Soul of Change*.

117. Pilgrim, D. (2009) Straight Talking Introduction to Psychological Treatments for Mental Health Problems (Straight Talking Introductions series – Bentall, R. and Sanders, P. series eds). Ross-on-Wye: PCCS Books, Ltd.

118. See, for example, The National Collaborative Centre for Mental Health (2009) *Depression: The Treatment and Management of Depression in Adults*. London: National Institute for Health and Clinical Excellence. For other good examples of NICE's undue confidence in the results of meta-analytic studies in talking therapy, see Guy, A., Thomas, R., Stephenson, S. and Loewenthal, D. (2011) *NICE Under Scrutiny: The Impact of the National Institute for Health and Clinical Excellence Guidelines on the Provision of Psychotherapy in the UK, June 2011*. Roehampton: UK Council for Psychotherapy.

119. Charlton, B. (2005) 'Infostat, Cargo-cult Science and the Policy Sausage Machine: NICE, CHI and the Managerial Takeover of Clinical Practice', in Hampton, M.J.R. and Hurwitz, B. (eds), *NICE, CHI and the NHS Reforms: Enabling Excellence or Imposing Control?* London: Aesculapius Medical Press.

120. Charlton, B. (1996) 'The Uses and Abuses of Meta-analysis', *Family Practice* 13(4): 397–401.

CHAPTER 5   'I'M NOT ILL, I'M HURT …' – THE HIDDEN INJURIES OF INEQUALITY

1. Adam, D. (2003) 'I am a Cliché', *Variant* 2(18): 25–6.

2. Wilkinson, R. and Pickett, K. (2010) *The Spirit Level: Why Equality is Better for Everyone*, 2nd edn. London: Penguin.

3. Office of National Statistics (2010) *Life Expectancy at Birth and at age 65 by Local Areas in the United Kingdom, 2004–06 to 2008–10*. London: HMSO. For the broader picture in respect of the western industrialised world, see Wilkinson and Pickett, *The Spirit Level*.

4. Organization for Economic Cooperation and Development (2011) *Society: Governments Must Tackle Record Gap Between Rich and Poor, says OECD* <http://www.oecd.org/newsroom/societygovernmentsmusttacklerecordgap betweenrichandpoorsaysoecd.htm> retrieved 11 February 2013.

5. Lelliot, P., Tulloch, S., Boardman, J., Harvey, S., Henderson, M. and Knapp, M. (2008) *Mental Health and Work*. London: Royal College of Psychiatrists; Mental Health Foundation (2012) *Mental Health Statistics* <http://www. mentalhealth.org.uk/help-information/mental-health-statistics/> retrieved 12 October 2012.

6. Centre for Mental Health (2010) *The Economic and Social Costs of Mental Health Problems in 2009/10*. London: Centre for Mental Health. See also

O'Brien, N. (2012) 'The Remarkable Rise of Mental Illness in Britain', *Daily Telegraph*, 30 October 2012 <http://blogs.telegraph.co.uk/news/neilobrien1/100186974/the-remarkable-rise-of-mental-illness-in-britain/> retrieved 11 February 2013.

7. Kessler, R., Bergland, P., Demler, O., Jin, R. and Walters, E.E. (2005) 'Lifetime Prevalence and Age-of-onset Distributions of DSM-IV Disorders in the National Comorbidity Survey Replication. *Archives of General Psychiatry* 62: 593–602.

8. Gore, F. et al. (2011) 'Global Burden of Disease in Young People Aged 10–24 Years: A Systematic Analysis', *The Lancet*, 377(9783): 2093–102, 18 June.

9. Lelliot et al., *Mental Health and Work*.

10. Horwitz, A.V. and Wakefield, J.C. (2007) *The Loss of Sadness: How Psychiatry Transformed Normal Sorrow into Depressive Disorder*. Oxford and New York: Oxford University Press.

11. Boyle, M. (2007) 'The Problem with Diagnosis', *The Psychologist* 20(5): 290–92.

12. Szasz, T. (1974) *The Myth of Mental Illness: Foundations of a Theory of Personal Conduct*. New York: Harper and Row.

13. Davies, D. (1997) *Counselling in Psychological Services*. Milton Keynes: Open University Press.

14. Hollingshead, A.B. and Redlich, F.C. (1954) 'Schizophrenia and Social Structure', *American Journal of Psychiatry* 110: 695–701; Ryan, J. (1971) *Blaming the Victim*. New York: Random House.

15. Crisis (2011) *Homelessness: A Silent Killer. A Research Briefing on Mortality Amongst Homeless People*. December. London: Crisis.

16. Fazel, S., Kosla, V. and Geddes, J. (2008) 'The Prevalence of Mental Disorders among the Homeless in Western Countries: Systematic Review and Meta-Regression Analysis', *PLoS Med* 5(12): e225 <http://www.plosmedicine.org/article/info%3Adoi%2F10.1371%2Fjournal.pmed.0050225> retrieved 11 February 2013.

17. Goodman, L., Dutton, M.A. and Harris, M. (1995) 'Episodically Homeless Women with Serious Mental Illness: Prevalence of Physical and Sexual Assault', *Journal of Orthopsychiatry* 65(4): 468–78.

18. Fazel, Kosla and Geddes, 'The Prevalence of Mental Disorders among the Homeless in Western Countries'.

19. Pilgrim, D. and Rogers, A. (2010) *A Sociology of Mental Health and Illness* (4th edn). Basingstoke: McGraw Hill Educational/Open University Press.

20. Melzer, D., Fryers, T. and Jenkins, R. (2004) *Social Inequalities and the Distribution of the Common Mental Disorders*, Maudsley Monograph 44. Hove and New York: Psychology Press.

21. Payne, S. (1995) *Poverty, Social Exclusion and Mental Health: Findings from the 1999 PSE Survey*, Working Paper Number 15. Bristol: Townsend Centre for International Poverty Research.

22. Boardman, A.P., Hodgson, R.E., Lewis, M. and Allen, K. (1997) 'Social Indicators and the Prediction of Psychiatric Admission in Different Diagnostic Groups', *British Journal of Psychiatry* 171: 457–62.

23. Payne, *Poverty, Social Exclusion and Mental Health*.

24. Joseph, J. (2003) *The Gene Illusion: Genetic Research in Psychiatry and Psychology under the Microscope*. Ross-On-Wye: PCCS Books, Ltd.

25. Joseph, J. and Ratner, C. (2013) 'The Fruitless Search for Genes in Psychiatry and Psychology: Time to Re-Examine a Paradigm', in Krimsky, S. and Gruber, J. (eds), *Genetic Explanations: Sense and Nonsense*. Cambridge, MA: Harvard University Press.

26. Horwitz and Wakefield, *The Loss of Sadness*.

27. Ibid.

28. Hidakh, B.H. (2012) 'Depression as a disease of modernity: explanations for increasing prevalence', *Journal of Affective Disorder* 140(3) (November): 205–14.

29. Hawton, K. and van Heeringen, K. (2009) 'Suicide', *The Lancet* 373(9672): 1372–81.

30. Scull, A. (2009) *Hysteria: A Biography*. Oxford: Oxford University Press.

31. Boyle, M. (2002) *Schizophrenia: A Scientific Delusion?* (2nd edn). London: Routledge.

32. Prinz, J. (2012) *Beyond Human Nature: How Culture and Experience Shape Our Lives*. London: Allen Lane.

33. Horgan, J. (1993) 'Eugenics Revisited', *Scientific American* 268(6): 122–31; Joseph, J. (2011) 'The Crumbling Pillars of Behavioural Genetics', *GeneWatch*, 24(6): 4–7.

34. Kagan, J. (2012) *Psychology's Ghosts*. New Haven, CT and London: Yale University Press, p. 53.

35. Ibid.

36. Ingleby, D. (2004) 'Understanding Mental Illness', in Ingleby, D. (ed.), *Critical Psychiatry: The Politics of Mental Health*. New York: Free Association Books, p. 39.

37. Read, J. (2010) 'Can Poverty Drive you Mad? Schizophrenia, Socio-Economic Status and the Case of Primary Prevention', *New Zealand Journal of Psychology* 39(2): 7–19.

38. See, for example, the studies selected by Melzer, Fryers and Jenkins, *Social Inequalities and the Distribution of the Common Mental Disorders*.

39. Scott, S., Craig, G. and Geddes, S. (2012) *Experiences of Forced Labour in the UK Food Industry*. York: Joseph Rowntree Foundation. For a journalistic account, see Ehrenreich, B. (2001) *Nickled and Dimed: Undercover in Low Wage USA*. London: Granta.

40. Tombs, S. (2004) 'Workplace Injury and Death: Social Harm and the Illusions of Law', in Hilyard, P. et al. (eds), *Beyond Criminality: Taking Harm Seriously*. London: Pluto Press. For crime and neighbourhood effects, see Dorling, D. and Thomas, B. (2011) *Bankrupt Britain: An Atlas of Social Change*. Bristol: The Policy Press.

41. Road Safety Analysis Group (2010) *Child Casualties 2010: A Study Into Resident Risk of Children on Roads in Great Britain 2004–08*. Gloucestershire: Road Safety Analysis Ltd.

42. Tomlinson, M. and Walker, R. (2009) *Coping With Complexity: Child and Adult Poverty*. London: Child Poverty Action Group.

43. Downey, L. and Van Willingen, M. (2005) 'Environmental Stressors: The Mental Health Impacts of Living Near Industrial Activity', *Journal of Health Social Behavior* 46(3) (September): 289–305.

44. Phillips, D. (1968) 'Social Class and Psychological Disturbance: The Influence of Negative and Positive Life Events', *Social Psychiatry* 3: 41–6.

45. Freidli, L. (2009) *Mental Health, Resilience and Inequalities*. Copenhagen: World Health Organization.
46. Bauman, Z. (2004) *Work, Consumerism and the New Poor*. Berkshire: Open University Press.
47. Marmot, M. and Stafford, S. (2003) 'Neighbourhood Deprivation and Health: Does It Affect Us All Equally?', *International Journal of Epidemiology* 32(3) (June): 357–66.
48. Orford, J. (2008) *Community Psychology: Challenges, Controversies and Emerging Consensus*. London and Chichester: John Wiley and Sons Ltd; Rogers, A. and Pilgrim, D. (2003) *Social Inequality and Mental Health*. London: Palgrave Macmillan.
49. NSPCC (2008) *Child Protection Research Briefing: Poverty and Child Maltreatment*. London: NSPCC.
50. Ussher, J. (2011) *The Madness of Women: Myth and Experience*. Hove, East Sussex: Routledge.
51. Rogers, A. and Pilgrim, D. (2003) *Social Inequality and Mental Health*. London: Palgrave Macmillan.
52. Widom, C.S. (1998) 'Child Victims: Searching for Opportunities to Break the Cycle of Violence', *Applied & Preventive Psychology* 7: 225–34.
53. Rogers and Pilgrim, *Social Inequality and Mental Health*. London: Palgrave Macmillan.
54. Stoppard, J. (1998) *Understanding Depression: Feminist Social Constructionist Approaches*. London: Routledge.
55. Malik, K. (2009) *Strange Fruit*. London: Oneworld Publications.
56. Ibid.
57. Pilgrim, D. (1997) *Psychotherapy and Society*. London: Sage.
58. Ibid.
59. Beliapa, J. (1991) *Illness or Distress? Alternative Models of Mental Health*. Newcastle upon Tyne: Confederation of Indian Organisations (UK).
60. Ibid.
61. Department of Health (2005) *Delivering Race Equality in Mental Health Care: An Action Plan for Reform Inside and Outside Services*. London: Department of Health.
62. Lloyd, C. (1995) *The Irish Community in Britain: Discrimination, Disadvantage and Racism*. London: University of North London Press.
63. Fernando, S. (2002) *Mental Health, Race and Culture* (2nd edn). London: Palgrave Macmillan.
64. Lipsdge, M. and Littlewood. R. (1997) *Aliens and Alienists: Ethnic Minorities and Psychiatry* (3rd edn). London: Routledge.
65. Tinghog, P., Hemmingson, T. and Lundberg, I. (2007) 'To What Extent may the Association Between Immigrant Status and Mental Illness be Explained by Socioeconomic Factors?', *Social Psychiatry and Psychiatric Epidemiology* 42: 990–96.
66. Pilgrim, D. and Rogers, A. (2010) *A Sociology of Mental Health and Illness* (4th edn). Buckinghamshire: McGraw Hill Educational, Open University Press.
67. Sayad, A. (2004) *The Suffering of the Immigrant*, trans. David Macey. London: Polity Press Ltd.
68. Fernando, *Mental Health, Race and Culture*.
69. Tinghog, P., Hemmingson, T. and Lundberg, I. (2007) 'To What Extent may the Association Between Immigrant Status and Mental Illness be Explained

by Socioeconomic Factors?', *Social Psychiatry and Psychiatric Epidemiology* 42: 990–96.

70. Phinney, J.S., Horenczyk, G., Leibkind, K. and Vedder, P. (2001) 'Ethnic Identity, Immigration and Wellbeing', *Journal of Social Issues* 57(3): 493–510.

71. Jahoda, M. (1982) *Employment and Unemployment: A Social-Psychological Analysis*. Cambridge: The Press Syndicate of the University of Cambridge.

72. Platt, S. (1984) 'Unemployment and Suicidal Behaviour: A Review of the Literature', *Social Science & Medicine* 19(2): 93–115.

73. Whooley, M., Kiefe, C., Chesney, M., Markovitz, J., Matthews, K. and Hulley, S. (2002) 'Depressive Symptoms, Unemployment, and Loss of Income. The CARDIA Study', *Arch Intern Med* 162: 2614–20.

74. Fryer, D. (1995) 'Benefit, Labour Market Disadvantage, Deprivation and Mental Health', *The Psychologist* 8: 265–72.

75. Ibid.

76. Paul, K.I. and Moser, K. (2009) 'Unemployment Impairs Mental Health: Meta-analyses', *Journal of Vocational Behavior* 74(3): 264–82.

77. Lampard, R. (1994) 'An Examination of the Relationship between Marital Dissolution and Unemployment', in Gallie, D., Marsh, C. and Volger, C. (eds), *Social Change and the Experience of Unemployment*. Oxford: Oxford University Press.

78. Marmot, M. and Wilkinson, R. (2006) *Social Determinants of Health* (2nd edn). Oxford: Oxford University Press; Ashby, K. (2010) *At Work on a Low Income. A Qualitative Study of Employees' Experiences*. London: The Work Foundation.

79. Walker, C. and Fincham, B. (2011) *Work and the Mental Health Crisis in Britain*. Chichester: Willey-Blackwell.

80. Marmot, M. (2004) *Status Syndrome: How Your Social Standing Directly Affects Your Health*. London: Bloomsbury.

81. Sennett, R. (2006) *The Culture of the New Capitalism*. New Haven, CT and London: Yale University Press.

82. Wainright, D. and Calnan, M. (2002) *Work Stress: The Making of a Modern Epidemic*. Buckinghamshire: Open University Press.

83. Channel 4 News (2011) 'Teacher Suicide Rates Rises by 80 Percent' (16 June) <http://www.channel4.com/news/teachers-suicide-rates-double-in-a-year> retrieved 30 July 2012.

84. Rogers and Pilgrim, *Social Inequality and Mental Health*.

85. Department of Health and Social Security (1980) *Inequalities in Health: Report of a Research Working Group*. London: DHSS, 1980.

86. Wilkinson and Pickett, *The Spirit Level*.

87. Wilkinson, R. (1996) *Unhealthy Societies: The Afflictions of Inequality*. London: Routledge, p. 107.

88. Orwell, G. (2012) *Charles Dickens* <http://orwell.ru/library/reviews/dickens/english/e_chd> retrieved 4 May 2012.

89. Wilkinson, and Pickett, *The Spirit Level*.

90. Runciman, W.G. (1966) *Relative Deprivation and Social Justice*. London: Routledge and Kegan Paul.

91. Sennett, R. and Cobb, J. (1972) *The Hidden Injuries Of Class*. New York: W.W. Norton.

92. Charlesworth, S.J. (1999) *A Phenomenology of Working-Class Experience*. Cambridge: Cambridge University Press.

93. Morgan, A. (2008) 'The Authority of Lived Experience', in Morgan, A. (ed.), *Being Human: Reflections on Mental Distress in Society*. Ross-on-Wye: PCCS Books Ltd.

94. Navarro, V. (ed.) (2002) *The Political Economy of Social Inequalities: Consequences for Health and Quality of Life*. New York: Baywood Publishing Company.

95. Muntaner, C. and Lynch, J. (2002) 'Income Inequality, Social Cohesion, and Class Relations: A Critique of Wilkinson's Neo-Durkheimian Research Program', in Navarro, *The Political Economy of Social Inequalities*.

96. Wainright and Calnan, *Work Stress*.

97. Sayer, A. (2005) *The Moral Significance of Class*. Cambridge: Cambridge University Press.

98. Gifford, R. (2008) 'The Consequences of Living in High Rise Buildings', *Architectural Science Review* 50(1): 1–20.

99. Davidson, J. (2000) 'A Phenomenology of Fear: Merleau-Ponty and Agoraphobic Life-worlds', *Sociology of Health and Illness* 22(5): 640–60.

100. Gunnel, B. (2004) 'Why Privacy is a Matter of Money', *New Statesman*, 19 January: 29–30.

101. Muntaner and Lynch, 'Income Inequality, Social Cohesion, and Class Relations', p. 330.

102. Bunting, M. (2004) *Willing Slaves: How the Overwork Culture is Ruling Our Lives*. London: HarperCollins; Walker, C. and Fincham, B. (2011) *Work and the Mental Health Crisis in Britain*. London: Wiley-Blackwell.

103. Muntaner, C., Borrell, C., Benach, J., Pasarin, M.I. and Fernandez, E. (2003) 'The Associations of Social Class and Social Stratification with Patterns of General and Mental Health in a Spanish Population', *International Journal of Epidemiology* 32: 950–58.

104. Borrell, C., Muntaner, C., Benach, J. and Artazcoz, L. (2004) 'Social Class and Self-reported Health Status Among Men and Women: What is the Role of Work Organisation, Household Material Standards and Household Labour?', *Social Science and Medicine* 58: 1869–87.

105. Muntaner, C., Li, Y., Xue, X., O'Campo, P., Chung, H.J. and Eaton, W.W. (2006) 'County Level Socioeconomic Position, Work Organization and Depression Disorder: A Repeated Measures Cross-classified Multilevel Analysis of Low-income Nursing Home Workers', *Health and Place* 12: 688–700.

106. Holmes, G. (2012) 'Introductory Paper: If We are to Have Mental Health Services, Let's Centre Them on Concepts of Trauma, not Illness', *Journal of Critical Psychology, Counselling and Psychotherapy* 12(3): 127–30.

CHAPTER 6   SWEET MEDICINE – TALKING THERAPY AS CONTROL

1. Engels, F. (2009) *The Condition of the Working Class in England*. London: Penguin, p. 74.

2. Reiff, P. (1966) *Triumph of the Therapeutic*. New York: Harper & Row.

3. Lasch, C. (1984) *The Minimal Self: Psychic Survival in Troubled Times*. New York: Norton.

4. Throop, E. (2009) *Psychotherapy, American Culture, and Social Policy: Immoral Individualism*. New York: Palgrave Macmillan.

5. Furedi, F. (2003) *Therapy Culture: Cultivating Vulnerability in an Uncertain Age*. London: Routledge.

6. Dineen, T. (1998) *Manufacturing Victims: What the Psychology Industry is Doing to People*. London: Constable.

7. Illouz, E. (2008) *Saving the Modern Soul: Therapy, Emotions and the Culture of Self-help*. Berkeley and London: University of California Press.

8. Cameron, D. (2000) *Good to Talk? Living and Working in a Communication Culture*. London: Sage.

9. Johnstone, L. (2000) *Users and Abusers of Psychiatry* (2nd edn). London: Routledge.

10. Illouz cites a wide range of laboratory research from social and cognitive psychology, which shows that people make poorer judgements and decisions when they are forced to substitute the ideas of experts for their own: Illouz, *Saving the Modern Soul*.

11. Department for Education and Skills (2005) *Social, Emotional Aspects of Learning – Guidance*. London: DfES.

12. Ecclestone, K. and Hayes, D. (2008) *Therapeutic Education*. London: Routledge.

13. Churches, R. and West-Burnham, J. (2008) *Leading Learning Through Relationships: The Implications of Neuro-linguistic Programming for Personalisation and the Children's Agenda in England*. Berkshire: CfB Educational Trust.

14. Throop, *Psychotherapy, American Culture, and Social Policy*; Emler, N. (2001) *Self-esteem: The Costs and Causes of Low Self-worth*. London: Joseph Rowntree Foundation.

15. Reay, D. (2006) 'The Zombie Stalking English Schools: Social Class and Educational Inequality', *British Journal of Educational Studies* 54(3) (September): 288–307.

16. Davies, N. (2000) *The School Report*. London: Vintage. For an American perspective, see Marsh, J. (2011) *Class Dismissed. Why We Cannot Teach or Learn Our Way out of Inequality*. New York: Monthly Reveiw Press.

17. Furedi, F. (2004) *Where Have All the Intellectuals Gone? Confronting 21st Century Philistinism*. London: Continuum.

18. Summerfield, D. (2007) 'The Invention of Post-Traumatic Stress Disorder and the Social Usefulness of a Psychiatric Category', *BMJ* 322: 95–8.

19. Bracken, P. (2002) *Trauma: Culture, Meaning and Philosophy*. London and Philadelphia, PA: Wurr. See also Summerfield, D. (2004) 'Cross-cultural Perspectives on the Medicalisation of Human Suffering', in Rosen, G. (ed.), *Posttraumatic Stress Disorder: Issues and Controversies*. New York: John Wiley.

20. Watters, E. (2010) *Crazy Like Us: The Globalization of the American Psyche*. New York: Free Press.

21. Pupavac, V. (2001) 'Therapeutic Governance: Psycho-social Intervention and Trauma Risk Management', *Disasters* 25(4): 358–72.

22. Polman, L. (2010) *War Games: The Story of Aid and War in Modern Times*. London: Viking.

23. Garland, D. (2002) *The Culture of Control: Crime and Social Order in Contemporary Society*. Oxford: Oxford University Press.

24. See Worrell, A. (2004) 'What Works and the Globalisation of Punishment Talk', in Mair, G. (ed.), *What Matters in Probation*. Cullompton: Willan Publishing.

25. Smith, D. (2004) 'The Uses and Abuses of Positivism; in Mair (ed.), *What Matters in Probation*.

26. Quoting from a senior probation officer, in Kendall, K. (2004) 'Dangerous Thinking: A Critical History of Correctional Cognitive Behaviourism', in Mair (ed.), *What Matters In Probation*, p. 53.

27. Fraser, D. (2006) *A Land Fit for Criminals*. London: Book Guild Ltd, p. 189.

28. Farrall, S. (2004) 'Supervision, Motivation and Social Context: What Matters Most When Probationers Desist?', in Mair (ed.), *What Matters in Probation*.

29. Mair, G. (2004) 'The Origins of What Works in England and Wales: A House Built on Sand?', in Mair (ed.), *What Matters in Probation*.

30. Fraser, *A Land Fit for Criminals*.

31. Vennard, J., Sugg, D. and Hedderman, C. (1997) 'Part I. The Use of Cognitive Behavioural Approaches with Offenders – Messages from the Research', in *Changing Offenders' Attitudes and Behaviour: What Works?* Home Office Research Study 171. London: Home Office Research and Statistics Directorate, p. 33.

32. Smith, 'The Uses and Abuses of Positivism'.

33. Laub, J.H. and Sampson, R.J. (2003) *Shared Beginnings, Divergent Lives: Delinquent Boys to Age 70*. Cambridge, MA: Harvard University Press, p. 279.

34. Dorling, D. (2010) *Injustice: Why Social Inequality Persists*. Bristol: Policy Press; Wilkinson, R. and Pickett, K. (2012) *The Spirit Level* (2nd edn). London: Penguin.

35. In England and Wales, a young black person is 30 times more likely than a white person to be stopped and searched by the police under Section 60: 'Stop and Search "Racial Profiling" by the Police Increases, Claims Study', *Guardian*, 14 January 2012 <http://www.guardian.co.uk/law/2012/jan/14/stop-search-racial-profiling-police> retrieved 8 January 2013.

36. Hilyard, P. and Tombs, S. (2004) 'Beyond Criminology?', in Hilyard, P., Pantazis, C., Tombs, S. and Gordon, D. (eds) *Beyond Criminology: Taking Harm Seriously*. London: Pluto Press.

37. Morrell, G. et al. (2011) *The August Riots in England: Understanding the Involvement of Young People*. London: National Centre for Social Research.

38. Porter, R. (1999) *The Greatest Benefit to Mankind: A Medical History of Humanity*. New York and London: W.H. Norton and Co.

39. Ogden, J. (2012) *Health Psychology: A Textbook* (5th edn). Berskhire: Open University Press.

40. Coyne, J.C. (2010) Editorial: 'Current Issues and New Directions in *Psychology and Health*. The Role of the Critic in Health Psychology: The Healthy Scepticism Project', *Psychology and Health* 25(6) (July): 647–50, at 648.

41. Coyne, J.C. and Thomb, B.D. (2010) 'Ain't Necessarily So: Review and Critique of Recent Meta-Analyses of Behavioural Medicine Interventions in *Health Psychology*', *Health Psychology* 29(2): 107–16.

42. Newson, L. and Flint, B. (2011) 'Applied Psychology and Obesity Management', in Obesity Working Group (eds), *Obesity in the UK: A Psychological Perspective*. Leicester: BPS.

43. Flegal, K.M and Graubard, B.I (2009) 'Estimates of Excess Deaths Associated with Body Mass Index and Other Anthropometric Variables', *American Journal of Clinical Nutrition* 89: 1213–19.

44. The Emerging Risk Factors Collaboration (2012) 'Separate and Combined Associations of Body-mass Index and Abdominal Adiposity with Cardiovascular Disease: Collaborative Analysis of 58 Prospective Studies', *The Lancet* 377(9771): 1085–95.

45. Lyons, R (2012) *Panic on a Plate: How Society Developed an Eating Disorder.* London: Civitas.

46. Campos, P. (2004) *The Obesity Myth.* New York: Gotham.

47. Monaghan, L. (2008) *Men and the War on Obesity.* London: Routledge.

48. Campos, *The Obesity Myth*; Aphromor, L. (2005) 'Is a Weight-Centred Health Framework Salutogenic? Some Thoughts on Unhinging Certain Dietary Ideologies'. *Social Theory and Health* 3(4): 315–40. See also Lyons, *Panic on a Plate* and Monaghan, *Men and the War on Obesity.*

49. Myslobodsky, M. (2004) *The Fallacy of Mother's Wisdom: A Critical Perspective on Health Psychology.* Singapore: World Scientific.

50. Radley, A. (2004) 'Suffering', in Murray, M. (ed.), *Critical Health Psychology.* London: Palgrave, p. 42.

51. Crossley, M. (2000) *Rethinking Health Psychology.* Buckingham: Open University Press.

52. Graham, H. (1998) 'Health at Risk: Poverty and National Health Strategies'. in Doyal, L. (ed.), *Women and Health Services.* Buckingham: Open University Press.

53. Becker, M.H. (1986) 'The Tyranny of Health Promotion', *Public Health Review* 14: 15–23.

54. Thaler, T.H. and Sustein, C.R. (2008) *Nudge: Improving Decisions about Health, Wealth and Happiness.* New Haven, CT: Yale University Press.

55. BBC News (2004) 'Government Unit "Urges Fat Tax"', 19 February <http://news.bbc.co.uk/2/hi/health/3502053.stm> retrieved 8 January 2013.

56. Wintour, P. (2010) 'David Cameron's "Nudge Unit" Aims to Improve Economic Behaviour', *The Guardian*, 10 September, p. 14.

57. Basham, P. (2010) *Are Nudging and Shoving Good for Public Health?* London: Democracy Institute.

58. Ibid.; Wilkinson and Pickett, *The Spirit Level.*

59. Furedi, F. (2008) *Paranoid Parenting: Why Ignoring the Experts May be Best for Your Child.* London: Continuum, pp. 186–7.

60. See, for example, Argyle, M., Trower, P. and Bryant, B. (1978) *Social Skills and Mental Health.* London: Methuen.

61. Paterson, C. (2011) *Parenting Matters.* London: CentreForum.

62. Critics of the Coalition government shortened its name to the 'Con-Dem government'. See, for example, Toynbee, P. and Walker, D. (2012) *Dogma and Disarray: Cameron at Half-Time.* London: Guardian Branded.

63. Craig, A. (2012) 'Can Good Parenting Classes Ever Work?', *Daily Telegraph*, 15 May <http://www.telegraph.co.uk/women/mother-tongue/9264712/Can-good-parenting-classes-ever-work.html> retrieved 8 January 2013.

64. Derbyshire, S. (2011) 'The Pseudoscience of the Parent-bashers', pp. 2–3 <http://www.spiked-online.com/index.php/site/article/11051/> retrieved 31 January 2013

65. Gillies, V. (2005) 'Raising the "Meritocracy": Parenting and the Individualization of Social Class', *Sociology* 39(5): 835–53.

66. Furedi, *Paranoid Parenting*.

67. See, for example, White, M. (1996), 'Single Mothers and Welfare Surveillance'. *The Journal of Critical Social Policy* (Summer 1996): 34–56.

68. *Observer* (2012) Editorial: 'Parenting Classes are a Good Idea. But Families Need So Much More', 20 May <http://www.guardian.co.uk/commentisfree/2012/may/20/editorial-cameron-childcare-plans-welcome> retrieved 22 May 2012.

69. Katrin Benhold, N.I. (2012) 'Cuts in UK Raise Risks for Women' <http://www.asafeworldforwomen.org/economics-poverty/ec-europe/2292-cuts-in-uk-raise-risks-for-women.html> retrieved 16 May 2012.

70. Tzu, L. (1997) *Tao Te Ching*. Kaufman, W. (ed.); Legge, J. (trans) Dover (Thrift Edition); originally published Oxford: Oxford University Press, 1891.

71. Throop, *Psychotherapy, American Culture, and Social Policy*, p. 53.

CHAPTER 7 THEORY INTO PRACTICE – THE PROGRAMME FOR IMPROVING ACCESS TO PSYCHOLOGICAL THERAPIES

1. Galeano, E. (2009) *Mirrors: Stories For Almost Everyone*. Philadelphia, PA: Nation/Perseus.

2. Clark, M. (2011) 'Implementing NICE Guidelines for the Psychological Treatment of Depression and Anxiety Disorders: The IAPT Experience', *International Review of Psychiatry* 23 (August): 375–84.

3. Barnett, A. (2000) 'Corporate Populism and Partyless Democracy', *New Left Review*, 11(3): 217–86.

4. Layard, R. (2005) *Happiness: Lessons from a New Science*. London: Allen Lane, Penguin.

5. Ibid.

6. Patel, N. (2007) 'Torture, Psychology and the "War on Terror": A Human Rights Framework', in Roberts, R. (ed.), *Just War: Psychology and Terrorism*. Ross-On-Wye: PCCS Books, Ltd.

7. He had not listened to equally compelling arguments that CBT 'is a very broad church indeed', see Loewenthal, D. and House, R. (2010) 'Conclusion', in Loewenthal, D. and House, R. (eds), *Critically Engaging CBT*. Berkshire: McGraw Hill, Open University Press, p. 177.

8. Pollock, A. (2005) *NHS Plc: The Privatisation of Our Health Care*. London: Verso.

9. Centre for Economic Performance's Mental Health Policy Group (2006) *The Depression Report: A New Deal for Depression and Anxiety Disorders*. London: London School of Economics and Political Science. See also, Layard, R. (2005) *Therapy for all on the NHS*. http:///www.scm.org.uk/ retrieved July 9, 2008.

10. Layard, R. (2005) *Therapy for all on the NHS*.

11. Centre for Economic Performance's Mental Health Policy Group (2006) *The Depression Report*, p. 1.

12. Clark, 'Implementing NICE Guidelines for the Psychological Treatment of Depression and Anxiety Disorders'.

13. Richards, D. and Suckling, R. (2008) 'Improving Access to Psychological Therapy: The Doncaster Demonstration Site Organisational Model', *Clinical Psychology Forum* 181: 9–16; Care Services Improvement Partnership. National Institute for Mental Health in England. *IAPT Outline Service Specification* <www.iapt.nhs.uk/silo/files/iapt-outline-service-specification.pdf> retrieved 8 January 2013.

14. Anekwe, L. (2008) 'Talking Therapies Scheme is Working, Evaluation Finds', *Pulse*, 24 November <http://www.pulsetoday.co.uk/talking-therapies-scheme-is-working-evaluation-finds/10993152.article#.UOsDSqzvYaw> retrieved 8 January 2013.

15. Ibid.

16. The Midlands Psychological Group. Our Big Fat Multi-Million Pound Psychology Experiment. *Clinical Psychology Forum*. No. 181, January 2008, 34–7.

17. Easton, M. (2008) 'A Lift for Those who are Down', *BBC News: Mark Easton's UK*, 28 October <http://www.bbc.co.uk/blogs/thereporters/markeaston/2008/10/a_lift_for_those_who_are_down.html> retrieved 28 June 2009.

18. Richards and Suckling, 'Improving Access to Psychological Therapy'.

19. HM Government/DoH (2011) *No Health Without Mental Health. A cross-government Mental Health Outcomes Strategy for People of All Ages.* London: DoH.

20. Marzillier, J. and Hall, R. (2009) 'The Challenge of the Layard Initiative', *The Psychologist* 22(5) (May): 396–9, at 396.

21. Kline, P. (1987) *Psychology Exposed: or The Emperor's New Clothes*. London: Routledge.

22. See discussion of experimental methodology in Esptein, W. (2006) *Psychotherapy as Religion: The Civil Divine in America*. Reno: University of Nevada Press.

23. Boyle, M. (2002) *Schizophrenia: A Scientific Delusion?* (2nd edn). London: Routledge.

24. Pilgrim, D. and Bentall, R. (1999) 'The Medicalisation of Misery: A Critical Realist Analysis of the Concept of Depression', *Journal of Mental Health* 8(3): 261–74.

25. Horwitz, A. and Wakefield, J.C. (2012) *All We Have to Fear: Psychiatry's Transformation of Natural Anxieties into Mental Disorders*. Oxford: Oxford University Press.

26. National Institute for Clinical Excellence (2004) *Clinical Guideline 23: Management of Depression in Primary and Secondary Care*. London: NICE, p. 8.

27. See Patient Health Questionnaire (2012) <http://www.patient.co.uk/doctor/Patient-Health-Questionnaire-%28PHQ-9%29.htm> retrieved 18 September 2012.

28. The 'GAD' is used as a short-hand reference to Generalised Anxiety Disorder Assessment, a self-administered patient questionnaire, used again as a screening tool, but this time for generalised anxiety disorder. See <http://www.patient.co.uk/doctor/Patient-Health-Questionnaire-%28PHQ-9%29.htm> retrieved 18 September 2012. Also, the outcomes for clients deemed to be suffering from other specific diagnosed problems – such as obsessive compulsive disorder, or PTSD for example – are measured in terms of their

scores on additional questionnaires, used alongside the GAD and the PHQ, and designed to tap the symptoms of their disorder.

29. Centre for Economic Performance's Mental Health Policy Group, *The Depression Report*, p. 1.

30. Layard appears to have a lot of faith in the CBT therapists, whose ministrations are 'not so different, you know, from what Jesus or any other great healer did for people' – quoted in Leader, D. (2008) 'A Quick Fix for the Soul', *Guardian*, 9 September <http://www.guardian.co.uk/science/2008/sep/09/psychology.humanbehaviour> retrieved 30 September 2010.

31. Midlands Psychology Group (2008) 'Our Big Fat Multi-Million Pound Psychology Experiment', *Clinical Psychology Forum* 181: 34–7.

32. Pilgrim, D. (2009) 'CBT in the British NHS: Vague Imposition or Imposition of Vagueness?', *European Journal of Psychotherapy, Counselling and Health* 11(3) (September): 323–39; Fletcher, P.K. (2007) 'Treating Depression with the Evidence Based Psychotherapies: A Critique of the Evidence', *Acta Psychiatr Scand* 2007: 352–9.

33. For example, Smail, D. (1978) *Psychotherapy: A Personal Approach*. London: Dent; Van Deurzen, E. (1998) *Passion and Paradox in Psychotherapy*. London: Johnathon Wiley; Spinelli, E. (2001) *The Mirror and the Hammer: Challenges to Therapeutic Orthodoxy*. London: Macmillan.

34. Hall, K. and Iqbal, F. (2010) *The Problem with Cognitive Behavioural Therapy*. London: Karnac.

35. National Institute for Clinical Excellence (2007 (2004 Clinical Guideline 23 (amended)) *Depression: Management of Depression in Primary and Secondary Care*, p. 10.

36. Richards and Suckling, 'Improving Access to Psychological Therapy'.

37. Richards, B. (1995) 'Psychotherapy and the Hidden Injuries of Class', *BPS Psychotherapy Section Newsletter* 17: 21–35; Williamson, H. (2004) *The Milltown Boys Revisited*. London: Berg.

38. National IAPT Programme Team (2011) *The IAPT Data Handbook*. Version 2.0. London: National IAPT Programme Team.

39. Epstein, W. (2006) *Psychotherapy as Religion: The Civil Divine in America*. Reno, NV: University of Nevada Press.

40. Rosen, T. (2011) *The Positive Power of Imagery: Harnessing Client Imagination in CBT and Related Therapies*. Chichester: Wiley-Blackwell.

41. *Chambers Dictionary* (2009) (11th edn). London: Chambers Harrap Publishers, Ltd.

42. Jopling, D. (2008) *Talking Cures and Placebo Effects*. Oxford: Oxford University Press.

43. Midlands Psychology Group (2010) 'Welcome to NICEworld', *Clinical Psychology Forum* 212: 52–6.

44. Duncan, B.L., Miller, S.D., Wampold, B.E. and Hubble, M.A. (eds) (2010) *The Heart and Soul of Change. Delivering What Works in Therapy* (2nd edn). Washington, DC: American Psychological Association.

45. Winter, D. (2007) 'Improving Access or Denying Choice?', *Mental Health and Learning Disabilities Research and Practice* 4(2): 73–82.

46. Priest, P. (2011) 'This is CBT (I'm Still Waiting for Magic Therapy to Put Things Right)', *Clinical Psychology Forum* 227 (November).

47. Winter, 'Improving Access or Denying Choice?', p. 78.

48. Robinson, L. (1994) *Psychology for Social Workers: Black Perspectives*. London: Routledge.

49. Weinstein, J. (2012) 'Social Work and Mental Health – A Paper Dealing with the Oppression of People with Mental Illness Under Neoliberalism', *Black Triangle Campaign: Anti-Defamation Campaign in Defence of Disability Rights* <http://blacktrianglecampaign.org/2012/05/17/social-work-and-mental-health-by-jeremy-weinstein-a-paper-dealing-with-the-oppression-of-people-with-mental-illnesses-under-neoliberalism> retrieved 8 January 2013.

50. Glover, G., Webb, M. and Evison, F. (2010) 'Improving Access to Psychological Therapies: A Review of the Progress Made by Sites in the First Roll Out Year', *North Eastern Public Health Observatory*, July <http://www.iapt.nhs.uk/wp-content/uploads/iapt-year-one-sites-data-review-final-report.pdf> retrieved 10 September 2012.

51. Gordon, P. (1998) *Face to Face: Therapy as Ethics*. London: Constable.

52. Mickle, A. (2009) 'IAPT Programme Fills Gap in Mental Health Provision', *Community Care*, 13 August <http://www.communitycare.co.uk/articles/07/08/2009/112312/is-the-roll-out-of-talking-therapies-fast-enough.htm> retrieved 8 January 2013.

53. Gilbert, M.C. and Evans, K. (2000) *Psychotherapy Supervision: An Integrative Rational Approach to Psychotherapy Supervision*. Buckingham: Open University Press.

54. Hemmings, A. (2009) 'A Response to Critiques of CBT in *Against and For CBT Towards a Constructive Dialogue*', in Hemmings, A. and Field, R. (eds), *Counselling and Psychotherapy in Contemporary Practice*. Hove: Routledge, p. 44, quoted in Weinstein, 'Social Work and Mental Health.

55. *Therapy Today* (2010) 21 (10) 'NHS Psychological Therapists Enable Four in 10 to Recover', retrieved January 15 2013.

56. Glover, Webb, and Evison, 'Improving Access to Psychological Therapies'. See also Barry McInnes's critique, from which these figures are drawn: McInnes, B. (2011) 'Nine out of ten people helped by IAPT?' Letters Section. *Therapy Today* 22 (1) http:www.therapytoday.net/article/show/2266/ retrieved January 20 2013.

57. McInnes, ibid.

58. See Furedi, F. (2003) 'How Did We Get here?', in idem, *Therapy Culture: Cultivating Vulnerability in an Uncertain Age*. London: Routledge.

59. Dorling, D. and Thomas, B. (2011) *Bankrupt Britain: An Atlas of Social Change*. Bristol: The Policy Press.

60. See Walker, C. and Fincham, B. (2011) *Work and the Mental Health Crisis in Britain*. London: Wiley-Blackwell. In contradiction to the official message that work is good for all, see Chartered Institute of Personnel and Development (2011) *Stress and Mental Health at Work*. London: CIPD.

61. On the personal consequences of low-pay employment, see, for example, Abrahams, F. (2002) *Below the Breadline: Living on the Minimum Wage*. London: Profile Books.

62. Stewart, H. (2012) 'George Osborne's Hidden Cuts Will Take Away 30% of Income for Poorest Families', *Observer*, 25 November <http://www.guardian.co.uk/society/2012/nov/25/hidden-cuts-hit-poorest-families> retrieved 26 November 2012.

63. Miller, D.S. (2012) 'Revolution in Swedish Mental Health Practice: The Cognitive Behavioural Therapy Monopoly Gives Way', 13 May <http://scottdmiller.com/about-scott/> retrieved 8 September 2012.

64. Ibid.

65. *British Medical Journal* (2003) Cover note: Bakker von Eeklo, 326(29 March): 695.

CHAPTER 8   THE THERAPY MARKET – FROM THE THIRD WAVE TO 'HAPPINESS'

1. Sebald, W.G. (1998) *The Rings of Saturn*. London: Vintage, p. 86.

2. Brown, G.S. and Minami, T. (2010) 'Outcomes, Management, Reimbursement, and the Future of Psychotherapy', in Duncan, S., Miller, S.D., Wampold, B.E. and Hubble, M.A. (eds), *The Heart and Soul of Change: Delivering What Works in Therapy*. Washington, DC: American Psychological Association, p. 281.

3. Ibid., p. 292.

4. Wotjas, O. (1999) 'Listening and Learning', *Times Higher Education Supplement*, 20 August <http://www.timeshighereducation.co.uk/story.asp?storyCode=147638&sectioncode=26> retrieved 11 May 2011.

5. Sorenson, J. (2005) *Relapse Prevention in Bipolar Disorder: A Treatment Manual And Workbook for Therapist and Client*. Hertfordshire: University of Hertfordshire Press.

6. 'NPD' stands for Narcissistic Personality Disorder. See Dimeff, M.A. and Koerner, K. (eds) (2007) *Dialectical Behavior Therapy in Clinical Practice: Applications Across Disorders and Settings*. New York: The Guilford Press.

7. See Michael Billig's review (2001) of *The Interpretation of Dreams*, in *Journal of Community and Applied Social Psychology* 11(63): 63–73.

8. Michael Elkin, PhD Director, Center for Collaborative Solutions. Quoted on the website of Ross Cohen, Licensed Professional Counselor <http://www.ross-cohen.com/emdr.html> retrieved 21 October 2012.

9. See Justman, S. (2011) 'The Power of Rhetoric: Two Healing Movements', *Yale Journal of Biology and Medicine* 84: 15–25.

10. Moerman, D. (2002) *Meaning, Medicine, and the 'Placebo Effect'*. Cambridge: Cambridge University Press.

11. Vaknin, S. (2011) *The Big Book Of NLP Techniques: 200+ Patterns & Strategies of Neuro Linguistic Programming* (4th edn). Inner Patch Publishing.

12. Behavioural Tec LLC (2012) *Training: Guidelines for Individuals and Teams New to DBT* <http://behavioraltech.org/training/guidelines_new.cfm> retrieved 5 February 2012.

13. Pollock, A. (2010) *NHS Plc: The Privatization of Our Healthcare* (2nd edn). London: Verso.

14. Leys, C. (2012) 'After the Health Bill: The End of the NHS as We Know It', *Red Pepper*, April <http://www.redpepper.org.uk/the-end-of-the-nhs-as-we-know-it/> retrieved 11 February 2013.

15. Smail, D. (2006) 'Is Clinical Psychology Selling its Soul (Again?)', *Clinical Psychology Forum* 168: 17–20. And in the case of psychiatry, see St John, P. et al. (2009) 'The Trouble with NHS Psychiatry in England', *The Psychiatrist* 33: 219–25. For the problems with IT systems, see Campbell, D. (2011) 'NHS Told to Abandon Delayed IT project', *Guardian*, 22 September, p. 4.

16. Westwood, N. (2006) 'What can the NHS Learn from 'The Lean Machine' Toyota?'. NHS Institute for Innovation and Improvement <http://www.institute.nhs.uk/images//documents/institute_documents/PDF/NHS_Institute_2_May_visit.pdf> retrieved 27 January 2013.

17. Watchman, G. (2012) 'Toyota recalls 700,000 vehicles in US amid safety concerns', *Guardian*, 8 March, p. 31.

18. Department of Health (2012) *Payment by Results Guidance for 2012–13*. London: Department of Health.

19. Sutherland, S. (1992) *Irrationality: The Enemy Within*. London: Constable.

20. Orford, J. (2011) 'Time to speak out on NHS reform', *The Psychologist*. Letters Section, 24(10): 713.

21. Harper, D. (2011) 'Staying Quiet?', *The Psychologist*. Letters Section, 24(7): 474.

22. The BPS eventually did so, in response to a petition, signed by 98 of its more concerned members. See Harper, ibid. However, the response fell far short of acknowledging the concerns raised by Harper and colleagues – that the Bill represented privatisation by stealth and the likely erosion of key mental health and social care services. See BPS (2012) *Society Statement: Health and Social Care Bill* <http://www.bps.org.uk/news/society-statement-health-and-social-care-bill> retrieved 22 February 2012.

23. Priest, P. (2013) 'The Tour de NICE and the Art of Deception', *Clinical Psychology Forum*.

24. Hagan, T. and Donnison, D. (1999) 'Social Power: Some Implications for the Theory and Practice of Cognitive Behaviour Therapy', *Journal Of Community & Applied Social Psychology* 9: 119–35. For a thoroughly mainstream (CBT practitioner's) acknowledgement of the limitations of CBT as a silver bullet for misery, see Sanders, F. and Wills, D.J. (2012) *Cognitive Behaviour Therapy: An Introduction*. London: Sage.

25. Hayes, S.C. (2004) 'Acceptance and Commitment Therapy, Relational Frame Therapy, and the Third Wave of Behavioural and Cognitive Therapies'. *Behaviour Therapy* 35: 639–65.

26. Humphries, C. (1985) *Buddhism*. Harmondsworth: Penguin.

27. Mace, C. (2008) *Mindfulness and Mental Health: Therapy, Theory and Science*. London: Routledge.

28. Ibid.

29. Ibid.

30. Hayes, S., Stroshal, K.D. and Wilson, K.G. (1999) *Acceptance and Commitment Therapy: An Experiential Approach to Behaviour Change*. New York: Guilford Press.

31. Choudhury, S. and Slaby, J. (2011) *Critical Neuroscience: A Handbook of the Social and Cultural Contexts of Neuroscience*. London: Wiley-Blackwell; Segal, Z.V., Williams, J.M.G. and Teasdale, J.D. (2002) *Mindfulness-based Cognitive Therapy for Depression: A New Approach to Preventing Relapse*. New York: Guilford Press.

32. Lineham, M.M. (1993) *Cognitive-behavioural Treatment of Borderline Personality Disorder*. New York: Guilford Press.

33. Olenchek, C. (2008) 'Dialectical Behavior Therapy – Treating Borderline Personality Disorder', *Social Work Today* 8(6): 22.

34. Jacobsen, N. and Christensen, A. (1996) *Acceptance and Change in Couple Therapy: A Therapist's Guide to Transforming Relationships*. New York: Norton.

35. Roemer, L. and Orisillo, S.M. (2009) *Mindfulness- and Acceptance-based Behavioral Therapies in Practice*. New York: Guilford Press.

36. Falb, M. and Pargament, K.I. (2012) 'Relational Mindfulness, Spirituality, and the Therapeutic Bond', *Asian Journal of Psychiatry* 5(4) (December): 351–4.

37. Hutchinson, T.A. and Dobkin, P.L. (2009) 'Mindful Medical Practice: Just Another Fad?', *Canadian Family Physician* 55(8) (August): 778–9.

38. Mental Health Foundation (2012) *Be Mindful Online* <http://www.bemindfulonline.com/the-benefits> retrieved 23 January 2012.

39. Baer, R. (2003) 'Mindfulness Training as a Clinical Intervention: A Conceptual and Empirical Review', *Clinical Psychology: Science and Practice* 10(2) (Summer): 125–43.

40. Mace, *Mindfulness and Mental Health*.

41. Lomas, P. (1996) *Cultivating Intuition*. London: Ashgate.

42. Gendlin, E.T. (1996) *Focusing-Oriented Psychotherapy: A Manual of the Experiential Method*. New York: Guilford Publications.

43. Laing, R.D. (1967) *The Politics of Experience and the Bird of Paradise*. London: Penguin.

44. Harrington, N. and Pickles, C. (2009) 'Mindfulness and Cognitive Behavioral Therapy: Are They Compatible Concepts?', *Journal of Cognitive Psychotherapy* 23(4): 315–23.

45. Smith, M. and Gore, N.J. (2012) 'Outcomes of a "Train the Trainers" Approach to an Acceptance Based Stress Intervention in a Specialist Challenging Behaviour Service', *International Journal of Positive Behaviour Support* 2(1): 39–48.

46. For some insights into the emotional strain that can be experienced both by staff and by the users of challenging behaviour services (which can include inpatient care), see Emerson, E. and Enfield, S.L. (2011) Challenging Behaviour (3rd edn). Cambridge: Cambridge University Press.

47. Smith and Gore, 'Outcome of a "Train the Trainers" Approach ... Behaviour Service', p. 46, emphasis added.

48. For a discussion of how employees often learn to 'talk the talk' required by managers in order to get by in their jobs, see Bradley, H., Erickson, M., Stephenson, C. and Williams, S. (2000) 'The Myth of Lean Production', in idem, *Myths at Work*. London: Polity; Schmidt, G. (2000) *Disciplined Minds: A Critical Look at Salaried Professionals and the Soul-Battering System that Shapes their Lives*. New York: Rowman and Littlefield.

49. Holmes, D.S. (1984) 'Meditation and Somatic Arousal Reduction. A Review of the Experimental Evidence', *American Psychologist* 39(1): 1–10; Holmes, D.S. (1988) 'The Influence of Meditation Versus Rest on Physiological Arousal: A Second Evaluation', in West, M.A. (ed.) *The Psychology of Meditation*. Oxford: Clarendon Press.

50. Austin, J.H. (2011) *Meditating Selflessly: Practical Neural Zen*. Cambridge, MA: MIT Press.

51. Choudhury, S. and Slaby, J. (2011) *Critical Neuroscience: A Handbook of the Social and Cultural Contexts of Neuroscience*. London: Wiley-Blackwell.

52. Sanders, L. (2009) 'Trawling the Brain. New Findings Raise Questions About Reliability of FMRI as Gauge of Neural Activity', *Science News*, 19 December, 176(13): 16.

53. Blackmore, S. (2009) *Ten Zen Questions*. Oxford: One World Publications.

54. Crook, J.H. (1980) *The Evolution of Human Consciousness*. Oxford: Oxford University Press; Buswell, R.E. (1992) *The Zen Monastic Experience*. Princeton, NJ: Princeton University Press.

55. The Midlands Psychology Group (2010) 'Post Qualification Training in Selective Ignorance: A Report from Two Recent National Conferences for Therapeutic Psychologists', *Clinical Psychology Forum* 212: 46–51.

56. Bruckner, P. (2011) *Perpetual Euphoria: On the Duty to Be Happy*. Princeton, NJ: Princeton University Press.

57. See the *Journal of Happiness Studies: An Interdisciplinary Forum on Subjective Well-Being* <http://www.springer.com/social+sciences/well-being/journal/10902> retrieved 1 May 2012.

58. Ecclestone, K. and Hayes, D. (2008) *The Dangerous Rise of Therapeutic Education*. London: Routledge.

59. Stratton, A. (2010) 'David Cameron Aims to Make Happiness the New GDP', *Observer*, 14 November <http://www.guardian.co.uk/politics/2010/nov/14/david-cameron-wellbeing-inquiry#history-link-box> retrieved 2 January 2011.

60. Van Deurzen, E. (2009) *Psychotherapy and the Quest for Happiness*. London: Sage.

61. Seligman, M.E.P. and Czíkszentmihályi, M. (2000) 'Positive Psychology: An Introduction', *American Psychologist* 55(1): 5–14.

62. Layard, R. (2006) *Happiness: Lessons from a New Science*. London: Penguin.

63. James, O. (2007) *Affluenza: How to Be Successful and Stay Sane*. London: Vermillion.

64. Czíkszentmihályi, M. (1990) *Flow: The Psychology of Optimal Experience*, New York: Harper and Row.

65. For example, James, *Affluenza*; de Botton, A. (2005) *Status Anxiety*. London: Penguin.

66. Layard, *Happiness*, p. 188.

67. Ibid., pp. 8–9.

68. Seligman, M.E.P. (2002) *Authentic Happiness: Using the New Positive Psychology to Realize Your Potential for Lasting Fulfillment*. New York: Free Press.

69. Ibid., p. xiv.

70. Kagan, J. (2012) 'Happiness Ascendant', in idem, *Psychology's Ghosts: The Crisis in the Profession and the Way Back*. New Haven, CT and London: Yale University Press.

71. Centre for Economic Performance (2006) *The Depression Report: A New Deal for Depression and Anxiety Disorders*. London: London School of Economics

72. James, *Affluenza*; James, O. (2009) 'Family Under the Microscope: Turn to Freud's Psychoanalysis for Postnatal Depression', *Guardian*, 3 October <http://www.guardian.co.uk/lifeandstyle/2009/sep/26/oliver-james-postnatal-depression> retrieved 23 May 2010.

73. Becker, D. and Marececk, J. (2008) 'Positive Psychology: History in the Remaking?', *Theory Psychology* 18(5): 591–604, at 593.

74. Layard, R. (2003) 'Happiness – Has Social Science a Clue?' The Lionel Robbins Memorial Lectures, 2002–03, delivered 3–5 March 2003 at the London School of Economics. London: London School of Economics. Also see, for example, Alesina, A. et al. (2001) 'Inequality and Happiness: Are Americans and Europeans Different?', *Journal of Public Economics* 88: 2009–42. In both cases, the authors are quoting a question asked of the American public every two years, in the US government's General Social Survey.

75. See the discussion of these issues in Kagan, J. (2012) *Psychology's Ghosts: The Crisis in the Profession and the Way Back*. New Haven, CT: Yale University Press.

76. See, for example, Grimshaw, A. (1992) *Servants of the Buddha: Winter in a Himalayan Convent*. London. Open Letters; Thompson, F. (1978) *Lark Rise to Candleford*. Harmondsworth: Penguin.

77. Charlesworth, S.J. (1999) *A Phenomenology of Working-Class Experience.* Cambridge: Cambridge University Press.

78. Ibid., p. 280.

79. Ibid., p. 292.

80. Rapley, M. (2004) *The Social Construction of Intellectual Disability.* Cambridge: Cambridge University Press.

81. Ehrenreich, B. (2008) *Bait and Switch*. London. Granta.

82. Ehrenreich, B. (2010) *Bright-Sided*. London. Granta.

83. Myslobodsky, M. (2004) *The Fallacy of Mother's Wisdom: A Critical Perspective on Health Psychology*. Hackensack, NJ:World Scientific.

84. Freidli, L. (2012) 'What We've Tried, Hasn't Worked: The Politics of Assets-based Public Health', *Critical Public Health* <http://www.tandfonline.com/doi/pdf/10.1080/09581596.2012.748882>. And for a discussion of the likely influence of the immune system on mood and optimism, rather than the other way round, see Trivers, R. (2011) 'The Immunology of Self-deception', in idem, *Deceit and Self-Deception: Fooling Yourself the Better to Fool Others*. London: Allen Lane, Penguin.

85. Neiman, S. (2002) *Evil in Modern Thought: An Alternative History of Philosophy*. Princeton, NJ: Princeton University Press, p. 83.

86. Ralston Saul, J. (1992) *Voltaire's Bastards: The Dictatorship of Reason in the West*. New York: Vintage.

87. Neiman, S. (2008) *Moral Clarity: A Guide for Grown-Up Idealists.* New York: Harcourt Trade Publishers. For an astute discussion of the psychological consequences of avoiding thought about hard issues like these in one's life, see Van Durzen, E. (2011) *Psychotherapy and the Quest for Happiness*. London: Sage.

88. Healy, D. (2012) *Pharmageddon*. Berkeley: University of California Press.

89. *Guardian* (2010) Editorial: 'Tony Blair Sold the Iraq War on his Judgement. His Judgement was Wrong', 31 January <http://www.guardian.co.uk/commentisfree/2010/jan/31/tony-blair-sold-iraq-war-on-his-judgement/print> retrieved 20 February 2010.

90. Unison (2011) 'UNISON Bullying Survey Reveals Real Impact of Government Cuts' <http://www.unison.org.uk/asppresspack/pressrelease_view.asp?id=2334> retrieved 20 April 2012. See also Sennett, R. (1998) *The Corrosion of Character: The Consequences of Work in the New Capitalism*. New York: Norton.

91. Russell, B. (1930) *The Conquest of Happiness*. New York: W.W. Norton and Company.
92. See, for example, <http://allpoetry.com/poem/8619489-The_Way_You_Think-by-Patience_Strong>. Retrieved 19 December 2012.
93. Orwell, G. (2003) *The Observer Years*. London: Grove Atlantic, p. 102.

CHAPTER 9   TOWARDS A PSYCHOLOGY THAT REFLECTS WHAT THE THERAPY INDUSTRY WILL NOT TELL US

1. Robertson, A.F. (2001) *Greed: Gut Feelings, Growth and History*. London: Polity, p. 222.
2. Masson, J. (1998) *The Assault on Truth: Freud's Suppression of the Seduction Theory*. New York: Pocket Books.
3. Webster, R. (2005) *Why Freud Was Wrong: Sin, Science and Psychoanalysis*. Oxford: The Orwell Press.
4. Manes, S. (1974) *Masks of Loneliness: Alfred Adler in Perspective*. New York: Macmillan and Co.
5. Horney, K. (1937) *The Neurotic Personality of our Time*. New York: Norton.
6. Sullivan, H.S. (1953) *The Interpersonal Theory of Psychiatry* (Swick Perry, H. and Ladd Gawell, M., eds). New York: W.W. Norton.
7. Totton, N. (2000) *Psychotherapy and Politics*. London: Sage.
8. Fromm, E. (1955) *The Sane Society*. New York: Henry Holt.
9. Kotowitz, Z. (1997) *R.D. Laing and the Paths of Anti-Psychiatry*. London: Routledge.
10. Miller, D. (2004) *R.D. Laing*. Edinburgh: Edinburgh Review, Edinburgh University Press.
11. Kotowitz, *R.D. Laing and the Paths of Anti-Psychiatry*.
12. Mullan, B. (1995) *Mad to be Normal: Conversations with R.D. Laing*. London: Free Association.
13. Quoted from Paul Gordon (2010) *An Uneasy Dwelling. The Story of the Philadelphia Association Community Houses*. Ross-On-Wye: PCCS Books, Ltd, p. 7.
14. Mullan, *Mad to be Normal*.
15. Laing, R.D. (1960) *The Divided Self: An Existential Study in Sanity and Madness*. Harmondsworth: Penguin.
16. Laing, R.D. and Esterson, A. (1964) *Sanity, Madness and the Family*. London: Penguin Books.
17. Itten, D. and Young, C. (2012) *R.D. Laing and the Divided Self: Fifty Years On*. Ross-on-Wye: PCCS Books Ltd.
18. Johnstone, L. (2000) *Users and Abusers of Psychiatry* (2nd edn). London: Routledge.
19. Mullan, *Mad to be Normal*.
20. Laing, R.D. (1967) *The Politics of Experience and the Bird of Paradise*. Harmondsworth: Penguin.
21. Kotowicz, *R.D. Laing and the Paths of Anti-Psychiatry*.
22. Doggett, P. (2007) *There's A Riot Going On: Revolutionaries, Rock Stars and the Rise and Fall of 60s Counter-culture*. Edinburgh: Canongate Books Ltd.

23. Boyd, J. (2004) *White Bicycles: Making Music in the 60s*. London: Serpents Tail, pp. 267–9.

24. Healy, D. (2012) *Pharmageddon*. Berkeley: University of California Press.

25. Harvey, D. (1990) *The Condition of Post-Modernity*. Malden, MA: Blackwell Publishing.

26. Shapiro, I. (2005) *The Flight from Reality in the Human Sciences*. Princeton, NJ and Oxford: Princeton University Press.

27. Harvey, *The Condition of Post-Modernity*.

28. See Gordon, *An Uneasy Dwelling*.

29. Kotowitz, R.D. *Laing and the Paths of Anti-Psychiatry*.

30. Johnstone, *Users and Abusers of Psychiatry*.

31. Pilgrim, D. and Rogers, A. (2010) *A Sociology of Mental Health and Illness* (4th edn) Basingstoke: Open University Press, McGraw Hill Educational.

32. See, for instance, Kotowitz, R.D. *Laing and the Paths of Anti-Psychiatry*.

33. Ingleby, D. (ed.) (1981) *Critical Psychiatry: The Politics of Mental Health*. Harmondsworth: Penguin.

34. Sedgwick, P. (1981) 'The Grapes of Roth', *New Society*, 30 April <http://www.critpsynet.freeuk.com/Grapes.htm> retrieved 13 August 2011.

35. Ingleby, D. (2006) 'Transcultural Mental Health Care: The Challenge to Positivist Psychiatry', in Double, D. (ed.), *Critical Psychiatry: The Limits of Madness*. London: Palgrave Macmillan.

36. Ingleby, D. (2004) 'Understanding Mental Illness', in Ingleby, D. (ed.), *Critical Psychiatry: The Politics of Mental Health* (2nd edn). London: Free Association Books.

37. Kovel, J. (1981) 'The American Mental Health Industry', in Ingleby (ed.), *Critical Psychiatry: The Politics of Mental Health*.

38. Conrad, P. (1981) 'On the Medicalization of Deviance and Social Control', in Ingleby (ed.), *Critical Psychiatry: The Politics of Mental Health*.

39. Ingleby, D. (1981) 'Understanding Mental Illness', in Ingleby (ed.), *Critical Psychiatry: The Politics of Mental Health*.

40. Morgan, A. (2008) 'The Authority of Lived Experience', in Morgan, A. (ed.), *Being Human: Reflections on Mental Distress in Society*. Ross-on-Wye: PCCS Books Ltd.

41. See *Critical Psychiatry Network* <http://www.criticalpsychiatry.co.uk> retrieved 16 August 2012.

42. See Double (ed.), *Critical Psychiatry: The Limits of Madness*.

43. Mental Health and Survivor's Movement (2012) *A History Organised by the Survivors History Group in Association with the Survivor History Internet Forum and Network and the Mental Health History Timeline* <http://studymore.org.uk/mpu.htm> retrieved 12 August 2012.

44. Fernando, S. and Keating, F. (2008) *Mental Health in a Multi-Ethnic Society: A Multidisciplinary Handbook*. London: Routledge.

45. Ingleby, D. (2008) 'Transcultural Mental Health Care: The Challenge to Positivist Psychiatry', in Double (ed.), *Critical Psychiatry: The Limits of Madness*.

46. Foucault, M. (1965) *Madness and Civilization: A History of Insanity in the Age of Reason*. New York: Random House, p. x.

47. See, for example, Sands, A. (2000) *Falling for Therapy*. London: Macmillan.

48. Wilson, T. and E. Dunne (2004) 'Self-Knowledge: Its Limits, Value, and Potential for Improvement', *Annual Review of Psychology* 55: 493–581.

49. Strawson, G. (2004) 'Tales of the Unexpected', *Guardian: Saturday Review*, 10 January, p. 15.

50. Babiker, G. and Arnold, L. (1997) *The Language of Injury: Comprehending Self Mutilation*. Leicester: BPS Books.

51. Irigaray, L. (2008) *Conversations*. London: Continuum; Orbach, S. (1978) *Fat is a Feminist Issue: The Anti-Diet Guide to Weight Loss*. London: Paddington Press; Chodorow, N. (1992) *Feminism and Psychoanalytic Theory* (2nd edn). New Haven, CT and London: Yale University Press.

52. Showalter, E. (1985) *The Female Malady: Women, Madness, and English Culture, 1830–1980*. New York: Pantheon Books.

53. Masson, J.M. (1988) *Against Therapy*. New York: Atheneum.

54. Ussher, J.M. (2011) *The Madness of Women: Myth and Experience*. London: Routledge.

55. Becker, D. (1995) *The Myth of Empowerment: Women and the Therapeutic Culture in America*. New York and London: New York University Press; Epstein, W. (2013) *Empowerment as Ceremony*. Piscataway, NJ: Transaction Publishers.

56. Leeming, D., Boyle, M. and MacDonald, J. (2009) 'Accounting for Psychological Problems: How User-friendly is Formulation?', *Clinical Psychology Forum* 200: 12–15.

57. Stenfert Kroese, B., Dagnan, D. and Loumidis, K. (eds) (1997) *Cognitive-Behaviour Therapy for People with Learning Disabilities*. London and New York: Routledge.

58. Stenfert Kroese, B. and Holmes, G. (2001) '"I've Never said 'No' to anything in my life": Helping People with Learning Disabilities who Experience Psychological Problems', in Newnes, C; Dunne, K. and Holmes. G. (eds), *This is Madness Too: A Critical Look at the Mental Health System*. Ross-on-Wye: PCCS Books Ltd, p. 79.

59. Kelly, P. and Moloney, P. (2013) 'Psychotherapy', in Cromby, D., Harper, D. and Reavey, P. (eds), *Psychology, Mental Health & Distress*. London: Palgrave Macmillan.

60. Clements, J. and Hassall, R. (2008) 'The Lost Patrol?', *Clinical Psychology Forum* 191: 15–19.

61. Newnes, C. and Radcliffe, N. (eds) (2005) *Making and Breaking Children's Lives*. Ross-on-Wye: PCCS Books Ltd.

62. Epstein, W. (2006) *Psychotherapy as Religion: The Civil Divine in America*. Reno, NV: University of Nevada Press.

63. Orford, J. (2008) *Community Psychology: Challenges, Controversies and Emerging Consensus*. London: Wiley.

64. Cox, R., Holmes, G., Moloney, P., Priest, P. and Ridley-Dash, M. (2013) 'Community Psychology', in, Cromby, Harper, and Reavey (eds), *Psychology, Mental Health & Distress*.

65. Holmes, G. (2010) *Psychology in the Real World*. Ross-on-Wye: PCCS Books Ltd. Holmes and colleagues also run a website which provides details of their activities and publications: <http://www.psychologyintherealworld.co.uk>.

66. Cox et al., 'Community Psychology', and Holmes, ibid.

67. Holland, S. (1995) 'Interaction in Women's Mental Health and Neighbourhood Development', in Fernando, S. (ed.), *Mental Health in a Multi-ethnic Society: A Multi-disciplinary Handbook*. London: Routledge, p. 142.

68. See, for example, Melluish, S. and Bulmer, D. (1999) 'Rebuilding Solidarity: An Account of a Men's Health Action Project', *Journal of Community and Applied Social Psychology* 9: 93–100.

69. This is a perennial problem for professions that try to act on behalf of the disadvantaged. See, for example, Gilbert, T. and Powell, J. (2010) 'Power and Social Work in the United Kingdom: A Foucauldian Excursion', *Journal of Social Work* 10(1) (January): 3–22.

70. Epstein, W. (2010) *Democracy without Decency: Good Citizenship and the War on Poverty*. University Park, PA: Pennsylvania State University Press; Epstein, W. (2002) *American Policy Making: Welfare as Ritual*. Lanham, MD: Rowman and Littlefield.

71. Orford, *Community Psychology: Challenges, Controversies and Emerging Consensus*.

72. Skinner, B.F. (1974) *About Behaviourism*. New York: Knopf.

73. Skinner, B.F. (1969) *Contingencies of Reinforcement: A Theoretical Analysis*. New York: Appleton-Century-Crofts.

74. Skinner, *About Behaviourism*, p. 233. Schlinger, H.D. (2004) 'Why Psychology Hasn't Kept Its Promises', *Journal of Mind and Behaviour* 25(2): 123–44.

75. Perez-Alvarez, M. and Sass, L.A. (2009) 'Phenomonology and Behaviourism: A Mutual Readjustment', *Philosophy, Psychiatry and Psychology* 15(3): 199–210.

76. Dewey, J. (1896) 'The Reflex Arc Concept in Psychology', *Psychological Review* July: 357–70.

77. Gross, D.M. (2006) *The Secret History of Emotion: From Aristotle's Rhetoric to Modern Brain Science*. Chicago, IL: University of Chicago Press.

78. Merleau-Ponty, M. (1971) *Sense and Nonsense*. Evanston, IL: Northwestern University Press.

79. Clarke, A. (1997) *Being There: Putting Brain, Body and World Back Together Again*. Cambridge, MA: MIT Press.

80. Noe, A. (2009) *Out of Our Heads: Why You Are Not Your Brain and Other Lessons from the Biology of Consciousness*. New York: Hill and Wang, p. 69.

81. Ibid.

82. Seligman, E.P. and Maier, S. (1967) 'Failure to Escape Traumatic Shock', *Journal of Experimental Psychology* 74(1) (May): 1–9.

83. Abramson, L.Y., Seligman, M.E.P. and Teasdale, J.D. (1978) 'Learned Helplessness in Humans: Critique and Reformulation', *Journal of Abnormal Psychology* 87(1): 49–74.

84. Seligman, M.E. (1990) *Learned Optimism: How to Change your Mind and Your Life*. New York: Pocket Books.

85. Cromby, J. and Harper, D. (2009) 'Paranoia: A Social Account', *Theory & Psychology* 19(3): 335–61.

86. Minton, J. (2012) *Ground Control: Fear and Happiness in the Twenty-First Century City* (2nd edn). London: Penguin.

87. Damassio, A. (1994) *Decartes' Error: Emotion, Reason and the Human Brain*. New York: Putnam.

88. Knight, T. (2004) 'Can the Mental Health System Cause Paranoia?', *Asylum* 13(2): 6–7, at 6.

89. See Tolman, C. (1994) *Subjectivity and Society: An Introduction to German Crtical Psychology*. London: Routledge.

90. Vidal, G. (1993) 'Rich Kids', in Vidal, *United States: Essays 1952–1992*. New York: Broadway, p. 635.
91. See Charlesworth, S. (1998) *A Phenomenology of Working Class Experience*. Cambridge: Cambridge University Press.
92. Pilgrim, D. and Bentall, R. (1999) 'The Medicalisation of Misery: A Critical Realist Analysis of the Concept Depression', *Journal of Mental Health* 8(3): 261–74.
93. Cromby, J. (2004) 'Depression: Embodying Social Inequality', *Journal of Critical Psychology, Counselling and Psychotherapy* 4(3): 176–87.
94. Bannister, D. (ed.) (1975) *Issues and Approaches in the Psychological Therapies*. London: Wiley; Pilgrim, D. (ed.) (1983) *Psychology and Psychotherapy*. London: Routledge & Kegan Paul.
95. Smail, D. (1978) *Psychotherapy: A Personal Approach*. London: Dent.
96. Ibid.
97. Smail, D. (1993) *The Origins of Unhappiness: Towards a New Understanding of Personal Distress*. London: Constable.
98. See Smail, D. (2005) *Power, Interest and Psychology*. Ross-On-Wye: PCCS Books Ltd.
99. Bourdieu, P. et al. (1999) *The Weight of the World: Social Suffering in Contemporary Society*. London: Polity.
100. Smail, D. (1991) 'Towards a Radical Environmentalist Psychology of Help', *The Psychologist: Bulletin of the British Psychological Society* 2: 61–5, at 64.
101. Ibid.
102. For a more detailed (but accessible) summary of the main elements of this approach, see Midlands Psychology Group (2012) 'Draft Manifesto for a Social Materialist Psychology of Distress', *Journal of Critical Psychology, Counselling and Psychotherapy* 12(2): 93–107. The Midlands Psychology Group also runs a website with downloadable publications, news updates and links to other relevant websites: <http://www.midpsy.org/>.
103. Sedgwick, P. (1981) *Psychopolitics*. London: Pluto.
104. Albee, G.W. and Joffe, J.M. (1977) 'The Issues: An Overview of Primary Prevention', in Albee and Joffe (eds), *The Issues: An Overview of Primary Prevention*. Hanover, NH: University Press of New England, p. 379.

Index

Compiled by Sue Carlton